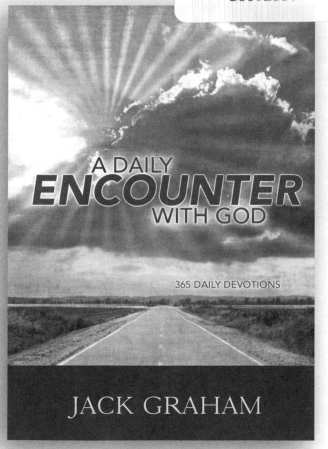

A DAILY
ENCOUNTER
WITH GOD

365 DAILY DEVOTIONS

JACK GRAHAM

DAD,

WITH ALL MY HEART & SOUL.

YOUR SON,

QUINN

A DAILY
ENCOUNTER
WITH GOD

G R A H A M

P.O. Box 799070
Dallas, Texas 75379

A DAILY ENCOUNTER WITH GOD

A DAILY
ENCOUNTER
WITH GOD

Fifteen years ago, God placed an extraordinary dream in my
heart—to spread the Gospel beyond the walls of our local church
to the world at large. And thus, PowerPoint Ministries was born.

Since our first broadcast in 1994, PowerPoint has grown into
an expansive network of local, national, and international
television and radio broadcasts, and God has used this ministry
to impact thousands and thousands of lives for eternity.

How I praise Him for this amazing work!

Today, we celebrate what God has done through PowerPoint
Ministries with this special 365-day devotional, A Daily
Encounter with God.

Through this devotional, my prayer is that God will use what
you read each day to help you get a glimpse of just what an
extraordinary God He is. And as you do, I believe that your
day-to-day life will be transformed in ways you didn't think
possible!

Jack Graham
January 2009

Day 1

I can do all things through him who strengthens me.
—Philippians 4:13

Which mode are you living in today? Are you simply in survival mode… just getting by… just trying to make it to Friday? Or are you in success mode… always striving for personal and financial achievement?

Or… do you live in significance mode… knowing who you are in Christ and discovering His destiny for your life?

Sadly, most people… and many followers of Christ… would have to admit that they live most of the time in survival or success mode. But living in significance mode is the only way to see God's plan for your life fulfilled before your very eyes!

Now, a great example of someone who lived life in the significance mode is Joseph. But what gave his life significance? Purpose. Joseph was a man of significance because he was a man of purpose.

God put a dream in Joseph's heart when he was a young man and he never forgot God's dream for his life. Joseph would not let that dream die. He was driven by that dream… and he was consumed by the call of God upon his life.

Joseph saw every problem as an opportunity… a possibility for God to work in his life.

So let me ask you, what mode are you living in today? I encourage you to live like Joseph… with significance and with purpose.

People of purpose are not paralyzed by their problems. Because people of purpose who know the Lord Jesus Christ, know that there's no panic in heaven… only plans!

LOOK AT EVERY PROBLEM AS AN OPPORTUNITY FOR GOD TO DO SOMETHING GREAT IN YOUR LIFE.

Day 2

Therefore, if anyone is in Christ, he is a new creation. The old has passed away; behold, the new has come.

—2 Corinthians 5:17

I'd like to talk to you today about repentance. So many people, even Christians, misunderstand what repentance is really all about.

First of all, repentance is not remorse. Remorse is simply being sorry for our sin. Many people are sorry because they got caught. Even the rich young ruler was sorrowful when he walked away from Jesus after deciding not to follow Him. He was remorseful... but he wasn't repentant.

Second, repentance is not regret. Regret is the experience of wishing that something didn't happen. Much like when Pilate... who knew Jesus was a guiltless man... washed his hands of the whole deal in remorse. Yet he was guilty of the blood of Jesus Christ. So repentance isn't regret.

Third, repentance is not resolve. We all know what it is to make New Year's resolutions... to resolve to do better and promise to be better. But, resolving or reforming is not true repentance.

True repentance literally means to change your mind. To change your mind about your sin, to change your mind about yourself, and to change your mind about Jesus Christ. It's true repentance when we come to faith in Jesus Christ... and our direction and affections are changed.

Repentance is a radical transformation of the human heart away from sin and toward a loving God! So if you find yourself caught in sin, I urge you to repent. Sure, it's fine to be remorseful, regretful, and to resolve not to sin again. But you really won't be transformed until you truly repent!

TURN FROM YOUR SIN TO JESUS CHRIST FOR A NEW LIFE OF HOPE, LOVE, AND TRANSFORMATION.

Day 3

Lead me in the path of your commandments, for I delight in it.
—**Psalm 119:35**

Do you have any roots of bitterness in your life today? I want you to really think about this for a moment. Are you harboring any negative feelings, animosity, or even hatred towards another person?

Now, perhaps you have been hurt greatly. Perhaps you were sexually, physically, or verbally abused as a child. Maybe you've been devastated by rejection in a relationship. Perhaps you've been unsuccessful in school... or in your current career. I know that every one of us faces hurt and rejection in life.

But I also know that Satan laughs when there's a conflict that's caused by bitterness. Why does he laugh? Because he knows that a spirit of bitterness gives him a foothold in your life... which will make you unable to pray, unable to witness, and unable to serve God effectively.

You say, "Well, Pastor, you don't understand how much I've been hurt. You don't know how deeply I've been wounded. You don't know my story." And you know what? You're right. I don't.

But I do know what happened to Jesus when He was taken into the hands of cruel and violent men... Roman soldiers who saw Him as nothing but a piece of flesh to be executed on a cruel Roman cross. They beat Him, mocked Him, pulled out His beard, spat in His face, and nailed Him to a cross.

And yet Jesus said, "Father, forgive them, for they know not what they do."

That's what Christ has done for you! And as a believer, the Spirit of Christ lives within you, enabling you... by His power... to respond to others with forgiveness.

If you will ask God to take away your bitterness, He will do it. He will bring you to a place in your life where His grace and peace replaces the animosity, hurt, and anger that you feel today.

**ASK GOD TO TAKE AWAY THE BITTERNESS
IN YOUR LIFE SO YOU CAN DISCOVER THE POWER
OF FORGIVENESS.**

Day 4

The saying is trustworthy and deserving of full acceptance, that Christ Jesus came into the world to save sinners, of whom I am the foremost.

—1 Timothy 1:15

Jesus Christ came to add to life, not to subtract from life. He said in John 10:10, "I came that they may have life and have it abundantly."

It's been said that Jesus will not only add years to your life, but life to your years. The cross of the Lord Jesus Christ is God's plus-sign to the world to say, "I love you and I've come to give you this abundant, overwhelmingly good life."

Some people think if they give their life to Jesus Christ, He's going to take away all those things that they enjoy. But remember that the only thing God asks you to give up are those things that harm and hurt you! Psalm 84:11 promises us, "For the Lord God is a sun and shield. No good thing does he withhold from those who walk uprightly."

You know, we don't deserve and we didn't earn the favor and the love of the Father. But by His mercy and grace, and because of His great love, He sent us His Son to die in our place on the cross.

And through Christ… as believers… we have everything we need! So why should we ever be disappointed? Why should we be discouraged? Why should we be distressed? Who minds the journey if the journey leads home?

The old hymn says, "Tis so sweet to trust in Jesus." And how sweet it is! To be loved unconditionally… and eternally provided for… makes for a truly abundant life!

If you will ask God to take away your bitterness, He will do it. He will bring you to a place in your life where His grace and peace replaces the animosity, hurt, and anger that you feel today.

TRUSTING IN JESUS CHRIST IS WHERE TRUE HAPPINESS AND JOY IS FOUND.

Day 5

You shall love the LORD your God with all your heart and with all your soul and with all your might.
—Deuteronomy 6:5

What… or who… do you worship? I'd like you to think about that for a moment, because we all worship something.

Why? Because God made us that way! He designed us to worship… but not to worship just anything. He hardwired us to worship Him!

Solomon tells us in Ecclesiastes chapter 3 that God "has put eternity into man's heart." We're made for beyond the here and now. We're made to experience and enjoy the living presence of our God today and every day.

And how do you experience the presence of God in your life today? Paul tells us in Romans 12:1. He says to "present your bodies as a living sacrifice, holy and acceptable to God, which is your spiritual worship."

Worship is so much more than the songs you sing in church— although praising God in song is vitally important.

Remember those two men who walked with the risen Christ along the road to Emmaus? They didn't recognize Him at first. But after they had experienced His presence and realized that they had been with the living Lord, they said, "Did not our hearts burn within us while he talked to us on the road…?"

You see, that is worship! Worship is giving yourself to God each step of the way… every day. It's surrendering yourself to the Lord in every area of your life.

It's my prayer that you will learn what it means to become a dynamic worshiper of the Lord Jesus Christ by giving yourself as a living sacrifice. When you do, you will experience His power and His presence in your life each day.

EXPERIENCE THE AMAZING POWER AND PRESENCE OF GOD BY SURRENDERING YOURSELF TO THE LORD EVERY DAY.

Day 6

Your word is a lamp to my feet and a light to my path.
—Psalm 119:105

In Ephesians 6:10-12, Paul says, "Finally, be strong in the Lord and in the strength of his might. Put on the whole armor of God, that you may be able to stand against the schemes of the devil. For we do not wrestle against flesh and blood, but against the rulers, against the authorities, against the cosmic powers over this present darkness, against the spiritual forces of evil in the heavenly places."

A vital part of standing firm in the spiritual battle is to take up the Sword of the Spirit, which is the Word of God. Becoming a fully committed follower of the Lord Jesus Christ begins by picking up your sword each day!

Second Timothy 3:16 says, "All Scripture is breathed out by God and profitable for teaching, for reproof, for correction, and for training in righteousness."

The Bible is not a human book. It's a God-given book! And it is sufficient for your every need.

That's why I want to encourage you to have a daily time of devotion and discipline when you open God's Word... when you pray and ask God to speak to you through the Scriptures.

I want to also encourage you to take your Bible with you when you gather with other believers in worship. Take your Bible to church! And take a pen with you so you can underline or highlight some Scriptures and take a few notes and really engage! Don't be a passive listener; be a proactive learner!

Just like your physical health, your spiritual health will deteriorate if you neglect it.

So... as 1 Timothy 4 encourages us... take the time and the trouble to be spiritually fit! It's the only way you'll be strong in the Lord and in the power of His might... able to withstand the attacks of our enemy, the devil. It's the only way you'll be able to stand strong in the spiritual battle you face every day!

YOUR BEST DEFENSE AGAINST THE ATTACKS OF THE ENEMY IS GOD'S WORD... SO PICK IT UP AND USE IT!

"Ah, Lord GOD! It is you who have made the heavens and the earth by your great power and by your outstretched arm! Nothing is too hard for you."

—Jeremiah 32:17

Today, you may find yourself in a rut. Maybe you're in a place where you're thinking, "Well, this is as good as it gets." And perhaps you've settled for mediocrity. Mediocrity in your marriage… mediocrity with your children… mediocrity in your career.

But God has so much more for you!

"Well," you say, "I've got all kinds of problems… all kinds of issues in my life you don't know about." You know, that may be true, but God is bigger than your problems. As 1 John 4:4 says, "He who is in you is greater than he who is in the world."

So let me ask you today: What are you asking God to do in your life? Because God wants to do supernatural things in you… things you could never imagine!

Think about what God tells us in Isaiah 43:19: "Behold, I am doing a new thing; now it springs forth, do you not perceive it? I will make a way in the wilderness and rivers in the desert."

In other words, God is saying, "Look! Can't you see it? Can't you taste it? Can't you feel this new thing that I'm doing?"

God takes barren places in our lives and uses them for His glory. That's when He does the brand new thing in our lives! And God wants to do something new in you.

Do you believe that God can do greater things in your own life… right now… than you ever imagined possible? I believe God can do and will do what you believe He can do.

Now, you say, "That's impossible!" Let me remind you what the Scripture says in Romans 8:31, "If God is for us, who can be against us?"

If you're a child of God, He is for you. So don't doubt that He wants to do great things in your life today!

GOD WANTS TO DO GREAT THINGS IN YOU AND THROUGH YOU, SO TURN TO HIM TODAY FOR WHAT YOU THINK IS IMPOSSIBLE.

"Ask, and it will be given to you; seek, and you will find; knock, and it will be opened to you."

—**Matthew 7:7**

God has called you not to just make a living, but to make a life. God has called you not to just take up space in this world, but to make our world a better place in which to live!

Yes, God wants you to make a difference!

Now, the people God uses to make a difference in this world are people who are vulnerable to Him, who are dependent on Him, and who are available to Him. If you desire and seek a courageous faith... and if you ask God to give you a compassionate heart... then anything is possible. I'm telling you, you can change the world!

I believe it's time to make an impact on this generation and the coming generations for Christ. It's time for us to fulfill our calling before He comes again. It's time for God's Church to rise up and shake off the past and shake the world for Christ. It's time for God to do a new thing... a brand new thing in the hearts of His people! And that means you!

The story of Nehemiah is a compelling illustration of how God uses people... all kinds of people... for His glory.

Someone put it this way: "A zealous man in religion is preeminently a man of one thing. It is not enough to say he is earnest, hardy, uncompromising, thoroughgoing, wholehearted, firm in spirit. He only sees one thing. He cares for one thing. He lives for one thing. He is swallowed up in one thing. And that one thing is to please God."

Let that be the passion and the prayer of our hearts and of our lives! God is looking for men and women who have a heart for Him... men and women who want to take their lives to the next level, who want to live beyond all limits!

That's my prayer for you... and me... today. That we will want to move out of the maze of mediocrity in our lives and live for something bigger than ourselves. That we will move out of our comfort zones and into the life God has called us to live!

**MOVE OUT OF THE MAZE OF MEDIOCRITY
IN YOUR LIFE AND LIVE THE POWERFUL LIFE GOD
HAS CALLED YOU TO LIVE!**

Day 9

Do not be anxious about anything, but in everything by prayer and supplication with thanksgiving let your requests be made known to God.

—Philippians 4:6

To pray successfully, we must pray with conviction.

What does it mean to pray with conviction? In Nehemiah 1:5-6, Nehemiah prays, "O LORD God of heaven, the great and awesome God who keeps covenant and steadfast love with those who love him and keep his commandments, let your ear be attentive and your eyes open, to hear the prayer of your servant...."

In these verses, Nehemiah is praying with conviction because he knows that his God is in control. When it seemed like everything was out of control in Jerusalem, Nehemiah knew that God was still on His throne. Nehemiah knew that the Lord would answer his prayer because He was a great and awesome God. Because He was a wonderful God. Because He was a faithful God. Because He was a God who could meet all of Nehemiah's needs!

And in just the same way, God can handle any problem in your life. Do you believe that today?

God is bigger... God is greater... than any situation or crisis in your life. And the first thing Nehemiah did is the first thing that you ought to do when you have a problem, a crisis, or a need: You need to turn it over to God. You need to give it to God, not as your last chance, but as your first choice!

When you know that God is above all and that He has everything under control... and when you know that your place is surrendered under the lordship of Christ, then you can find your place and know your prayers will be answered!

TRUST THAT GOD CAN HANDLE ANY PROBLEM IN YOUR LIFE.

Day 10

"Only be strong and very courageous, being careful to do according to all the law that Moses my servant commanded you. Do not turn from it to the right hand or to the left, that you may have good success wherever you go."

—Joshua 1:7

Nehemiah was one of the great leaders of the Bible even though he wasn't a prophet, a priest, or a preacher!

Nehemiah described himself as a cupbearer to the king. He was just a guy who worked hard and had risen to some prominence in his day and time. Nehemiah was just a man… but he was a man whom God raised up!

As we look at his life, there are some steps that Nehemiah took that insured his success… steps that made him a very effective leader. They're the same steps you can take as a follower of Christ to ensure you're an effective leader in your sphere of influence as well.

Step number one is to pray fervently. We see this trait over and over again in the life of Nehemiah. He was a man of prayer. Real leaders understand that opportunity swings on the hinges of prayer.

Step number two is to proceed confidently and courageously. You accomplish this by living what Proverbs 3:5-6 says: "Trust in the LORD with all your heart, and do not lean on your own understanding. In all your ways acknowledge him, and he will make straight your paths."

Step number three to being an effective leader is to plan wisely. Too often we have an idea… we have a dream… and we just go at it arms flailing, rather than taking time to plan. But there's a beautiful balance here. There's the divine side of praying and then there's the human side of planning. There is agonizing and then there is organizing.

This is why Nehemiah was such a great leader. He not only prayed, he not only proceeded with confidence and trust in the Lord, he planned effectively.

These same steps… when applied to your life as a Christian… will help you become the effective leader God intends for you to be!

**BECOME THE EFFECTIVE LEADER GOD
WANTS YOU TO BE BY PRAYING FERVENTLY,
PROCEEDING CONFIDENTLY, AND PLANNING WISELY.**

Day 11

For as in one body we have many members, and the members do not all have the same function, so we, though many, are one body in Christ, and individually members one of another. Having gifts that differ according to the grace given to us, let us use them...
—Romans 12:4-6

Everybody is somebody in the Body of Christ. Every member is a minister. You don't have to resign from your job for God to have a ministry for you. And when we work together... cooperating in God's Church among God's people... the force is amazing.

Now, Nehemiah leaves a very sad commentary in Nehemiah chapter 3 when he talks about a group of people called the Tekoites. These people were farmers who helped repair the wall of Jerusalem. In Nehemiah 3:5, Nehemiah says, "And next to them the Tekoites repaired, but their nobles would not stoop to serve their Lord."

The nobles thought they were too good! They wouldn't stoop down. They didn't want to get their hands dirty. They thought they were above working on a wall, just shoving bricks around. So what did they do? They sat out while others worked!

It's always been an amazing thing to me that some believers watch while others work. That some believers sit while others serve! To me, a non-serving Christian is a contradiction in terms.

Perhaps today, you'd admit that you've been sitting on the sidelines... watching while others get their hands dirty doing the work of the Lord. And who knows, maybe you have a list a mile long as to why you're not involved in some kind of ministry in your church or elsewhere. Or maybe you don't think there's a place of ministry for you.

If so, I want to ask you to perform an experiment this week. I want you to call up your church and ask them if they need help in any area of ministry. Whether it's ushering, parking cars, working with children, or sweeping floors, just ask if there's some place where they need help. If you do this, I can promise you that God will use you in a mighty way... a way you never thought possible!

**MAKE YOURSELF AVAILABLE TO GOD
THROUGH SERVICE.**

Day 12

Therefore, since we are surrounded by so great a cloud of witnesses, let us also lay aside every weight, and sin which clings so closely, and let us run with endurance the race that is set before us, looking to Jesus, the founder and perfecter of our faith, who for the joy that was set before him endured the cross, despising the shame, and is seated at the right hand of the throne of God.

—Hebrews 12:1-3

How do you get up when you're down? Look up!

When you're down, look up. That's what Nehemiah did when there was opposition to the rebuilding of the wall of Jerusalem.

Listen to his prayer in Nehemiah 4:4: "Hear, O our God, for we are despised. Turn back their taunt on their own heads and give them up to be plundered in a land where they are captives."

Nehemiah didn't waste time or divert from the task at hand dealing with all the criticism he received from those who opposed him rebuilding the wall. Instead of trying to handle it all on his own, do you know what Nehemiah did? He went straight to the throne of God. Nehemiah recognized that God could do a better job of dealing with his enemies than he could, so he just gave it all to God!

The next time you're down... the next time you're discouraged... let me give you the best piece of advice that you could ever hear: Run to God! Cry out to Him!

And yet, so often we try to figure out everything on our own. We try to fix things ourselves. And then we come to the end and say, "Well, I guess it's come to this; I guess I'm just going to pray now."

Don't make prayer your last chance... make it your first choice!

Somebody said if you look behind you, you'll be defeated. If you look ahead of you, you'll be distressed. If you look around you, you'll be discouraged. But if you look above you, you will be determined.

So when problems come... with people, with pressures, with whatever... take it to the top! Go to the Lord and tell Him all about it. Look to Him... and overcome the disappointments you face in life!

**WHEN PROBLEMS COME... TAKE THEM
TO GOD FIRST, NOT LAST.**

Day 13

Whoever trusts in his riches will fall, but the righteous will flourish like a green leaf.

—Proverbs 11:28

D o you want to free yourself from financial bondage? Well, the first step is to know exactly what financial bondage really looks like!

You're in financial bondage...
1. When you charge daily expenditures due to the lack of funds.
2. When you put off paying a bill until next month.
3. When you borrow money to pay fixed expenses such as your mortgage, insurance, or energy payment.
4. When you become unaware of how much you owe your creditors.
5. When you have creditors call or write to you about past-due bills.
6. When you take money from savings to pay your current bills.
7. When you take out new loans to pay off old loans.
8. When you and your spouse argue about money.
9. When you consider being dishonest about your finances.
10.When you find it difficult to return God's tithe to God's house on God's day.

If any one of these markers describes your life today, I want to offer you a word of encouragement: There is a way to escape financial bondage!

Number one, you need to confront the problem. When you have a problem, you have to be willing to be honest about it.

Number two, you need to take decisive action. Proverbs 21:5 says, "The plans of the diligent lead surely to abundance, but everyone who is hasty comes only to poverty." You need to have a plan if you're going to escape financial bondage. It's not just going to take care of itself on its own! This will probably involve such things as reducing your spending, putting away or tearing up your credit cards, and budgeting your income.

The last way to escape financial bondage is to focus on what you can give—not on what you can get. In Luke 6:38, Jesus says, "Give, and it will be given to you. Good measure, pressed down, shaken together, running over, will be put into your lap. For with the measure you use it will be measured back to you."

If you find yourself in financial bondage today, I encourage you right now to make the decision to free yourself. You will never be the blessing God intends as long as you are in bondage to money!

BY ESCAPING FINANCIAL BONDAGE, YOU CAN LIVE THE ABUNDANT LIFE GOD INTENDS FOR YOU.

Day 14

"The best of the firstfruits of your ground you shall bring into the house of the LORD your God."

—Exodus 23:19a

I want to ask you a very important series of questions today… questions every follower of Christ should ask themselves from time to time.

- If every member of your church were just like you, what kind of church would your church be?
- If every member prayed like you pray, what kind of prayer life would your church know?
- If every member served as you serve, what kind of ministry would your church have to hurting and broken people?
- If every member worshipped as you worship, what would the dynamic of your church's worship look like and feel like?
- If every member witnessed, invited, and encouraged others to come just like you witness, invite, and encourage others to come, what would the outreach of your church look like?
- Lastly, if every church member gave as you give, would your church have buildings to worship and serve our God?

Now, I know that asking people about money is a very touchy thing. When you get close to people's money, people get nervous! But the fact is that every follower of Christ has a duty before God… and accountability to one another to be a part of what He is doing in His Church.

And with this accountability comes a commitment of our finances to God. In Nehemiah 10:35, the people of Israel said, "We obligate ourselves to bring the firstfruits of our ground and the firstfruits of all fruit of every tree, year by year, to the house of the LORD."

The Israelites were committing to give God the very best… something we call "sacrifice."

So I want to ask you today, are you giving God the "firstfruits" of everything you have? Are you giving to His Church like He would have you to? Because it takes your sacrifice and stewardship to help the Church successfully and effectively reach others for Christ!

SACRIFICE AND STEWARDSHIP ARE MARKS OF TRULY FOLLOWING JESUS CHRIST.

Day 15

Your word is a lamp to my feet and a light to my path.

—Psalm 119:105

In Psalm 16:11, the psalmist says, "You make known to me the path of life; in your presence there is fullness of joy; at your right hand are pleasures forevermore."

When you and I get in the presence of God... when we open God's Word and let it speak to our hearts... when we gather as the people of God and He begins to revive our spirit and He begins moving through the proclamation and the revelation of His Word... then the joy that Jesus gives fills our lives.

God's Word is an amazing gift that He has given to each of us. Yet so many times, we don't study, read, meditate, and live out God's Word like we should. The Bible is the most important tool a believer can have on this earth and it serves specific and strategic purposes in every believer's life.

God's Word offers us spiritual communion with God. When we study the Word of God, we get to know God's character. It's not just an ancient book, irrelevant to today's culture. God's Word is alive and it is there to change your life!

Maybe today you'd admit that you're struggling with sin... that you're about ready to give in to temptation. If so, turn to God's Word. Read it... meditate on it... pray about the verses you read, and strive to live it out day by day.

FAITHFULLY GET INTO GOD'S WORD AND YOUR LIFE WILL NEVER BE THE SAME!

Day 16

"Go therefore and make disciples of all nations, baptizing them in the name of the Father and of the Son and of the Holy Spirit, teaching them to observe all that I have commanded you."
—Matthew 28:19-20

In order to take the gospel to the world, we must first remember several important factors about it.

One, the gospel is universal in its application. It is for all people, all cultures and all countries. All people need to know Jesus as Savior. In Luke 18:19, Jesus states, "Why do you call me good? No one is good except God alone." As a result, there is no difference between the believer and non-believer. We all have a universal problem and that problem is the problem of sin. And the solution is Jesus.

Secondly, the gospel is universal in its invitation. John 3:16 says that whoever believes in Jesus should not perish but have eternal life. I believe that "whoever" or "whosoever" must be one of the favorite words of God. And the gospel is therefore universal because all people have the same need and all people need the same Savior. We've sung it since we were little children, "Red and yellow, black and white, they are precious in His sight." And the "whoever" is the invitation of the Church and the invitation of Christ.

Finally, the gospel is universal in its proclamation. We must go and be messengers. In Acts 1, verse 8, Jesus commands His apostles that they will be His witnesses, "…in Jerusalem and in all Judea and Samaria, and to the end of the earth." You may ask, "What can I do about world missions?" Get available, get usable, and get expendable. The gospel cannot go from land to land until it goes from life to life and lip to lip. And you're not only to go into the world at large, but you are to go to the world nearby, and across the street with the message of Jesus Christ.

STEP INTO YOUR OWN MISSION FIELD AND SHARE THE STORY OF GOD'S WONDERFUL PLAN OF SALVATION.

Day 17

Walk in wisdom toward outsiders, making the best use of the time. Let your speech always be gracious, seasoned with salt, so that you may know how you ought to answer each person.

—Colossians 4:5-7

God has called every Christian to share Jesus…and you and I must embrace that responsibility to personally share the Good News one-on-one with our friends and family members who don't know Him.

But the sad and tragic fact is that most Christians never lead another soul to Christ. For instance, when was the last time you individually shared Christ with someone else? How many people are going to be in heaven because you cared and because you dared to share the gospel?

Let's take a look at Psalm 126, verses 5 and 6: "Those who sow in tears shall reap with shouts of joy! He who goes out weeping, bearing the seed for sowing, shall come h)me with shouts of joy, bringing his sheaves with him."

Let me break this down into three parts for you: task, tears, and treasure. Our task is bringing people to Jesus. The psalmist is saying in verse 5 that sharing Jesus Christ is like planting a crop. And the only way to plant this crop is by sharing Christ personally with someone else. This is our task; this is our priority as followers of Jesus.

Next is our tears. Great men of God have always wept tears over the "lostness" of people. In Romans 9:2-4, Paul says "I have great sorrow and unceasing anguish in my heart…for the sake of my brothers, my kinsmen according to the flesh. They are Israelites, and to them belong the adoption, the glory, the covenants, the giving of the law, the worship, and the promises." What drove Paul was his deep burden because people are lost without Jesus Christ. This burden should continue to drive us today. And our concern for those lost around us should drive us to tears.

Then, finally, there's our treasure, for it says in Psalm 126:6, "He who goes out weeping, bearing seed for sowing, shall come home with shouts of joy, bringing his sheaves with him." The seed is the Word of God, and if we're faithful to take the Word of God to people, it's the Spirit's responsibility to drive it home to their hearts. We don't win people to Christ by our theories, or opinions. We bring people to Jesus Christ by the seed of the Word of God.

I pray you will care enough…to dare to share the gospel with someone you know today!

BE COURAGEOUS ENOUGH TO SHARE THE GOSPEL WITH SOMEONE IN YOUR LIFE TODAY!

Day 18

And he said to them, "Go into all the world and proclaim the gospel to the whole creation."

—Mark 16:15

People need the Lord. But they will never know the Lord unless you and I are willing to share Jesus with our world. It's what God has called every one of us to do.

Now in Luke 14, beginning in verse 15, Jesus tells a story, or parable, of a beautiful banquet that has been prepared. But when the master of the house says, "Invite the guests," all the guests begin to make excuses. They all reject the master's invitation. So the master says, "Fine, go tell the blind, the lame, the maimed; go into the highways and hedges, go into the streets, the lanes, the back alleys and invite all of those folks to come in."

As we learned today, this parable gives us important insight into our responsibility to share the gospel. First, verse 21 shows who is to go and extend the invitation to the banquet—the servants. If we are servants of the Lord Jesus Christ, it's our job to share Christ… to issue the invitation to his "banquet" of salvation.

Next, it shows how we are to go. Verse 22 says, "And the servant said, 'Sir, what you commanded has been done, and still there is room.' And the master said to the servant, 'Go out to the highways and hedges and compel people to come in.'" We're to go and share the gospel in every form and every fashion with every kind of method that we can use that honors God!

Third, we are shown who we are to go to. Verse 21 again shows us that we're to go and reach the poor—the physically poor, materially poor, spiritually poor. All are poor without the Lord Jesus Christ.

And when are we to go? Again, verse 21 says we're to go quickly. There's never been an opportunity better than right now.

Finally, we are told in verse 23, why are we to go…"That my house may be filled." Jesus is talking about His heavenly house, and He is looking for us to reach more and more people who need to hear the invitation of the Lord Jesus Christ to spend eternity with Him.

God has prepared the banquet of salvation. Are you willing to be His servant… going to a spiritually hungry world and extending His invitation to come and dine with Him for eternity? I hope your answer is YES!

MAKE IT YOUR PRIORITY TO ANSWER CHRIST'S CALL TO SHARE THE GOSPEL.

Day 19

For I am not ashamed of the gospel, for it is the power of God for salvation to everyone who believes, to the Jew first and also to the Greek.

—Romans 1:16

I want to share with you one of the most important things a believer in Jesus Christ can do... sharing your faith with someone else. Many of us don't know how to do that, but I want you to take a pencil and a piece of paper and simply write down A, B, C, D.

It starts with A... there's something to admit. Romans 3:23 says that, "All have sinned and fall short of the glory of God." And Romans 6:23 tell us, "The wages of sin is death." Before someone can be saved, they have to recognize that they're lost. They have to understand their condition without God.

Then there's B... something to believe. And what people need to believe if they're going to be saved is that Jesus is Lord. In Acts 16:31 Paul made it clear, "Believe on the Lord Jesus Christ and you will be saved." To believe in Jesus means to trust Him, to really give your life to Him.

Then there's C... something to consider. You need to consider what it means to give your life to Christ. As Paul says in Ephesians 4:21-24, "You were taught in him, to put off your old self, which belongs to your former manner of life and is corrupt through deceitful desires, and to put on the new self, created to be like God in true righteousness and holiness." This means a new way of living... and it means repenting and turning from those things that bury you spiritually.

Then there's D... something to do. And that something is to receive Jesus as your Lord and Savior. John 1:12 says, "To all who believed in his name, he gave the right to become children of God."

Admit, believe, consider, and do. You can share that little message, as I have, in just a few minutes. But it is a message that will change a person's life for eternity!

ADMIT, BELIEVE, CONSIDER, AND DO... AN EASY TO REMEMBER, LIFESAVING MESSAGE THAT CAN BRING OTHERS TO CHRIST.

Day 20

"But for this purpose I have raised you up, to show you my power, so that my name may be proclaimed in all the earth."

—Exodus 9:16

If you look at Acts 1, verse 8, Jesus is about to ascend into heaven after His resurrection. And He says to His disciples, "But you shall be witnesses unto Me after the Holy Spirit is come upon you. And you shall be witnesses in Jerusalem, Judea, Samaria, and to the uttermost parts of the earth."

Christ made it clear that God's plan for every Christian is a life of faithfulness to be a witness for Him. Unfortunately, most of us have this fear... or maybe reluctance... to share our faith. So how do we overcome these obstacles?

I believe there are two simple principles that will help you be the witness God desires you to be.

First, recognize the adequacy of Jesus Christ in you through His Holy Spirit. Jesus said, "You shall be my witnesses when the Holy Spirit is come upon you." See, the work of the Holy Spirit in our lives makes us more than adequate for everything we need as a witness. And when we recognize who we are in Christ, we overcome our reluctance to share our faith.

Second, you and I must also develop certain skills that will help us share our faith. Now God can use even the most limited witness, but you and I should want to fully develop our evangelism skills as followers of Jesus Christ. And as you learn the skills to share your faith with others, God will use you under any circumstances, wherever you are.

MAKE YOURSELF AVAILABLE TO SHARE THE GOOD NEWS OF JESUS CHRIST TO THOSE AROUND YOU.

Day 21

By faith Abraham obeyed when he was called to go out to a place that he was to receive as an inheritance. And he went out, not knowing where he was going.

—Hebrews 11:8

To this day, it amazes me that the God of the universe would use people…people like you and me…to accomplish great and mighty things for Him! I mean, I've been walking with the Lord for most of my life, and I still can't get over it!

God… uses… people. And He wants to use you!

"But, Pastor," you say, "you don't know my past. You don't know what I struggle with. How can God ever use someone like me?"

I'm here to tell you today that God can and will use you. How do I know? Because His Word is full of men and women who would have never thought God would use them! These are people like Noah. When God called him to build the ark, we might have heard him say, "Do what, God? Build an ark? That's impossible!"

Or what about Nehemiah? When the call of God came upon his life, he might have said something like, "Wait a minute, God. I'm comfortable here in Persia. I've got a great job. Why would you want someone like me to give up everything to rebuild a wall?"

Or think about Paul. When Jesus called him, we might have heard him say, "Wait a minute, Lord, I'm your chosen instrument? Do you know my past? Have you seen what I've done?"

Yet God called each of these men to do great things for Him! And not only did He call them, but God equipped them to do what He had called them to do.

And you know what? God can do the same for you! Philippians 2:13 says, "It is God who works in you, both to will and to work for his good pleasure."

So let me ask you, are you willing to let God use you? If so, I urge you to echo the words of Isaiah, who said to God, "Here am I! Send me"!

GOD HAS CALLED YOU AND WILL EQUIP YOU TO DO GREAT THINGS.

Day 22

"You are the light of the world. A city set on a hill cannot be hidden. Nor do people light a lamp and put it under a basket, but on a stand, and it gives light to all in the house. In the same way, let your light shine before others, so that they may see your good works and give glory to your Father who is in heaven."

—Matthew 5:14-16

Becoming a global Christian starts with a personal commitment. Each of us… every Bible-believing man, woman, and young person… needs to make and take our witness for Jesus Christ personally.

Acts 1:8 says, "'But you will receive power when the Holy Spirit has come upon you, and you will be my witnesses in Jerusalem and in all Judea and Samaria, and to the end of the earth.'"

If you want to live under the lordship of Christ… if you want to be an obedient, Spirit-filled Christian… then you must take seriously the commandment of Christ to be a personal witness for Him.

Now, everyone's a witness, of course. You're either a good witness or a bad witness. You're either witnessing positively for Christ or negatively for Christ. But we're all witnesses for Him!

But we're not only to witness with our lives… we're to witness with our lips. If we want to live a significant life and get beyond ourselves and our own little world, we will do what Jesus said to do… and that is to be salt and light.

Salt penetrates and light illuminates. And every one of us can be salt and every one of us can be light right where we live. "Well," you say, "I don't really have a witness. I really don't have that great of a testimony."

Christian, it doesn't matter how small you think your life is. You can penetrate the darkness for Jesus Christ. And besides that, you're called to do it! So make that a priority today!

MAKE AND TAKE YOUR WITNESS FOR JESUS PERSONALLY SO YOU CAN BE THE GLOBAL CHRISTIAN GOD HAS CALLED YOU TO BE.

Day 23

"For I know the plans I have for you, declares the LORD, plans for welfare and not for evil, to give you a future and a hope."
—Jeremiah 29:11

D Elton Trueblood, the noted 20th century American Quaker and theologian, wrote, "Faith is not belief without proof, but trust without reservation." Let me say that again: "Faith is not belief without proof, but trust without reservation."

For you and for me, there are times when we can't fully understand all that's going on in our lives. There are things that don't make sense to us. There are painful times that make us question God's plan for us.

But it is in those times that we must fully trust God. To have a faith that is without reservation!

And how do you do that? By understanding the truth of Romans 8:28-29: "And we know that for those who love God all things work together for good, for those who are called according to his purpose. For those whom he foreknew he also predestined to be conformed to the image of his Son, in order that he might be the firstborn among many brothers."

We get the word *synergy* from the word *work* in this passage. God is working synergistically in your life… taking the forces and circumstances and situations of your life and working them all together for your good. That's why you can fully trust God… even when things are not going as you had hoped.

Yes, God does have an incredible plan for your life… and that plan is indeed your purpose.

TRUST GOD TO WORK EVERYTHING IN YOUR LIFE TOGETHER FOR YOUR GOOD.

O death, where is your victory? O death, where is your sting? The
sting of death is sin, and the power of sin is the law. But thanks be
to God, who gives us the victory through our Lord Jesus Christ.
— **1 Corinthians 15:55-57**

As followers of Christ, you and I are to keep ourselves under the umbrella of God's protection and provision every day of our lives. But how do you do that?

One way is by living for eternity. Or, as Steven R. Covey says, "Begin with the end in mind." That's how you and I are to live our lives as followers of Christ!

When everything around you is crumbling... when you're facing danger and difficulties and deception of all kinds... your outlook on life will be determined by your "up-look."

And if your up-look is to love Christ's return and to long for His appearing knowing that at any moment He could come for you... and that He has defeated death... then you are living in light of eternity and abiding in His love.

In 2 Timothy 4:8, the apostle Paul said this: "There is laid up for me the crown of righteousness, which the Lord, the righteous judge, will award to me on that Day, and not only to me but also to all who have loved his appearing."

When we are daily embracing our future with Him, that keeps us in the love of God!

EMBRACE GOD'S LOVE FOR YOU BY REALIZING THAT
YOUR ETERNITY IS SECURE IN HIM.

Day 25

"You shall love the Lord your God with all your heart and with all your soul and with all your mind."

—Matthew 22:37

Today is a good day for you to have a spiritual DTR—Defining The Relationship—talk with Christ. In fact, I believe every person who calls themselves a Christian should take stock and evaluate where they are with Jesus Christ on a regular basis.

Jesus is constantly calling us to commitment... to define our relationship with Him. He wants to know, as He often said, "Are you with Me or are you against Me? Are we really a thing or do you just date Me on Sundays? Am I just a friend or do we really have something that's real... something that's relational... something that's forever?"

So many people treat God as though He is a distant relative rather than a vital part of life. But Jesus refuses to let us get away with that in our relationship with Him!

You know, when people in the Bible came face to face with Jesus, they didn't walk away the same people. They were dramatically transformed... for good or for bad. Some received Him... some rejected Him... but everyone who came in contact with Christ was powerfully impacted by Him.

That rich young ruler had a DTR talk with Jesus when Jesus called him to follow Him fully. But that man went away sorrowfully... with a storm in his soul, rejecting Christ... because he couldn't handle the commitment.

So what about you? Is it time that you had a DTR talk with Jesus Christ?

Just like Jesus asked the disciples after He fed the multitudes in John chapter 6, He's asking you, "Are you with Me? Are you willing to walk with Me every day of the week... not just on Sundays?" My prayer is that your answer will be a resounding, "YES!"

DEFINE YOUR RELATIONSHIP WITH JESUS CHRIST TODAY BY COMMITTING YOUR LOVE AND YOUR LIFE FULLY TO HIM.

Day 26

Therefore, if anyone is in Christ, he is a new creation. The old has passed away; behold, the new has come.

—2 Corinthians 5:17

If you walk into any bookstore today, you'll find shelves and shelves of self-improvement books... books about how to change and improve your life.

So many of us fall into the trap of thinking that changing our jobs, changing our appearance, or changing our environment will make us happy. But it just isn't true!

All of these external changes may temporarily improve your life... they may better your life for a time... but none of them can change your life. You may move around. You may change cars. You may even change jobs. But you know what? Wherever you go, it's the same old you, right?

It's not that your circumstances or your surroundings need to change. It's your heart that needs to change. It's your heart that needs a new birth.

The Bible is pretty clear when it talks about our hearts. In Jeremiah 17:9, it says, "The heart is deceitful above all things, and desperately sick." The heart, according to the Bible, is not good!

Which means your heart needs a spiritual transformation. I'm not talking about a resolution... promising to be better, do better, or live better. I'm talking about a revolution!

It's something so radical, so dramatic, that it's like beginning life all over again! It's a new beginning! It's an inward change! Your heart undergoes a spiritual transformation when God takes it and transplants it with His love and His heart.

So my challenge to you today is... let God transform your heart. Realize that no external change can truly make you joyful or fulfilled. Only a heart transformed by God will. So let Him create a new beginning in you today!

IF YOU WANT TO REALLY IMPROVE YOUR LIFE... START BY LETTING GOD TRANSFORM YOUR HEART.

Day 27

"And you will feel secure, because there is hope; you will look around and take your rest in security."

—Job 11:18

I want you to think about Jesus' words, "Follow Me," for a moment. They were written in Matthew 9:9 as an imperative... a command.

Jesus didn't ask Matthew to follow Him if he felt like it. No. Jesus said, "Follow Me. Start today... and follow Me for the rest of your life. Don't ever stop following Me."

But I want you to notice too that the words Follow Me actually mean "to walk alongside the road with me." Jesus, the great God of the universe, told Matthew... a social outcast... to walk with Him!

And you know what? Jesus says the same thing to you today! The great God of the universe is saying to you, "Follow Me." Not, "Walk way behind Me," but "walk with Me." God wants to be your friend!

"But Pastor," you say, "there are things in my past... things that God could never forgive me for. It's too late for me."

I'm here to tell you today that Jesus Christ is passing your way. And He's calling your name and saying, "Follow Me"! This is a great deal! You can leave your sin and your past and walk into a brand new life and a brand new future with the Lord.

Take Jesus up on His offer to follow Him today! Your life will never be the same.

CHOOSE TO FOLLOW JESUS CHRIST TODAY AND WALK INTO A NEW LIFE OF JOY, HOPE AND PEACE.

Day 28

There is therefore now no condemnation for those who are in Christ Jesus. For the law of the Spirit of life has set you free in Christ Jesus from the law of sin and death.

—Romans 8:1-2

In the fifth chapter of the Gospel of Mark, we see a remarkable story about a madman who was set free by the Lord Jesus Christ from the evil that tormented his life.

And it's a great reminder of what Jesus has done for you and me! Without Christ, we're madmen who are addicted to sin… broken and bruised… self-destructive… hurting ourselves, our families, and our friends.

But when we ask Jesus into our lives, He doesn't just clean us up. He sets us free and gives us a brand new heart!

We read what God does for our hearts in Ezekiel 11:19-20 when He says, "I will give them one heart, and a new spirit I will put within them. I will remove the heart of stone from their flesh and give them a heart of flesh, that they may walk in my statutes and keep my rules and obey them. And they shall be my people, and I will be their God."

You see, being a Christian isn't about getting cleaned up and then trying to hang on for dear life! No, coming to Christ means you have the power of Jesus to overcome your habits, your addictions, and your sins. You're no longer on your own!

The apostle Paul reinforces this in 2 Corinthians 5:17 when he says, "Therefore, if anyone is in Christ, he is a new creation. The old has passed away; behold, the new has come."

It's not just getting the evil out. It's getting the power of God in! That's what changes you.

When Christ comes to live in you and clothes you with His brand new righteousness… the righteousness of God Himself… then the love of sin is replaced with a love of God! The love of sinful passion and sinful pleasure is replaced with a love for holy purposes and passions that honor God. The old you passes away… and the new you takes its place!

I pray this glorious promise encourages your heart today… and that you will take time to thank God for the incredible and powerful work He has done for you!

**IN JESUS CHRIST, YOU ARE A NEW CREATION…
FREE FROM THE BONDAGE OF SIN.**

Day 29

"But seek first the kingdom of God and his righteousness, and all these things will be added to you."

—Matthew 6:33

In Matthew chapter 15, we see how the Canaanite woman relentlessly pursued Jesus… how her faith in Christ was daring, desperate, and determined.

Which leads me to the question, what does your faith look like today? How relentless are you in your pursuit of Jesus Christ?

Think about that Canaanite woman for a moment. Think about all the obstacles she had to overcome to get to Jesus. She was a social outcast. The religious people of her day had turned their backs on her. More than likely, she was responsible for her daughter being possessed by a demon. And not only that, Jesus didn't respond to her the first time she called out to Him!

Yet she still came to Jesus. She still pursued Him. She still sought His blessing in her life. And as a result, Jesus said, "O woman, great is your faith!" And forever she is an example in God's Word of a person of relentless faith.

Maybe today, your kids have turned their backs on you or on God. Maybe your parents are far from God… with no desire to know Him personally. Maybe your friend doesn't know the Lord and is making all the wrong decisions in life. And maybe Satan is saying to you, "It's a lost cause! Give up! I've got them now!"

Don't you believe a word of it! Keep running relentlessly to Jesus! Keep crying out to the One who said, "Ask, and it will be given to you; seek, and you will find; knock, and it will be opened to you." Literally, keep on asking, keep on seeking, keep on knocking!

Psalm 37:4 says, "Delight yourself in the LORD, and he will give you the desires of your heart." Trust in this promise today… as you relentlessly pursue Jesus Christ!

RELENTLESSLY PURSUE JESUS CHRIST WITH A DARING, DESPERATE AND DETERMINED FAITH.

Day 30

Turn to me and be saved, all the ends of the earth! For I am God, and there is no other.

—Isaiah 45:22

It doesn't matter who you are, what you've done, or where you've been, no one is too far gone for Jesus.

I think that statement's important enough that it's worth repeating: No one is too far gone for Jesus. No one! And there's no better evidence of this than the woman Jesus met at the well.

When Jesus meets this woman she has been used and abused. She has been divorced five times and is living with her boyfriend. She's a mess! At least, she was seen as a mess to the people around her. Even so, Christ reached out to her with the living water of eternal life. And her life was transformed instantly and eternally!

This woman… a woman who had been ravaged by regrets and failures and brokenness… this wasted, burned out woman…was made brand new because of the power of Jesus Christ, which began to change her! She wasn't too far gone for the Lord Jesus!

And the application in your life and my life is clear. No one around us… no matter how wasted, burned out, or strung out they may seem… is too far gone for Jesus Christ.

And you know what else? Neither are you!

In John 4:13, Jesus says, "Everyone who drinks of this water will be thirsty again, but whoever drinks of the water that I will give him will never be thirsty again.The water that I will give him will become in him a spring of water welling up to eternal life."

Jesus says whoever drinks of the water that He gives will have eternal life! Like I said before, it doesn't matter who you are, what you've done, or where you've been. None of us is ever too far gone for Jesus Christ.

It's my prayer that no matter what your past may hold, you will turn to God today!

NO ONE ON THIS EARTH IS TOO FAR GONE FOR JESUS.

Day 31

In the beginning was the Word, and the Word was with God, and the Word was God.

—John 1:1

What does "the Word was God" in today's verse mean? It means "face to face with God." It describes the most intimate kind of communion and union.

Christ left the intimacy and "face-to-faceness" with God... He left the glory of heaven and the majesty of God's presence... and came to earth.

Think about that for a moment. Jesus left heaven to be born in a stable... to walk among men on the dirty streets of Galilee. He lived and died and rose again as a human being.

Isn't it amazing that God would walk among us? But why would He do this?

He did it because He loves you and me... and He wants you and me to come into a personal relationship with Him. But because we are separated from God by our sin, we can't know God or experience God or get near to God in His absolute holiness. So God came near. He came down in the person of Jesus Christ and paid the price for our sin by dying on the cross.

So let me ask you, how have you responded to Jesus Christ in your life?

If you've accepted Him as your personal Lord and Savior, I praise God that you've made the best decision you will ever make. But if you haven't made this decision, what's stopping you from accepting God's free gift of eternal life right now?

If you'd like to know how to accept Christ, call PowerPoint Ministries at 1-800-414-7693. Please contact us today!

GOD CAME TO EARTH IN THE PERSON OF JESUS CHRIST AND PAID THE PRICE FOR OUR SIN BY DYING ON THE CROSS.

Day 32

And from his fullness we have all received, grace upon grace.

—**John 1:16**

As human beings, you and I sin. We mess up. In fact, you've probably already messed up today!

But the Scripture contains an amazing promise for you and me. It's found in today's verse.

Do you know what "grace upon grace" means? It means that as believers, God's grace keeps flowing into our lives like the waves of the sea that just keep coming again and again and again. It's grace upon grace upon grace upon grace upon grace upon grace!

It's not as though we received God's grace five years ago and we're still trying to hang on to that grace. No. We keep receiving grace, grace, grace, grace and more grace… His marvelous grace. We never run out of the grace of God because His grace is infinite!

God gives us His grace the moment we're saved… and He continues to give us His grace each day… for daily strength and endurance to face the trials and temptations of life.

Lamentations 3:21-23 promises us, "The steadfast love of the LORD never ceases; his mercies never come to an end; they are new every morning; great is your faithfulness."

God's grace is new every morning! And it's my prayer today that you'd be encouraged to know you have this daily grace as a follower of Jesus Christ. Walk in this light today… and every day… as you faithfully follow Him!

**GOD GIVES US HIS GRACE TO FACE THE TRIALS
AND TEMPTATIONS WE FACE EACH DAY.**

Day 33

There was a man sent from God, whose name was John. He came as a witness, to bear witness about the light, that all might believe through him. He was not the light, but came to bear witness about the light.

—John 1:6-8

As believers, you and I can learn so much from God's man, John the Baptist.

He was sent from God to introduce Christ to the world. And in just the same way, you and I are to be witnesses... to introduce men, women, boys, and girls to faith in Jesus Christ before He comes again.

Now, a witness is someone who steps aside, someone who gets out of the spotlight, someone who removes themselves from the scene. And a witness for Christ is someone who does nothing but point others to Christ. That's what John the Baptizer did. He was willing for his great life to be eclipsed by the greater life of Christ. He was willing to say, "I'm not the light, but Jesus Christ is the light."

John the Baptist was a passionate and powerful witness for Jesus Christ.

Now let me ask you, are you a passionate and powerful witness for Jesus Christ? If not, why not?

Today, it's my prayer that you would understand God's call on your life to be a witness in this generation for Jesus Christ... like John the Baptist was for his generation.

Live your life in such a way that you point people to the one true Savior... Jesus!

YOU AND I ARE TO INTRODUCE MEN, WOMEN, BOYS, AND GIRLS TO FAITH IN JESUS CHRIST BEFORE HE COMES AGAIN.

Day 34

Jesus said to her, "Everyone who drinks of this water will be thirsty again, but whoever drinks of the water that I will give him will never be thirsty again. The water that I will give him will become in him a spring of water welling up to eternal life."
— **John 4:13-14**

God's primary way of bringing people to Jesus Christ is through people. And if you're going to be an effective witness, you must make sure that you treat people differently… just like Jesus did.

We have to remember that people are at all sorts of different places in their spiritual journey. Some people are seekers, some are skeptics, some are ready, ripe, and responsive. Then there are those who are recalcitrant and rebellious, and it might take a little longer for them to come to Christ!

That's why you and I have to be real and transparent. And we have to build bridges into people's lives. Just like Jesus did!

A good example is how Jesus spoke to the woman at the well (see John 4). She was a Samaritan, a race of people with whom Jews typically didn't associate. She was an adulteress, a woman whose lifestyle was obviously unholy and unwholesome. Yet Jesus spoke with her and treated her with dignity. He spoke of the source of real satisfaction of the heart that would last forever. And she placed her faith in Christ that day!

We all come to Jesus differently. And if you're going to be effective in your witness for Christ, you must be willing to go out of your way to meet people where they are. Just like Jesus did!

So let me ask you, are you waiting for that golden opportunity to share your story of grace with someone? Are you waiting for someone to ask you about Christ simply because of the way you live?

While this does happen every now and then, more often people meet Christ because someone like you got out of their comfort zone… took the initiative… and struck up a conversation with them. Someone like you took the time to ask someone else how they were really doing… offered a word of biblical encouragement… or simply just showed that they cared.

It's my prayer that you will meet people where they are today… just like Jesus did!

IF YOU'RE GOING TO BE EFFECTIVE IN YOUR WITNESS FOR CHRIST, YOU MUST BE WILLING TO GO OUT OF YOUR WAY TO MEET PEOPLE WHERE THEY ARE.

Day 35

We are afflicted in every way, but not crushed; perplexed, but not driven to despair; persecuted, but not forsaken; struck down, but not destroyed.

—2 Corinthians 4:8-9

As a follower of the Lord Jesus Christ, I can say with integrity that every day with Him has been sweeter than the day before... just as the old hymn says.

Now, when I say that, please listen to what I'm not saying. I'm not saying that my life hasn't had its share of valleys. I'm not saying that I haven't experienced times of grief, illness, distress, or stress. I'm not saying that!

What I am saying is that I may have been afflicted in every way, but I've never been crushed. I may have been perplexed, but I've never been driven to despair. I may have been persecuted, but I've never been forsaken. I may have been struck down, but I've never been destroyed.

And you know why I can say this? Because of the work of Jesus Christ in my life. He's never let me be crushed. He's never let me be driven to despair. He's never forsaken me. And He's never let me be destroyed!

But perhaps today you'd say, "Pastor Graham, that's great for you, but you don't know what I've been through. You don't know how hard my life has been. You don't know how many of my prayers have gone unanswered. You don't know how disappointed I am in God."

You know, I don't know. But you know what I do know? That we serve a God who is bigger than whatever it is you're holding onto. He's bigger than your past sins... your past hurts. And He's even bigger than your disappointments.

But more than that, He sympathizes with you... right where you are. The writer of Hebrews tells us, "For we do not have a high priest who is unable to sympathize with our weaknesses, but one who in every respect has been tempted as we are, yet without sin. Let us then with confidence draw near to the throne of grace, that we may receive mercy and find grace to help in time of need" (Heb. 4:15).

Today... if your life has bottomed out... listen to me: The love and mercy of Christ reaches deeper than where you are right now. So draw near to His throne of grace... so that you can receive His mercy to help you in your time of need!

GOD IS BIGGER THAN YOUR SINS, YOUR HURTS, AND YOUR DISAPPOINTMENTS.

Day 36

Or do you not know that your body is a temple of the Holy Spirit within you, whom you have from God? You are not your own, for you were bought with a price. So glorify God in your body.

—1 Corinthians 6:19-20

Are you honest with God? I mean, judgment-day-honest with God?

Think about it. We all sin. But are you actively dealing with the sins in your life that only you and God know about? Are you getting real with God by admitting your weaknesses… your compulsive thoughts or worries… or your past secrets?

The great need is for the Church of Jesus Christ to be revived. And the only way that will happen is when individual men and women of God get real, admit their junk, and ask God for a spiritual breakthrough where there has been a spiritual breakdown.

The only way for God's people… you and me…to change the world is for us to make sure our lives are real…honest… and genuine. And through the power of God living in and through us, we can live that kind of life.

It's an amazing thought that as believers in Jesus Christ, God dwells in us through His Holy Spirit… as we see in today's verse. If you're a follower of Christ, God lives in you. He lives in me. And through that indwelling power you can get beyond your compulsive thoughts… your worries… and the bondage of your past secrets.

In the power of the Holy Spirit, get real with God today. And ask God for that spiritual breakthrough where there has only been spiritual breakdown.

I pray you will get honest with God today… and determine to glorify Him in your life today… and every day!

ASK GOD FOR A SPIRITUAL BREAKTHROUGH IN YOUR LIFE WHERE THERE HAS BEEN SPIRITUAL BREAKDOWN.

Day 37

Now there was a man of the Pharisees named Nicodemus, a ruler of the Jews. This man came to Jesus by night and said to him, "Rabbi, we know that you are a teacher come from God, for no one can do these signs that you do unless God is with him." Jesus answered him, "Truly, truly, I say to you, unless one is born again he cannot see the kingdom of God."

—John 3:1-3

Just like Nicodemus, hearing that you have to be born again to have eternal life may be startling to you.

You may think of yourself as religious, you may go to church, you may live a good and respectable life. You may even see yourself as a good person... an intelligent person. But I say to you with the words of Christ, "unless one is born again he cannot see the kingdom of God."

Nicodemus' greatest need was to see his need for Christ. Which is the same need for every human being on the face of this earth! Including you. But as long as you're chasing something, you will never get to the bottom line of your real need for God.

The world offers so many things that seem like they will satisfy... so we chase after those things thinking the yearning in our hearts will be fulfilled. It might be riches... or getting married...or having children... or a successful career. But even when you achieve these things... in your heart there's still something missing, there's still a nagging emptiness.

Proverbs 27:20 tells us, "Never satisfied are the eyes of man." The heart of man has an insatiable appetite that is never satisfied by the things we can do, gain, or accomplish.

That great and aching need of the human heart was what Jesus was talking to Nicodemus about. And God is talking to you today about that same need... your need for a supernatural birth from above... a spiritual birth that is called salvation in Jesus Christ.

THE HEART OF MAN HAS AN INSATIABLE APPETITE THAT IS NEVER SATISFIED BY THE THINGS WE CAN DO, GAIN, OR ACCOMPLISH.

Day 38

And he said to them, "Follow me, and I will make you fishers of men."

—Matthew 4:19

There are many, many reasons why people reject Jesus Christ. And one of the most popular excuses people give for rejecting Him is because of hypocrisy in the Church.

Yes, there are hypocrites in the Church of Jesus Christ. Think about it. Jesus had 12 disciples and one of them was even a hypocrite! So yes, there are—unfortunately—people who say they are Christians, and yet don't live like Christians.

But did you ever consider that the devil may put a hypocrite in your path just to keep you from Jesus Christ? The devil can do that. Let me help you understand why.

Have you ever considered that when people want to counterfeit something, they don't counterfeit gum wrappers? They counterfeit $20 bills, $100 bills... something that's real! So for people to counterfeit the Christian faith... and for the devil to put those counterfeits in your path... only indicates that Christianity is real!

Again, the fact that there are hypocrites in the Church doesn't lessen the credibility of the Christian faith. You need to make a distinction between sin and hypocrisy. All Christians sin.

But not all sinful Christians are hypocrites. Just because a Christian may sin doesn't mean that Christianity is phony. And... look again at today's verse. Jesus said, "Follow me." He didn't say, "Follow that person" or "Follow that church." He said, "Follow me"!

Jesus Christ isn't a hypocrite. When you follow Jesus Christ, you're following Someone who always keeps His promises... and you're following Someone who never sinned.

So Christianity doesn't stand or fall by the way a so-called Christian may act. Christian faith is in Jesus Christ! I hope this encourages you in your faith today.

THE FACT THAT THERE ARE HYPOCRITES IN THE CHURCH DOESN'T LESSEN THE CREDIBILITY OF THE CHRISTIAN FAITH.

Day 39

"Go therefore and make disciples of all nations, baptizing them in the name of the Father and of the Son and of the Holy Spirit."

—Matthew 28:19

Baptism should be important to followers of the Lord Jesus Christ because it was important to Him, plain and simple!

Not only was Jesus baptized at the outset of His ministry, He concluded His ministry with baptism. So don't you think we should make it a priority too? I think so!

If you are a believer in Jesus Christ, and you have never been baptized, then I want to challenge you today to do so. Let me share with you why.

First, baptism is a sign of your commitment to Jesus Christ. If you are truly committed to Jesus, then you need to make a public statement of that commitment, much like a wedding ring is a public expression of the commitment of a husband or wife.

Second, baptism is a symbol of your salvation. You need to publicly symbolize the sacrifice of Christ on your behalf and your submission to Him in your life.

Third, baptism is a sign of obedience. While there are many things you and I cannot do like Jesus Christ did, baptism is one thing that we can do exactly like He did! And when you are baptized, you are publicly declaring your obedience to Him.

Finally, baptism is a statement of your faith. When you're baptized, you're declaring to the world that you believe and belong to Jesus Christ. You are saying to everyone that you love Christ and want to follow Him with your whole heart.

Now, understand that being baptized doesn't save you. But I would encourage you today… if you're a believer and you've never been baptized… to prayerfully consider following Christ in this step of obedience. Through it, you will give a beautiful testimony of your faith in Him.

JESUS MADE BAPTISM A PRIORITY… AND SO SHOULD WE!

Jesus said to her, "Everyone who drinks of this water will be thirsty again, but whoever drinks of the water that I will give him will never be thirsty again. The water that I will give him will become in him a spring of water welling up to eternal life."

—John 4:13-14

What would it take to make you genuinely happy? What would it take to really satisfy you?

Would it be more money, more pleasure, greater success, better relationships, or a better physique? What would it take?

Unfortunately, the world screams that these are the things that will bring you ultimate satisfaction. And it's so easy to buy into the notion that these things will truly satisfy.

But take another look at today's verse. Jesus told the woman at the well that the things of this life won't ever really satisfy us… only He will.

So many people today chase the dream of personal achievement… and find that it doesn't really satisfy. Others think, "I'll be happy if I can just find Mr. Right," or "I'll be fulfilled if I can just find Mrs. Right." But even the best man or the best woman can't satisfy the deepest longings of the human heart!

I can guarantee you that nothing… no human relationship… no job promotion… no amount of money in your bank account… will satisfy you like Jesus can.

If you've lost sight of this fact, I encourage you to ask God to help you realign your priorities today!

**NOTHING IN LIFE WILL TRULY SATISFY YOU
EXCEPT JESUS CHRIST.**

Day 41

"Look, I tell you, lift up your eyes, and see that the fields are white for harvest."

—John 4:35

If you are a follower of Christ... if you claim the Lord Jesus as your personal Lord and Savior... you are called to share your faith with others.

Yet, if you find sharing your faith difficult, I want to offer you a word of encouragement today: In spite of your weaknesses, in spite of your past mistakes or struggles, you can be an effective and successful witness for the Lord Jesus Christ. You can share your faith!

First, ask God to give you a passion for people. That's where it all begins! Sharing your faith isn't so much a program or technique as it is a passion of the heart. So ask God to give you a burden... a desire... a passion... to talk to your friends and family about Jesus.

Second, be authentic. Most people can identify with the ordinary, real experiences you've had in your life. So don't be afraid to let people know how God is working in those ordinary, everyday experiences! Remember... people aren't looking for perfection. They're looking for someone who's real.

Third, love people unconditionally. This is a hard one! But this is what Jesus did... and it's what you and I are to do as well. No matter how people may mistreat or misuse you.

Finally, share Jesus now! This is why Jesus says in today's verse, "Lift up your eyes, and see that the fields are white for harvest." It's the responsibility of every Christian to introduce as many people as possible to Jesus. Today! Right now!

It's my prayer that you will get out of your comfort zone this week... and begin sharing your story of grace with those who need to hear it!

SHARING YOUR FAITH ISN'T SO MUCH A PROGRAM OR TECHNIQUE AS IT IS A PASSION OF THE HEART.

Day 42

So Jesus said to him, "Unless you see signs and wonders you will not believe."

—**John 4:48**

Y ou know, it's funny. Human nature really hasn't changed much since Jesus walked the earth 2,000 years ago.

Back then, people wanted a sign... a miracle... from Jesus. They wanted something tangible, something they could see, to believe in Him. And today, people are the same way! So many men and women say they would believe in Christ if only He would show Himself physically... if only He would come through miraculously in their lives.

But when Jesus said, "Unless you see signs and wonders you will not believe," He was saying, "Don't wait for a sign to believe and trust in Me. Don't wait on some miracle. Don't demand that I perform for you in order for you to believe in Me."

You may be struggling to trust Christ today in your life. While I don't know what you may be facing, I want to challenge you to trust Him even if you can't see Him in your circumstances right now.

Jesus had no confidence in the kind of faith that demands sight. Because faith that demands sight is not real faith! It's just doubt expecting evidence!

I know it's hard to come to grips with this fact, but oftentimes, you just can't figure God out. There will be times when you cannot see in the dark. There will be times when you just have to keep clinging, singing, and bringing your heart to God by faith. And this may be that kind of time in your life.

Trust me, I know it's hard. But Jesus wants to get you to that place in your life where it's not about the miracle... but all about Him. Where you are willing to trust Him, regardless of the outcome.

So, if you find yourself in a place today where you need a miracle, look to Jesus. As the writer of Hebrews says, "Let us run with endurance the race that is set before us, looking to Jesus, the founder and perfecter of our faith, who for the joy that was set before him endured the cross, despising the shame, and is seated at the right hand of the throne of God. Consider him who endured from sinners such hostility against himself, so that you may not grow weary or fainthearted" (Heb. 12:2-3).

It's my prayer that this encourages you to trust Jesus today, no matter what you face. Because He is fully trustworthy!

TRUST CHRIST TODAY... EVEN IF YOU CAN'T SEE HIM IN YOUR CIRCUMSTANCES.

Day 43

Jesus looked at them and said, "With man it is impossible, but not with God. For all things are possible with God."
— **Mark 10:27**

A re you facing an impossible situation in your life right now?

Maybe your relationship with your spouse or child seems like it's damaged beyond repair. Or perhaps you feel like your financial situation will never recover. Or maybe you're questioning whether your health will ever be the same as it once was.

Whatever you may be going through today, let me assure you of this: God delights in using impossible situations like yours to display His power and glory.

Today… if you're in a dead-end, nowhere-to-run, hopeless, impossible, helpless situation… you're a prime candidate for the power of God to move in your life. Don't say, "My life, my home, my family, my future is impossible," because as Jesus says in today's verse, "All things are possible with God."

Remember the man who Jesus healed at the pool in Bethesda? He had been paralyzed for 38 years! Nothing anyone had done in all that time had helped this poor, crippled man. Can you imagine the feelings of despair and hopelessness that this man must have struggled with all that time?

Yet in Jesus' divine and perfect plan, He chose to do something powerful and wonderful in this man's life. And He can do the same in yours!

In the midst of hopeless situations, there's nothing that would please the evil one more than for you to throw up your hands in despair… for you to say, "That's it, I quit!" But remember what Galatians 6:9 says: "Let us not grow weary of doing good, for in due season we will reap, if we do not give up."

No matter what you may be going through today, please don't grow weary. Please don't give up. Wait on the Lord… and remember that all things… even the most hopeless things… are possible with God!

**IF YOU'RE IN A HOPELESS SITUATION TODAY,
YOU'RE A PRIME CANDIDATE FOR THE POWER OF GOD
TO MOVE IN YOUR LIFE!**

Day 44

Therefore, if anyone is in Christ, he is a new creation. The old has passed away; behold, the new has come. **—2 Corinthians 5:17**

Did you know that each and every one of us will give an account of our lives to a holy God one day? It's true. That's why it's worth thinking about the kind of life you're leading.

Accountability and judgment play a vital role in every aspect of life. Every employee is evaluated on their job performance. Sports teams are judged on their ability and performance. The leaders of our government are held accountable by the people who elected them. And the same is true for you as a Christian!

If you're a believer, you've been given new life in Christ. Which means that you will be evaluated and rewarded according to what you've done with the life God has given you.

Does this mean you could lose your salvation as a result of what you do or don't do after you accept Christ as your personal Lord and Savior? Absolutely not. Because that was settled at the cross.

What it does mean, however, is that what you do with the life God's given you on earth will have repercussions for eternity in heaven. So let me ask you today, what are you doing with your life for Jesus? Are you just living for the pleasures of the day or are you living for Him?

What are you doing with the spiritual gifts Christ has put in your heart by the Holy Spirit? Are you serving Christ with those gifts?

What about the talents that God has uniquely given to you? Are you using those to bring Him glory and extend His kingdom… or are you letting them go to waste?

Today, ask God to help you honestly evaluate how well you're utilizing the life He has given you. If you can say that you're living for His glory, praise God. But if you're not, it's my prayer that you will begin… today… to use your unique set of gifts and talents to bring honor and glory to the Lord Jesus Christ.

WHAT YOU DO WITH THE LIFE GOD'S GIVEN YOU ON EARTH WILL HAVE REPERCUSSIONS FOR ETERNITY IN HEAVEN.

Day 45

Jesus said to him, "I am the way, and the truth, and the life. No one comes to the Father except through me."

—John 14:6

At one point or another, every person has to come to grips with the question, "Who is Jesus Christ?" And today I want to help you answer that question in your own heart and life.

It's true that the miracles of Jesus identify Him as God. They give Him credibility that He was who He said He was. But Jesus didn't perform them as publicity stunts. He performed them to show you and me something about who He was and what His supernatural power can accomplish in our lives.

Maybe today, you can relate to the disappointment of the couple in the Bible who ran out of wine at the wedding in Canaan (John 2:1-12). By turning water into wine, Jesus was saying to them... and He's saying to you today, "I am the answer for life's disappointments... I can turn your disappointments into joy."

Or perhaps today you're in need... like the thousands of people Jesus fed with two fish and five loaves of bread (John 6:1-15). In feeding them, Jesus showed them... and He's showing you today... that He is the answer to your needs and your desires.

And lastly, maybe today you're going through a dark time of life... and you'd admit that you're fearful of what the future holds. If so, think about when Jesus walked on the water in the middle of the night (John 6:16-21). By doing this, Jesus showed Peter... just like He shows you and me...that He is the answer in the dark times of life.

The point of the miracles of Jesus Christ for you is this: Whatever you're going through today, He is your answer... just as we see in today's verse.

It's my prayer that you will look to Jesus as the answer to whatever you are facing today!

JESUS PERFORMED MIRACLES TO SHOW YOU SOMETHING ABOUT WHO HE IS AND WHAT HIS SUPERNATURAL POWER CAN ACCOMPLISH IN YOUR LIFE.

Day 46

For the moment all discipline seems painful rather than pleasant, but later it yields the peaceful fruit of righteousness to those who have been trained by it.

—Hebrews 12:11

You know how it goes. Just about the time you think you've got it together in life, the wheels start coming off as another challenge comes along. That's just the way life is!

And the Christian life is no different. Just about the time we get comfortable in our Christian lives… just about the time we think we've arrived spiritually… God brings along another test to raise the bar a little bit higher.

Now, believe me, I know… sometimes it feels like all of life is a series of tests. Today, you may even be wondering how much more character-building you can stand! But trust God's heart on this. He tests you because He loves you. He tests you because He wants to stretch your faith and to build you up—not because He wants to beat you down or wear you out.

Think about the process of weight lifting. It's a physiological reality that you have to tear your muscles down in order to build them back up to make them stronger. That's why you're always sore after a workout. And it's the same process in the Christian life!

If you're going through a test today, remember what today's verse says. There are very few things as discouraging in the Christian life as thinking that God is out to get you… that He somehow isn't on your side. Which is exactly what the devil wants you to think when you're going through a test or trial!

Today, I want to encourage you to recognize the lie of Satan that says God is letting you be tested because He doesn't care about you. Then believe the promise that God will use your trials to produce something good in you… if He hasn't done so already.

And finally, claim a verse like James 1:12, which says, "Blessed is the man who remains steadfast under trial, for when he has stood the test he will receive the crown of life, which God has promised to those who love him."

**GOD TESTS YOU BECAUSE HE WANTS
TO STRETCH YOUR FAITH AND BUILD YOU UP—NOT
BECAUSE HE WANTS TO BEAT YOU DOWN OR
WEAR YOU OUT!**

Day 47

Immediately he [Jesus] made the disciples get into the boat and go before him to the other side, while he dismissed the crowds.

—Matthew 14:22

I want you to think about today's verse for a moment. Jesus made the disciples get into that boat, knowing that a storm was coming their way.

Yet Jesus didn't send them into the teeth of a storm to be malicious or mean. He did it to help build the disciples' faith! And by doing this, Jesus also showed that He was in complete control.

You know, outside of salvation itself, the most liberating, life-producing, joy-producing, peace-giving truth is the fact that Jesus Christ is sovereignly in control of your life. This means no matter what storm you're in or what storm you're going to be in (because you'll always be in one of those two places), God has you there for a reason.

So you can give Him thanks… not necessarily for the circumstance or the crisis itself… but for the Christ who reigns and rules in your heart and in your daily experiences. And you can thank God for loving you enough to be willing to send storms into your life to either perfect you or correct you.

There's a song by Babbie Mason that says, "God is too wise to be mistaken, God is too good to be unkind. So when you don't understand, when you don't see His plan, when you can't trace His hand, trust His heart."

The same God who took you into the storm is the same God who will bring you out of it! So trust His heart… and His love for you… today.

OUTSIDE OF SALVATION ITSELF, THE MOST LIBERATING, LIFE-PRODUCING, JOY-PRODUCING, PEACE-GIVING TRUTH IS THE FACT THAT JESUS CHRIST IS SOVEREIGNLY IN CONTROL OF YOUR LIFE.

Day 48

When I saw him [Jesus], I fell at his feet as though dead.

—Revelation 1:17

There are many things we can learn from today's verse, which describes John's initial reaction to seeing Jesus in all His glory.

As husband and father, I've seen a lot of amazing sights over the course of my life. The sight of my bride walking down the aisle... the births of all three of my children. But as great and wonderful as those experiences were, none of them caused me to fall to the ground like a dead man!

Yet when John saw Jesus, it was too much for his mind...too much for his body... to bear. And as a result, he crumbled like a leaf at the feet of Jesus.

Today I want to ask you, what is your initial reaction to the Lord Jesus Christ in your life?

In Galatians 2:20, Paul says, "I have been crucified with Christ. It is no longer I who live, but Christ who lives in me." Is this the cry of your heart today? Because Jesus can't take His rightful place as Lord of your life until you die to yourself... until self is conquered and laid at the feet of Jesus, dead.

Are there areas in your life that you haven't died to... that you haven't truly laid at the feet of Jesus? I would encourage you to pray Psalm 139:23-24 today, "Search me, O God, and know my heart! Try me and know my thoughts! And see if there be any grievous (or wicked) way in me, and lead me in the way everlasting!"

It's my hope that you will begin to truly give up control of every area of your life to Christ today... so He will lead you in the everlasting way.

JESUS CAN'T TAKE HIS RIGHTFUL PLACE AS LORD OF YOUR LIFE UNTIL YOU TRULY DIE TO YOURSELF.

Day 49

"But I have this against you, that you have abandoned the love you had at first. Remember therefore from where you have fallen; repent, and do the works you did at first. If not, I will come to you and remove your lampstand from its place, unless you repent."

—Revelation 2:4-5

I remember the day I got my first car like it was yesterday. Now, that old jalopy wasn't much to look at to some people. But to me, it looked like a brand new Rolls Royce!

What's funny, though, is after a while, that new car feeling just sort of wore off. The more I drove it, the more I got used to it. What was once a new, exciting thing in my life eventually became everyday and ordinary.

And sadly, that's how a lot of Christians view their relationship with Jesus. When they first got saved, man, they were on fire for Christ! Their eyes were wide open, their ears were ready to hear the Word of God, they were excited about their faith! They were in love with the Lord Jesus.

But somehow… over time… that newfound love for Christ wore off. What was once new, exciting, and fresh became old, mundane, and stale. Can you relate?

The fact is Jesus never changes. You and I do… whether it's a result of busyness, distraction, or outright sin in our lives.

But today, I've got some good news for you if you'd admit that your love for Jesus has grown cold: Jesus longs for your fellowship! He wants to spend time with you!

All it takes to revitalize your relationship with Christ is to remember what it was like when you first met the Lord, repent of any of those sins that are keeping you at a distance from Him, and repeat those things that keep you at His feet… things like reading His Word each day and regular prayer.

Today, it's my prayer… if your heart is cold or if you've fallen into a casual, mechanical, comfortable routine in your Christian walk… that you will rekindle the fire and revive your relationship with Jesus Christ. Because He's waiting for you to do it right now! Today!

JESUS LONGS FOR YOUR FELLOWSHIP! HE WANTS TO SPEND TIME WITH YOU!

Day 50

Blessed is the man who remains steadfast under trial, for when he has stood the test he will receive the crown of life, which God has promised to those who love him.

—James 1:12

L ike it or not, suffering is a required course in God's curriculum. He had one Son who was without sin, yet suffered. So why should we live life thinking we should be exempt from suffering? It is impossible to pass through this life as a believer without passing through dark valleys.

Now, those valleys look different for each person and they look different depending on the culture in which we find ourselves. But all Christians will suffer. The question is how do you respond when life gets hard?

Some people… when the heat is on… fold up their tents and go home. They can't take it. It's not what they bargained for… and they turn their backs on God.

Other people… and I pray that you fall into this camp… look at their suffering as a time of learning… as a time of testing and proving of their faith. It's not that these people like to suffer or would choose to suffer… it's just that their peace and contentment in God is disconnected from their circumstances in life.

Today, I pray… no matter where you find yourself in life… that you will remember that Jesus has His eye on the clock and His hand on the thermostat! He won't let you suffer beyond what you can bear.

So cheer up, knowing that He's in control and that He only wants what's ultimately best for you.

JESUS HAS HIS EYE ON THE CLOCK AND HIS HAND ON THE THERMOSTAT! HE WON'T LET YOU SUF-FER BEYOND WHAT YOU CAN BEAR.

Day 51

"Therefore repent. If not, I will come to you soon and war against them with the sword of my mouth. He who has an ear, let him hear what the Spirit says to the churches. To the one who conquers I will give some of the hidden manna, and I will give him a white stone, with a new name written on the stone that no one knows except the one who receives it."

—Revelation 2:16-17

We live in an age of compromise. You see it in every level of government, industry, and unfortunately... you see it in the Church as well.

But today... instead of focusing on the compromise you see in others... I want to ask you... are you a compromising Christian? Are you living a double standard? Are there areas in your life, be it in your marriage... your professional life... or your thought life... where you are compromising?

Maybe you're thinking about cheating on your spouse. Perhaps you've turned a blind eye to something unethical at work. Or maybe you allow yourself the leeway to think lustful or hateful thoughts.

Whatever it is, let me assure you of this: God takes the sin of compromise seriously! Revelation 2:16 says it clearly, "Therefore repent. If not, I will come to you soon and war against them with the sword of my mouth." Jesus is not only saying that He'll deal with any church that compromises with sin... He's saying it to any Christian too... including you and me!

Jesus wants you to stop compromising, admit your sin, and deal with it. He wants you to get right with Him.

And you know what's great about repentance? When we repent... when we genuinely change our mind and attitude about our sin... Jesus says in Revelation 2:17, "To the one who conquers I will give some of the hidden manna...." Jesus says to the one who repents, He will give a taste of heaven!

There is blessing and there is reward when you quit compromising. And it's my prayer that you will ask God to help you see any area of your life where the world has crept in... and that you will turn from your sin to a life of freedom in Christ!

JESUS WANTS YOU TO STOP COMPROMISING, ADMIT YOUR SIN, AND DEAL WITH IT. HE WANTS YOU TO GET RIGHT WITH HIM!

Day 52

Jesus said to her, "Go, call your husband, and come here." The woman answered him, "I have no husband." Jesus said to her, "You are right in saying, 'I have no husband'; for you have had five husbands, and the one you now have is not your husband. What you have said is true."

—**John 4:16-18**

Being intolerant of sin is one of the most practical ways to really love someone… as Jesus shows us many times in the Scripture.

Now, does that mean that we should be intolerant of sinners? Absolutely not! Christ frequently interacted with the worst "sinners" of His day.

But He didn't just interact with those who were caught in the grip of sin. He loved them enough to tell them that they were heading down a dead-end road.

But we live in a culture where anyone who stands for truth is seen as intolerant. People are expected to be tolerant of everything and everyone except those who are willing to stand for what is right!

The fact is, what this world needs… what the Church needs… and what your sphere of influence needs is a Christian who will say, "You know, I'm going to take a stand for the truth of God's Word. I'm going to buck the system of this world and in love, I'm going to call right, right and I'm going to call wrong, wrong."

You know, it doesn't take a thousand people to start a revival. It only takes a few! It only takes a few who will be willing to be used by God to start that fire.

So let me ask you… are you willing to be used by God? Are you willing to take a stand for what's right… even if it comes at great personal cost to you?

God is looking for a few good men and women… a remnant… who are willing to pay the price for Him. It's my prayer that you will be one of those brave men or women who takes a stand for God's truth in the face of our godless culture!

BEING INTOLERANT OF SIN IS ONE OF THE MOST PRACTICAL WAYS TO REALLY LOVE SOMEONE.

Day 53

"Wake up, and strengthen what remains and is about to die, for I have not found your works complete in the sight of my God. Remember, then, what you received and heard. Keep it, and repent. If you will not wake up, I will come like a thief, and you will not know at what hour I will come against you."

—Revelation 3:2-3

Would you describe your faith as supernatural... or superficial? This is a question every child of God needs to ask themselves from time to time.

And today, if you'd admit that your faith is more superficial than supernatural, I want to tell you what Jesus told the church in Sardis in Revelation 3:2-3.

First of all, Jesus says to wake up. Come face to face with your sin problem. Admit the diagnosis of the Spirit of God upon your life... and wake up!

Second, Jesus says to "strengthen what remains" of your faith. This means to start reading your Bible again. Start praying again. Start meeting together with other believers again. Strengthen what remains of your faith.

Then, Jesus says to look back. Remember that moment you met Christ... how excited you were about your faith! And then remember again what the Lord Jesus did for you... how He cleansed you from your sin and saved your soul from hell. Remember the grace of God in your life! Look back.

But not only do you need to look back and remember, you need to hold on. In other words, keep on keeping on! Obey God's Word! Keep His commandments! Consistently strive to apply the Scripture to your daily life.

Finally, Jesus says to repent. That means to let go of the past, to do an about-face, to turn around, and come back to Him. If you realize that your faith is more fluff than substance, just admit it to God! Agree with Him that you've been a hypocrite... that you've been a phony.

If you're like most people, there are few things that irk you more than someone who's a hypocrite. And you know what? Jesus feels the same way! Which is why I pray you will come clean today if you realize your faith is, in fact, more superficial than supernatural.

IF YOU REALIZE THAT YOUR FAITH IS MORE FLUFF THAN SUBSTANCE, JUST ADMIT IT TO GOD!

Day 54

JACK GRAHAM ❖

Now to him who is able to do far more abundantly than all that we ask or think, according to the power at work within us, to him be glory in the church and in Christ Jesus throughout all generations, forever and ever. Amen.

—Ephesians 3:20-21

Jesus is in the business of opening doors for faithful Christians. Even in the most impossible of circumstances.

Today, you may feel how the Israelites felt when they were trapped against the Red Sea... with the Egyptian army behind them, and the mountains on either side of them. Talk about an impossible situation!

But what did God do? With a brush of His hand, He parted the waters and paved a highway right through the Red Sea... allowing the Israelites to escape Pharaoh's army. He opened a door for them... and God can do the same thing for you!

"But wait, Pastor," you say. "You don't know how far in debt I am." Or, "You don't know how badly I've messed up my marriage." And you know what? I don't know. But what I do know is that the size of your God will determine the size of the way He blesses and delivers you from whatever Red Sea you may be facing today.

Ephesians 3:20 reminds us that God "is able to do far more abundantly than all that we ask or think, according to the power at work within us." Do you really believe this?

Maybe you've been waiting for God to part the waters in your life for a while now... and you're starting to lose patience. If so, stay faithful. Keep your eyes on Christ. As I've said before, if you're a child of God, He's got His eye on the clock and His hand on the thermostat. He won't give you more than you can bear!

It's my prayer that whatever your situation, no matter what you may be facing today, you will faithfully look to God and trust Him to open that door for you!

JESUS IS IN THE BUSINESS OF OPENING DOORS FOR FAITHFUL CHRISTIANS.

Day 55

"Behold, I stand at the door and knock. If anyone hears my voice and opens the door, I will come in to him and eat with him, and he with me."

—Revelation 3:20

Today, I'd like to give you a test so you can evaluate where you are spiritually.

Question number one: Is prayer a passion in your life? If you're really fired up for the Lord, prayer will not be drudgery... it won't be a duty. It will be an ongoing, exciting conversation you have with God day by day.

Question number two: Do you love the Word of God? I believe if your heart is hot towards God, you'll look forward to meeting Him in the Scriptures. You'll look forward to hearing the Word of God preached. And you'll carve out time every day to read the Bible.

Question number three: Do you hate the sin in your life? Do you hate the things that God hates? When your heart is hot for God, you will weep at those things that make God weep... and you will rejoice over those things that cause God to rejoice.

Question number four: Do you long for the return of Christ? In the heart of every Christian who is passionately pursuing Christ is a longing for His return... there's a longing to see Him face to face. So are you excited about seeing Him? Or would you be ashamed if He returned today?

The fifth and final question: Do you obey Christ? Is it your heart's desire to please God in every single area of your life? In John 14:15, Jesus says, "If you love me, you will keep my commandments."

So let me ask you: What's your spiritual temperature? Are you hot... cold... or lukewarm?

Today... if you know that your heart is cold or lukewarm... it's my prayer—and my challenge—to you to answer that knocking at the door of your heart. Open that door... let Jesus in... and enjoy the personal relationship He's provided for you through His death and resurrection!

**WHAT'S YOUR SPIRITUAL TEMPERATURE?
ARE YOU HOT... COLD... OR LUKEWARM?**

For to me to live is Christ, and to die is gain.

—Philippians 1:21

There are five things that need to happen in your life and my life before true revival can occur.

These include things like striving to live out the Word of God every day, exalting Christ in your thoughts and actions, overcoming when it's tempting to give up, and admitting and confronting sin. It also includes looking forward with anticipation to Christ's return. We are to expect the Kingdom!

But let me ask you, what are you striving for today? Is it the next promotion, the next newer, bigger house? What is it? Do you long for the things of this world... or do you long for the things not of this world?

As the apostle Paul says in today's verse, "For to me to live is Christ, and to die is gain." Paul looked forward with anticipation to heaven... and so should we! Because when you live with your mind and affection focused on heaven, it puts a purpose to what you're doing here on earth.

Now, perhaps you'd say today, "Pastor, I don't look forward to going to heaven because I'm not sure I'd go there when I die." If so, you can be sure today that your eternal home will be with the Lord Jesus Christ in heaven.

WHEN YOU LIVE WITH YOUR MIND AND AFFECTION FOCUSED ON HEAVEN, IT PUTS A PURPOSE TO WHAT YOU'RE DOING HERE ON EARTH.

Day 57

"Call to me and I will answer you, and will tell you great and hidden things that you have not known." **—Jeremiah 33:3**

True and lasting fulfillment isn't found in any kind of man-made, man-centered philosophy. A life of vitality isn't based on what you think or how you feel. True success... true joy... and true happiness in this life can only be found in one place.

Now, it's easy to see why a book like *The Secret* has been so popular in our culture today... and why so many Christians are falling prey to its deception. Well-respected personalities like Oprah and Larry King endorse it. Millions of people have bought it. And it does contain some biblical truth.

But the fact is the real secret to life isn't found in a philosophy... or in a movie... or in a passing Hollywood fad. The real secret to this life is prayer the Jesus way!

Now you may be wondering why I'm saying that. Well, God lays it out for us in Jeremiah 33:3 when He says, "Call to me and I will answer you, and will tell you great and hidden things that you have not known." Yep. God alone is the One with the real secret! He alone is all-knowing and all-powerful!

I don't know about you, but when I'm faced with what looks like an impossible situation in life, I don't want to have to depend on my own wishful thinking to save myself!

I want to lean on the all-powerful God who answered Elijah's prayer when He sent rain from heaven. I want to depend on the sovereign God who answered Paul and Silas' prayers and broke them out of jail. I want to depend on the almighty God of the universe who raised the Lord Jesus Christ from the dead!

Remember that prayer changes things. It changes circumstances, and it can change history. So if you're stuck in an impossible situation today, please don't lean on yourself. Lean on God!

Cry out to Him and just see... in time... if He won't deliver you or give you the endurance and peace you need to make it through.

THE REAL SECRET TO THIS LIFE IS PRAYER THE JESUS WAY!

Day 58

"Our Father in heaven, hallowed be your name. Your kingdom come, your will be done, on earth as it is in heaven. Give us this day our daily bread, and forgive us our debts, as we also have forgiven our debtors. And lead us not into temptation, but deliver us from evil. For yours is the kingdom and the power and the glory, forever. Amen."

—Matthew 6:9-13

Today, I want to remind you that when you accept Jesus Christ as your Lord and Savior, you are given a life connection to the heavenly Father.

This means you are given the promise and privilege of knowing that when you do pray, God doesn't hear you as a stranger or even a subject. He hears you as His own child. What an incredible reality in the life of the believer!

And to help you in your own prayer life, I want to give you a simple acrostic: P-R-A-Y. This tool will help give your prayers structure and direction as you pray to God throughout each day.

The P in pray stands for PRAISE. That's why Jesus taught us to pray beginning with "Our Father in heaven, hallowed be Your name." Praising God in prayer says, "It's about You, Lord, Your kingdom, Your glory, Your greatness, Your name, Your honor."

The R in pray stands for REPENT. Yes, the penalty for your sins was paid for by Christ's death. But because we sin daily, we are to repent, or turn from, our sin daily.

The A in pray stands for ASK. This is when you come to God to ask Him for daily strength and to petition Him on behalf of others.

And finally, the Y in pray stands for YIELD. This is why Jesus ended His prayer, "For yours is the kingdom and the power and the glory, forever." Yielding yourself in prayer is the exact opposite of the popular "law of attraction" in our culture today that says you are the center of the universe. Rather, yielding is driven by getting God's will done on earth in your life.

So I encourage you today to…
P-PRAISE… **R**-REPENT… **A**-ASK… and **Y**-Yield.

WHEN YOU ACCEPT JESUS CHRIST AS YOUR LORD AND SAVIOR, YOU ARE GIVEN A LIFE CONNECTION TO THE HEAVENLY FATHER.

Day 59

Rejoice always, pray without ceasing, give thanks in all circumstances; for this is the will of God in Christ Jesus for you.

—1 Thessalonians 5:16-18

It's a good thing to take time out to give thanks during Thanksgiving, but of course, it shouldn't be a one-time event in your life. Gratitude should be part of your daily lifestyle! And the Bible reveals some godly habits you and I need to develop to truly be thankful people all year round.

The first habit is joyfulness. First Thessalonians 5:16 says, "Rejoice always." Now, it's important to remember that this kind of joy isn't found in your external circumstances. It's found by focusing on Jesus in the midst of your circumstances.

The second habit of a thankful person is prayerfulness. First Thessalonians 5:17 tells us to "pray without ceasing." Now, I know this sounds like a tall order! But the Scripture is telling you and me that we need to live life with a mindfulness of God's presence all the time. We do this by acknowledging Him throughout the day and developing a habit of talking to Him about every experience we have in life, whether it's good or bad.

The third habit of a thankful person is, well, being intentional about being thankful! First Thessalonians 5:18 says, "Give thanks in all circumstances...." This doesn't mean we'd call everything we see or experience in life good, necessarily, it means that in the midst of everything, God is good. And because God is good all the time, you have a reason to be thankful no matter what you're going through today!

Finally, being thankful requires the habit of hopefulness. Now, I'm not talking about wishful thinking here. I'm talking about believing what God says... that as a believer, you can become more and more like Jesus and that you will be with Him one day in heaven.

So what about you? Are you living in joyfulness... prayerfulness... thankfulness... and hopefulness? Remember, these habits are actually commands! So I challenge you today... and every day... to cultivate these important qualities in your life!

THANKSGIVING SHOULDN'T BE A ONE-TIME EVENT IN YOUR LIFE. IT SHOULD BE PART OF YOUR DAILY LIFE-STYLE!

Day 60

And without faith it is impossible to please him, for whoever would draw near to God must believe that he exists and that he rewards those who seek him.

—Hebrews 11:6

More often than not, I think we all have a tendency to make things in life more complicated than they really are. And this includes knowing God's will.

Because knowing God's will isn't a formula you have to figure out... nor is it a mystery that He's trying to keep you from solving. Knowing God's will in your life stems from your relationship with Him, your obedience to Him, your willingness to follow Him, and your faith to trust Him.

Today, let's break each of those down one by one.

First of all, think about the relationship principle. When you're connected to Jesus Christ... when His Spirit is living in you... you discover His will for your life as you walk with Him each day.

You see the path He has for you when you take the time to read the Scriptures... when you speak with Him regularly through prayer... and when you intentionally listen for the still, small voice that says, "This is the way, walk in it." Because when Christ rules your life, He will lead you!

Then, think about the obedience principle. Many people aren't happy to hear it, but God won't take you one step further than the measure of your obedience to Him. For some of us that means getting back in the center of God's will as we know it, and then letting God lead us the rest of the way!

Third, there's the willingness principle. So much of knowing and doing the will of God is just being willing to say, "Lord, I'm available. Lord, I'm accessible. Lord, I am willing." Now, you may say, "Well, I'm not there yet." But are you willing to be willing?

Last, there's the faith principle. I've discovered in my own life the will of God requires faith. As today's verse says, "Without faith it is impossible to please him." And Christian, God will do amazing things in your life if you are willing to act in faith and trust in Him!

KNOWING GOD'S WILL ISN'T A FORMULA YOU HAVE TO FIGURE OUT... NOR IS IT A MYSTERY THAT HE'S TRYING TO KEEP YOU FROM SOLVING.

Day 61

"But seek first the kingdom of God and his righteousness, and all these things will be added to you."

—Matthew 6:33

In today's verse, we see Jesus teaching us the principle of putting first things first. Which means before we ask for anything in prayer, we need to make sure we're putting first things first... seeking God's Kingdom and glory in every area of our lives.

So today I want to give you a little test. And I want you... as best you know how... to answer these questions honestly. It may be hard to admit some of your answers to yourself. But I truly believe this test will help you reorder your priorities... and as a result, reinvigorate your personal prayer life.

Question #1: Do you give God the first thoughts of your day? Even before your feet hit the floor, do you thank God for another day of life... of health... of family... of friendship? A great verse to quote to start your day is Psalms 118:24, "This is the day that the LORD has made; let us rejoice and be glad in it." I encourage you to memorize this verse today!

Question #2: Do you give God the first day of your week? God has set aside a day of the week to worship and honor Him with other believers. He's done this to give us strength and power in the midst of our crazy lives. Are you taking advantage of this awesome opportunity?

Question #3: Do you give God the first place in your life... stewarding well what God has given you? This not only includes your income, but also your family and your time. Stewardship is really a matter of Lordship!

Question #4: Are you giving God the first of all your desires? Because loving, serving, or worshipping anything more than Jesus Christ is idolatry, plain and simple.

As you answer these questions honestly, it's my prayer that God will reveal to you any priorities in your life that might be out of order. And... as He does this... it's my hope that you will begin putting first things first.

And by doing so, it's my hope that you will experience the joy of a powerful prayer life!

BEFORE WE ASK FOR ANYTHING IN PRAYER, WE NEED TO MAKE SURE WE'RE PUTTING FIRST THINGS FIRST.

Day 62

For while bodily training is of some value, godliness is of value in every way, as it holds promise for the present life and also for the life to come.

—1 Timothy 4:8

We all know that it's very important to eat right and exercise. According to the Scripture, our bodies are temples God have given us, and we need to take care of them. But being spiritually healthy is even more important.

And to be spiritually healthy, you need to exercise your faith. Just as you wouldn't expect to be able to run a marathon without any training, you can't expect to face the trials and tribulations of life without exercising your faith in God.

Exercising your faith requires discipline, dedication, and determination, which means being in God's Word, spending time in prayer, and obeying God's will for your life. Each of these disciplines will help you endure and enjoy the road ahead.

Life is often described in the Bible as a race. Some of us run the race well, some of us not so well, and others don't even finish the race at all! The goal as a believer in Jesus Christ is to run the race of life strong... and finish well. And you do this is by exercising your faith by spending time with God!

Now, there will be times in your life when you will be tempted not to spend that precious time with God. Things will come up, life will get in the way, and excuses will start to pile up. But if you make it a priority to exercise your faith and grow more intimately with God through reading His Word and spending time in prayer, you will be better equipped to face the problems of life. And when you have the appropriate eternal perspective that God wants you to have, your problems won't seem as big as they once were!

So do yourself a favor and begin working out your faith. If you do, you soon will become a spiritual athlete who runs the race of life strong... and you will finish well!

EXERCISING YOUR FAITH REQUIRES DISCIPLINE, DEDICATION, AND DETERMINATION, WHICH MEANS BEING IN GOD'S WORD, SPENDING TIME IN PRAYER, AND OBEYING GOD'S WILL FOR YOUR LIFE.

Day 63

Search me, O God, and know my heart! Try me and know my thoughts! And see if there be any grievous way in me, and lead me in the way everlasting!

—**Psalm 139:23-24**

As believers in Christ, you and I need to deal diligently with our character... which involves having a proper attitude about sin.

So what should that attitude be? For one, as believers we should be sensitive toward the sin in our lives. It's like getting something in your eye and not resting until you get it out! You should be so sensitive to the sin in your life that you can't rest until you get it out.

Now, believe me, I've heard all kinds of excuses over the years from people as to why they let sin remain in their lives. And some people do take some steps to remove the sin from their lives.

But I want to ask you today, are you doing everything you can to remove sin from your life? Are you using every resource God makes available to you in order to kill sin and grow in Christ-likeness?

Maybe it means disconnecting the internet at home. Maybe it means getting rid of your cable television. Maybe it even means admitting your sin to a close circle of fellow believers you trust so they can help hold you accountable.

I don't know what it specifically means for you, but I do know this: You and I are crazy if we don't take advantage of any chance to eliminate anything that pulls us away from Christ!

Today, to help you become more sensitive to the sin in your life, I encourage you to take some time to think and pray through today's verses.

May God bless you as you strive to become more like Him today!

AS A BELIEVER IN CHRIST, YOU SHOULD BE SENSITIVE TOWARD THE SIN IN YOUR LIFE.

Day 64

Now the law came in to increase the trespass, but where sin increased, grace abounded all the more, so that, as sin reigned in death, grace also might reign through righteousness leading to eternal life through Jesus Christ our Lord.
—Romans 5:20-21

It might come as a shock to you, but God delights in forgiving us of our sins… even when we come to Him with the same sin over and over again!

That's right, because we worship a God who is full of mercy and full of pardon. In fact, today's verses tell us that where sin increases, grace abounds all the more.

It really is an amazing day when you realize… when you finally embrace the truth… that God delights in forgiving you of your sin. As humans, offering forgiveness isn't a natural act. In most cases, it's extremely difficult to do. And as a result, I think many Christians assume that God begrudgingly offers forgiveness when we ask for it. But this simply isn't true!

The Scripture tells us that when we confess our sins with honesty and sincerity and brokenness, God is eager to forgive us. He loves to forgive you… even if you're coming to Him with the same sin for the 100th time in a row. There are no limits to His love!

I love the song by the Christian group Selah that says, "Before the throne of God above I have a strong and perfect plea. A great high Priest whose name is love, who ever lives and pleads for me. My name is graven on His hands, my name is written on His heart. I know that while in heaven He stands, no tongue can bid me thence depart… no tongue can bid me thence depart."

Christian, as a child of God, the blood of Jesus Christ cleanses you from all your sins! You can never, ever, exhaust the grace of God. So don't let Satan tempt you into believing that God wants nothing to do with you when you sin. Remember the promise from Hebrews 4:16, which tells us, "Let us then with confidence draw near to the throne of grace, that we may receive mercy and find grace to help in time of need."

GOD DELIGHTS IN FORGIVING YOU OF YOUR SIN WHEN YOU SINCERELY ASK FOR IT!

Day 65

And at the time of the offering of the oblation, Elijah the prophet came near and said, "O LORD, God of Abraham, Isaac, and Israel, let it be known this day that you are God in Israel, and that I am your servant, and that I have done all these things at your word. Answer me, O LORD, answer me, that this people may know that you, O LORD, are God, and that you have turned their hearts back." Then the fire of the LORD fell and consumed the burnt offering and the wood and the stones and the dust, and licked up the water that was in the trench. And when all the people saw it, they fell on their faces and said, "The LORD, he is God; the LORD, he is God."

—1 Kings 18:36-39

Elijah was just a man like you and me. He had the same kinds of flaws and failures as the rest of us. In fact, he became so fearful and depressed on one occasion that he ran into the desert and prayed that he would die!

But you know what's great about Elijah? Even though he was imperfect... even though he had his faults and failures... Elijah had an enduring faith that his God was alive. And because Elijah knew that God was alive, he wasn't afraid of men or what men might do to him!

Isn't that great?! Wouldn't you like to have the kind of faith that says, "I won't be intimidated by anything or anyone... ever!"? Or the kind of faith that says, "It doesn't matter what the culture around me says, I'm going to stand for the truth of God's Word, regardless of the cost!"?

Second Chronicles 16:9 says, "For the eyes of the LORD run to and fro throughout the whole earth, to give strong support to those whose heart is blameless toward him."

Christian, God is searching your heart today. And when He does, will He find a heart that's full of a living faith? Will He find a heart that's loyal and steadfast to Him?

Maybe today you'd admit that you've been practicing a religion more than you've been enjoying a relationship with Christ. If so, I want to encourage you... Jesus Christ is alive! And He wants to have a deeper relationship with you!

Today, it's my prayer that you will allow Christ to come alive in your life. Be open to Him... and just see if He won't use you... like he did Elijah... in extraordinary ways!

JESUS CHRIST IS ALIVE... AND HE WANTS A RELATIONSHIP WITH YOU!

Day 66

And Elijah came near to all the people and said, "How long will you go limping between two different opinions? If the LORD is God, follow him; but if Baal, then follow him."

—1 Kings 18:21

From the Old Testament to the New Testament, the Scripture is pretty clear when it comes to what our commitment to Christ should look like.

In today's verse, Elijah asks, "How long will you go limping between two different opinions?" Then in James 1:8 we read that a double-minded man is "unstable in all his ways." And in Revelation 3:15-16, Jesus says, "I know your works: you are neither cold nor hot. Would that you were either cold or hot! So, because you are lukewarm, and neither hot nor cold, I will spit you out of my mouth."

Today, I want to ask you, are you limping between two opinions? Are you lukewarm for Christ? Because if you say Jesus is your Lord, He deserves the entirety of your life... to truly be the Lord of your life!

Decide today to not be like so many Christians who are flirting with the world and the idols of this world... those who want to have one foot in the kingdom of this world and another in the Kingdom of God. Jesus is clear... He says to make up your mind because you can't serve two masters!

Now, I realize that I'm coming on pretty strong here today. But really, how much longer are the people of God going to limp along in their faith? How much longer are we going to wimp out in our commitment to Christ?

The story of Elijah is a constant reminder to me of what God can do through someone who's sold out, heart and soul, to Him. It's a testimony of what one man can accomplish when his heart is totally and completely God's. And you know, that's the kind of man I want to be... and I pray it's the kind of man or woman you want to be as well!

JESUS CHRIST DESERVES THE ENTIRETY OF YOUR LIFE TO TRULY BE THE LORD OF YOUR LIFE.

Day 67

Delight yourself in the LORD, and he will give you the desires of your heart.

—Psalm 37:4

I'd like to cut through the mystery and confusion about God's will today and remind you that there are specific ways you can discover God's will for your life!

If you're facing a major decision, personal dilemma, or relational challenge... let me share with you a five-point checklist you can use.

First, is what you're doing or thinking about doing consistent with the Scriptures? God will never ask you to do anything that is inconsistent with what He says in His Word.

Second, have you prayed about it faithfully? As today's verse says, "Delight yourself in the Lord, and He will give you the desires of your heart." I believe if you stay in communion and union with Christ in prayer, God will implant in your heart the right desires!

Third, have you sought the wisdom of godly friends and counselors? Proverbs 11:14 tells us that in "an abundance of counselors there is safety." If you're facing a big decision in life right now, be sure to seek counsel from godly friends... people who are passionately pursuing Christ and who understand the Scriptures.

Number four, what do the circumstances surrounding your decision look like? Are they lining up with what God wants you to do? Does it look like God is opening a door... or is He shutting a door? Pay attention to your circumstances.

And finally, number five, if you're dealing with a relational challenge... and you're not sure how or if to respond, what is the most loving thing to do? Sometimes the most loving thing to do is to keep your mouth shut. But sometimes, the most loving thing to do is to stand up and say, "Friend, I love you, but this isn't right... it doesn't line up with what God tells us to do in His Word."

I trust that you will run through this checklist whenever you're facing a decision or relational challenge. Determine what God wants you to do and then by faith, do it with all your heart, mind, soul, and strength!

DETERMINE WHAT GOD WANTS YOU TO DO AND THEN BY FAITH, DO IT WITH ALL YOUR HEART, MIND, SOUL, AND STRENGTH!

Day 68

I will meditate on your precepts and fix my eyes on your ways. I will delight in your statutes; I will not forget your word.

—Psalm 119:15-16

You know, it's pretty simple. To claim real victory over temptation and sin in our lives, you and I need to get in the Word of God and we need to stay in the Word of God.

There really is no excuse not to read the Bible! I mean, it's on the internet in every possible version and translation, you can download it on your iPod, and it's on CD! You can even listen to it on your way to work! There are more opportunities than ever to get into God's Word.

But there's more than just reading or listening to the Word of God. It must be applied to our lives. One of the best things you can do for your Christian walk is to memorize Scripture. Because when you memorize Scripture, it becomes a part of you… it becomes your way of life… and it becomes your defense against Satan. You will be amazed how God will use those verses you have memorized in your life!

But also, you must be obedient to God's Word. You must do what it says… you must be obedient to the counsel, guidance, and advice found in God's Word. Following Jesus Christ means obedience in every way… not just in some parts of your life, but obedience in every aspect of your life.

Maybe today you'd admit that you're struggling with sin… that you're about ready to give in to temptation. If so, turn to God's Word. Read it… meditate on it… pray about the verses you read, and strive to live it out day by day.

TO CLAIM REAL VICTORY OVER TEMPTATION AND SIN IN YOUR LIFE, YOU NEED TO GET IN THE WORD OF GOD AND STAY IN THE WORD OF GOD.

Day 69

Now faith is the assurance of things hoped for, the conviction of things not seen.

—Hebrews 11:1

What does genuine faith look like?

So many people in our society today put their faith in self-help gurus, books, programs... the list goes on and on! And some people think that just believing in the power of positive thinking can somehow accomplish things in their lives.

But none of these things are examples of genuine faith!

Christian, it's vitally important you're not deceived into putting your faith anywhere else but in the one true God. Because He is the only One who is worthy of putting your true faith and hope in this life!

Despite what our world says, genuine faith is not based on your feelings... your emotions... your life circumstances... or even in what you can see, as today's verse reminds us.

Maybe today you're struggling to put your faith in God. Maybe you have some intellectual questions that are keeping you from trusting in Him completely. If so, remember that it's natural to have questions. It's natural to want to understand as much as you can about God and the Christian faith.

But listen to me here: When you come to God with a genuine faith, your intellectual curiosities will be met and satisfied.

Please don't think I am saying you must have the faith of a giant and never struggle through the difficulties of life. In Matthew 17:20, Jesus said that faith the size of a grain of mustard seed is a great faith.

No matter where you are in your walk with Christ today, it's my prayer that you would develop a genuine and courageous faith in Jesus Christ... the only One who is worthy of your complete trust and hope!

GENUINE FAITH IS NOT BASED ON YOUR FEELINGS, YOUR EMOTIONS, YOUR LIFE CIRCUMSTANCES, OR EVEN IN WHAT YOU CAN SEE.

Day 70

Then Joshua said to the people, "Consecrate yourselves, for tomorrow the LORD will do wonders among you."
—Joshua 3:5

God wants to do incredible things in your life… even things you might consider impossible. Today's verse is proof of this!

The problem with a lot of believers these days is that most of us like to play it safe. We like living life in our little comfort zones. But being a believer in Jesus Christ is not always about playing it safe!

Sometimes, oftentimes, God calls us to step outside of our comfort zone to follow Him. And when you take that leap, what wonderful things He can do in and through you!

Now, you may think it's impossible that God could do something amazing through you. But trust me on this. All you have to do is take that first step of faith. God will never ask you to do anything that He won't give you the strength to do. He will make a path for you. He will direct your steps and blaze a trail before you!

Today, I want to challenge you to be spiritually, emotionally, and physically ready for the adventures God wants to take you on in your life. Take time to read and study His Word, talk to Him through prayer, and bottom line… seek after Him!

And when you're facing what seems impossible, remember what it says in Matthew 6:33, "But seek first the kingdom of God and his righteousness, and all these things will be added to you."

BEING A BELIEVER IN JESUS CHRIST IS NOT ALWAYS ABOUT PLAYING IT SAFE!

Day 71

"The thief comes only to steal and kill and destroy. I came that they may have life and have it abundantly."

—John 10:10

Whether you realize it or not, there is a spiritual battle being waged all around you right now. And the person waging the war... your enemy as a follower of Jesus Christ... is Satan himself. As it says in today's verse, the devil's only intent is to kill and destroy you!

Now, the good news is that the war was won when Jesus died for your sins and mine and rose again. When He did this, Satan was defeated. But that doesn't stop Satan from trying to defeat you and me in our day-to-day lives.

Even today, you might admit that you're tired of fighting the fight of faith. Maybe you feel like you're about to throw in the towel.

If so, I have a word of encouragement for you today: Be patient. I remember singing that song to my children so long ago. "Have patience, have patience, don't be in such a hurry. When you get impatient, you only start to worry...."

As you face the walls of discouragement, the walls of illness, the walls of financial insecurity, the walls of relational frustration, be patient. Keep doing what God is telling you to do.

Today lean on God to help you take that next step of faith. Then lean on Him to take the next step of faith. Keep marching patiently forward... and eventually... as you persevere and patiently pursue God's will for your life... He will see you through to a real victory.

THE WAR WAS WON WHEN JESUS DIED FOR YOUR SINS AND ROSE AGAIN. BUT THAT DOESN'T STOP SATAN FROM TRYING TO DEFEAT YOU IN YOUR DAY-TO-DAY LIFE.

Day 72

But thanks be to God, who gives us the victory through our Lord Jesus Christ.

—1 Corinthians 15:57

Any sin in our lives defeats. That's just the nature of sin! Yet God never intended for his children to be defeated. His desire is that you walk in spiritual victory each day!

Yet one of the greatest barriers to experiencing that daily spiritual victory is hidden sin in our lives. Because not only will hidden sin zap you spiritually, it will drain you physically and emotionally. Not only will it diminish your witness, but it will also impact your relationship with those you love.

The Scripture even says that before God can hear our prayers, we must deal with the sin in our lives. David tells us this in Psalm 66:18 when he says, "If I had cherished iniquity in my heart, the Lord would not have listened."

The only way to deal with sin in your life is to strike at it immediately before it gets you in its grip. You must treat sin as ruthlessly as it will treat you! The moment you are aware that there is an unclean desire in your heart or evil thought in your mind, strike back at it in the power of God and the power of prayer.

Remember, there is no sin that God can't forgive! No matter what you have done, God always forgives when we come to Him in true repentance. First John 1:9 says, "If we confess our sins, he is faithful and just to forgive us our sins and to cleanse us from all unrighteousness."

If there is something in your life that you are clinging to... be it a sinful habit or an ungodly attitude... my prayer is that you will deal with it and ask for true forgiveness. God is waiting with open arms to bring about a new beginning... a new hope in your life today!

GOD DESIRES THAT YOU WALK IN SPIRITUAL VICTORY EACH DAY!

Day 73

But Jesus looked at them and said, "With man this is impossible, but with God all things are possible."

—Matthew 19:26

As a Christian, your lifeline to God is prayer. It's how you grow more intimately with God and develop a deeper and more personal relationship with Him. But prayer is also how you face the enemy of your soul head-on with courage and hope!

God tells us not to be afraid of Satan and his forces. Because as a Christian, you have authority in Jesus Christ, who has conquered all the spiritual forces of darkness. When Jesus Christ died on the cross and rose again, He won the victory. And He wants you and me to live in that victory!

How? It starts with prayer... passionate, even presumptuous prayer... to a God who you know can overcome anything. So often we forget to pray boldly, thinking that God can't do what we are asking. But that is far from the truth, as today's verse tells us.

Now, it's important to remember that doesn't mean we have a blank check to ask God to do anything and everything we want Him to do. There is a powerful connection to God's Word and prayer. Scripture will guide you and teach you what things you should pray for. And God will always come through in His response based on what His Word says.

Let me put it this way: There is nothing that lies outside the reach of prayer except that which may lie outside the will of God.

If you are facing a battle with the enemy today, know that God is fighting for you... and your victory is sure in Jesus Christ. Your best weapon is prayer. Claim the promises God has for you in His Word, accept the victory, and live a life that exemplifies the power of our great God!

PRAYER IS HOW YOU FACE THE ENEMY OF YOUR SOUL HEAD-ON WITH COURAGE AND HOPE.

"For I know the plans I have for you, declares the LORD, plans for welfare and not for evil, to give you a future and a hope."
— **Jeremiah 29:11**

Wholeheartedly following after God can be such an adventure! God doesn't want you to live a mediocre life. He wants you to claim the wonderful promises He has given you... promises for a hope and a future.

Now, when you do choose to wholeheartedly follow the Lord, you will face battles in your life. You will face some opposition. But rest assured... with God's help, you can overcome it!

The first opposition you may face when you follow after Christ is the opposition thrown at you by your friends. They may tell you, "You can't do it" or "It's not worth it." Some friends might even doubt you. But some friends will stand with you... which is why it is so important to choose your friends wisely.

Time is another obstacle to overcome when following after God. It can be so hard waiting on the Lord, but you have to remember that His timing is perfect.

God could be delaying the delivery of His promise to you in order to strengthen and grow your faith and commitment to Him. He knows when you will be ready! Isaiah 40:31 is a great reminder of the strength that comes in waiting on the Lord: "But they who wait for the LORD shall renew their strength; they shall mount up with wings like eagles; they shall run and not be weary; they shall walk and not faint."

It's my prayer you will decide today to follow wholeheartedly after God. And as you do, remember that every obstacle is an opportunity for you to grow more like Christ. And remember that if you keep your eyes focused on the promises and purposes that God has for your life, you can overcome anything through Him!

EVERY OBSTACLE YOU FACE AS A CHRISTIAN IS AN OPPORTUNITY FOR YOU TO GROW MORE LIKE CHRIST.

Day 75

Do not be conformed to this world, but be transformed by the renewal of your mind, that by testing you may discern what is the will of God, what is good and acceptable and perfect.

—Romans 12:2

Life really is full of hard choices, but thankfully, we have God's Word to help us make those tough decisions. And today, if you have a tough choice to make, ask yourself these five questions:

Question #1: Is it helpful? Is the decision you are making encouraging you and moving you down the path to serve Jesus Christ? If it's not moving you towards accomplishing God's will for your life, maybe you shouldn't do it.

Question #2: Is it habit-forming? Anything that can potentially put you in its grip and not let go is something to avoid. As Christians, we are free in Jesus Christ to not sin. We aren't slaves to anything! So ask yourself if the decision you are making has the potential to engulf your life and enslave you.

Question #3: Would this decision hinder my witness for Christ? You never know who is watching you and you certainly don't want to be a stumbling block for someone who doesn't know the Lord. Remember what Romans 14:13 says, "Therefore let us not pass judgment on one another any longer, but rather decide never to put a stumbling block or hindrance in the way of a brother."

Question #4: Would this decision build me up in my faith? Would it make you stronger in your faith, make you a better Christian, and encourage you to witness to others for Christ. If not, you know which way to go!

And finally, question #5: Does this decision honor God? As it says in Colossians 3:17, "Whatever you do, in word or deed, do everything in the name of the Lord Jesus, giving thanks to God the Father through him." If you can't say for sure that your decision will honor God, then steer clear of it!

I pray today that this helps you make those tough decisions in your life!

**WE HAVE GOD'S WORD TO HELP US MAKE
HARD DECISIONS IN LIFE.**

Day 76

Rejoice always, pray without ceasing, give thanks in all circumstances; for this is the will of God in Christ Jesus for you.
—1 Thessalonians 5:16-18

I'd like to point out a few key words in today's verses... "give thanks in all circumstances."

It's easy to give thanks to God and have a grateful heart when things are going well in your life. But the hard part is being thankful when life gets hard!

I believe having a thankful response in all circumstances starts with having an appropriate perspective. It's easy to become narrow in your outlook and forget the big picture. When we become so focused on ourselves and our problems, the problem usually ends up being a lot bigger than it should be.

So today... I encourage you to take your eyes off your problems and, instead, look to God. Say a prayer of thanks to Him that He has created you and given you life... and look at today as a gift from God to start fresh.

As it says in Lamentations, "The steadfast love of the LORD never ceases; his mercies never come to an end; they are new every morning; great is your faithfulness."

Most often, we can't change our circumstances... but we can change our response to difficult times. If you allow every trial and tribulation to become an opportunity to thank God, He will always show up! When we come into the presence of God and sing praises to Him... He is always there!

God inhabits the praises of His people and can change your entire perspective on whatever it is you may be facing today.

HAVING A THANKFUL RESPONSE IN ALL CIRCUMSTANCES STARTS WITH HAVING AN APPROPRIATE PERSPECTIVE.

Day 77

For the word of God is living and active, sharper than any two-edged sword, piercing to the division of soul and of spirit, of joints and of marrow, and discerning the thoughts and intentions of the heart.

—Hebrews 4:12

God's Word is an amazing gift He has given to each of us. Yet so many times, we don't study, read, meditate, and live out God's Word like we should!

The Bible is the most important tool a believer can have on this earth and it serves specific and strategic purposes in every believer's life.

First, God's Word gives us spiritual counsel. There are so many decisions in life to make, some big and some small. And the Bible is there to give us guidance on these decisions.

Do you want to know God's will for your life? Then get into His Word. Psalm 119:105 promises us that God will guide us every step of the way. You can learn and live the will of God for your life through the promises and principles found in His Word.

God's Word also offers us spiritual correction. Perhaps you have fallen off the path God has for you and you want to get going in the right direction. Well, God's Word is there to lead you back.

Third, God's Word is there to enable us to face spiritual conflict. Satan and his team of evil forces are working all around us, all the time. And it's crucial that you be armed with the knowledge, truth, and power found in God's Word. The Bible enables us to conquer our spiritual problems as well as face the daily burdens that we all have in life!

And finally, God's Word offers us spiritual communion with God. When we study the Word of God, we get to know God's character. It's not just an ancient book, irrelevant to today's culture. God's Word is alive and it is there to change your life!

It's my prayer that as you faithfully read, study, memorize, meditate, obey, and share God's Word, your life will never be the same!

THE BIBLE IS THE MOST IMPORTANT TOOL A BELIEVER CAN HAVE ON THIS EARTH.

Day 78

"But seek first the kingdom of God and his righteousness, and all these things will be added to you."

—**Matthew 6:33**

A re you giving God your best in every area of life?

Giving God your best not only means giving Him the best of your time and talents… it means being a good steward of what He's given you as well!

You know, how you think about and handle money says a lot about who you trust and where you really find your significance. And it's an expression of our faith, our hope, and our love as believers.

So often we say we trust God to meet our needs… yet we are stingy with our money! It's easy to say, "When I make more money, I'll give to the church," or "I just need another raise, then I can start contributing to the work of God around the world." Start giving to God's Kingdom work now and trust that He will meet all your needs! I think today's verse says it best, "But seek first the kingdom of God and his righteousness, and all these things will be added to you."

Remember, as well, that giving God your best financially also expresses your hope for the future.

What good does it do to store up things on this earth? You came into this world with nothing and you will leave this world with nothing. But if you begin to invest in your future and in the Kingdom of God, then one day, when you stand before God and give an account of what you have done with your life, God can say, "Well done, My good and faithful servant."

Finally, remember that giving God your best also says a great deal about your love for Him. God doesn't want you giving out of guilt or because someone is making you. No, He wants you to give out of your love for Him and His church. Because God knows your heart and knows your motives, you can't really disguise a hardened heart by writing a big check.

The bottom line is that God doesn't need your money. What He really wants is your heart. So today, begin to look at giving to Him as a way of expressing your faith, hope, and love for Him!

HOW YOU THINK ABOUT AND HANDLE MONEY SAYS A LOT ABOUT WHO YOU TRUST AND WHERE YOU REALLY FIND YOUR SIGNIFICANCE.

"Look at the birds of the air: they neither sow nor reap nor gather into barns, and yet your heavenly Father feeds them. Are you not of more value than they?"

—Matthew 6:26

God often uses unlikely people, events, and circumstances to provide for us. Even when we think there is no way out or no hope... He always provides.

But here's the question I want to ask you today, do you honestly believe that God will meet your every need?

Many people know the story of the good Samaritan... how God strategically placed a Samaritan along the Jericho road to meet the needs of the Jewish man who was robbed and left for dead. The key thing I want you to remember here is that the one who helped the man was a Samaritan... a known enemy of the Jews.

Imagine if you will, that you're the Jewish man in the story, laying on the ground, severely beaten, and scared half to death. Now, imagine seeing your sworn enemy heading your way. You'd probably think you were about to get another beating! That's probably what the Jewish man in this story thought.

Instead, the Samaritan man showed compassion and love for his Jewish enemy. He took him in, cared for his wounds, and provided a safe place for him.

You know, I'm always amazed at the creativity of God... how He meets our needs through the most unlikely people or circumstances. Even when we think things couldn't get any worse, God always has a plan in mind.

Take a moment to reread today's verse.

You are more valuable than the birds of the air! And God is there to take care of you every step of the way, even through the most unlikely of situations. That's why... no matter what you're going through today... you can trust in God and fall into His arms of peace, safety, and rest.

EVEN WHEN WE THINK THERE IS NO WAY OUT OR NO HOPE, GOD ALWAYS PROVIDES.

Day 80

Love is patient and kind; love does not envy or boast; it is not arrogant or rude. It does not insist on its own way; it is not irritable or resentful; it does not rejoice at wrongdoing, but rejoices with the truth. Love bears all things, believes all things, hopes all things, endures all things. Love never ends.

—1 Corinthians 13:4-8

Love is one of the greatest gifts that God has given to each of us as believers. Not only does He love you and me, but He's gifted us with the ability to love others. And what an important ability that is!

As believers in Jesus Christ, we are called to love people, no matter their background, color, race, or religion. Why? Because God loves people and He called each of us to love as He loves.

And how do you love people like God loves people? One way is to look for a need and meet it. Maybe the person you sit next to at work needs some encouragement or just a simple, "How are you doing today?" And I don't mean a "How are you doing today?" that is just small talk, but really taking the time to listen to their answer and understand what they are going through.

Or, maybe a server you had at a restaurant this week needed to know you valued and appreciated their service. There are so many opportunities to show your love to people! I would encourage you to ask God to open your eyes to opportunities to love and serve those around you each day.

Over and over again in the Scripture, we see how Jesus loved those around Him… how He empathized and felt for those who were hurting or in need.

Today, I want to encourage you to go out of your way to offer a word of encouragement or to help someone in need… like Jesus did.

I know you're busy… I know you've got lots on your plate… but you never know… that someone you help or encourage might see the love of Jesus in you and come to know Him!

LOVE IS ONE OF THE GREATEST GIFTS THAT GOD HAS GIVEN TO EACH OF US AS BELIEVERS.

Day 81

"Awake, O sleeper, and arise from the dead, and Christ will shine on you."

—**Ephesians 5:14**

One of the best ways you can start your day is to spend time with God. With as much as you have going on these days… work, school, kids, chores, extra-curricular activities… those few precious moments in the morning can often set the tone for the rest of your day.

I would encourage you to spend a few moments, first thing in the morning, in God's Word and in prayer. There are so many instances in the Bible where godly men and women awoke early to spend time with God. In fact, Paul reminds us of this in today's verse!

One of the great benefits of coming to the Lord in the morning is that it prepares you for the challenges of the day and puts you in the right frame of mind. By spending time in God's Word, you refresh your spirit, nourish your soul, and refuel your body. You will be better prepared for whatever life throws your way!

Now, I don't know if you're a morning person or not but if you aren't, try to wake up just a few minutes earlier and I promise you will be amazed at the results.

As you spend time in His Word and in prayer, you will live in the fullness of Christ and the freshness of His renewing spirit. And the best part is… you will have more to give! Ordinary days will become extraordinary, boring days will become exciting, and you will be ready to give more of yourself to your family and friends.

It's my prayer that you would become diligent about spending time with God each and every day… starting your morning at the feet of Jesus. Make it a priority to spend time alone with God and come into His presence. Because there is no better place to be!

**ONE OF THE BEST WAYS YOU CAN START OFF
YOUR DAY IS TO SPEND TIME WITH GOD.**

Day 82

"For God so loved the world, that he gave his only Son, that whoever believes in him should not perish but have eternal life."

—John 3:16

G od wants to live in your heart and transform your life. You see, when you become a believer in Jesus Christ, a wonderful thing happens. The very Spirit of God enters your life and lives within you! And when the Holy Spirit lives within, you're never the same.

This is the best present of all! Nothing can compare to receiving the gift of Jesus Christ because His salvation is the ultimate gift of forgiveness and eternal life.

God loves you and me so much that He sent His Son, Jesus Christ, to earth as a baby. God sent Him so that we could have meaning, purpose, and a future with Him. God didn't walk away or give up on restoring our relationship with Him. No, He came to save us!

It's my prayer that you would remember God's love for you today and that you would be bold in sharing this gift with the world. It is the best present you could ever give someone!

**NOTHING CAN COMPARE TO
RECEIVING THE GIFT OF JESUS CHRIST
BECAUSE HIS SALVATION IS THE ULTIMATE GIFT
OF FORGIVENESS AND ETERNAL LIFE.**

Day 83

"You are the light of the world. A city set on a hill cannot be hidden. Nor do people light a lamp and put it under a basket, but on a stand, and it gives light to all in the house. In the same way, let your light shine before others, so that they may see your good works and give glory to your Father who is in heaven."

—Matthew 5:14-16

Jesus clearly states in the Scripture that believers in Him "are the light of the world." So my question for you is this: Are you letting the light of Jesus shine through you?

Far too often, followers of Christ forget that they influence other people. Whether it's for good or for bad, we do influence others! And as believers in Jesus Christ, we are called to shine the light of Jesus Christ in any circumstance in which we find ourselves. You and I are called to influence others for Him!

It might seem overwhelming at first to shine the light of Christ into such a dark world, but you have nothing to fear! You don't have to be afraid of the dark anymore because Jesus Christ has already overcome it. He will make a path for you and light the way. You just need to trust and follow Him.

Today, it's my prayer that you would take the light of Jesus Christ to those who don't know Him. Be responsible with the light God has given you… and help others live in the light like you do!

AS BELIEVERS IN JESUS CHRIST, WE ARE CALLED TO SHINE THE LIGHT OF JESUS CHRIST IN ANY CIRCUM- STANCE IN WHICH WE FIND OURSELVES.

Day 84

Now as they went on their way, Jesus entered a village. And a woman named Martha welcomed him into her house. And she had a sister called Mary, who sat at the Lord's feet and listened to his teaching. But Martha was distracted with much serving. And she went up to him and said, "Lord, do you not care that my sister has left me to serve alone? Tell her then to help me." But the Lord answered her, "Martha, Martha, you are anxious and troubled about many things, but one thing is necessary. Mary has chosen the good portion, which will not be taken away from her."

—Luke 1:38-42

Before you can be effective for Christ, you must first make it a practice to be still and experience His presence in your life each day.

In the story of Mary and Martha, we see two very different responses to Jesus. While Martha is busy getting the food ready, making sure the house is clean, and so on, we find Mary sitting at Jesus' feet... listening to His teaching.

This made Martha mad! There she was, frantically preparing a meal, running around, trying to make everything perfect in her house for Jesus, while her sister wasn't helping her at all!

Martha was so mad that she even made a comment to Jesus about the lack of help from her sister. But Jesus came back to Martha with a fascinating response... a response that most of us need to hear today. Jesus said, "Martha, Martha, you are anxious and troubled about many things, but one thing is necessary. Mary has chosen the good portion, which will not be taken away from her."

The one thing necessary that Jesus talks about here is spending time with Him. While serving others is important and something each believer is called to do, we can't make this our priority and forget to spend time with God every day!

So let me ask you... when it comes to your walk with God, are you a "Martha" or a "Mary"? It's my prayer that you and I would be a "Mary"... a person who makes spending time with the Lord Jesus our number one priority!

BEFORE YOU CAN BE EFFECTIVE FOR CHRIST, YOU MUST FIRST MAKE IT A PRACTICE TO BE STILL AND EXPERIENCE HIS PRESENCE IN YOUR LIFE EACH DAY.

Jesus looked at him and said, "So you are Simon the son of John? You shall be called Cephas" (which means Peter).

—John 1:42

When Jesus looked at Simon and called him Peter, which means "rock," most of Simon Peter's friends were shocked! Peter wasn't exactly someone you would have referred to as a rock... someone who was stable, strong, and a source of strength. But Jesus saw much more in Peter than his friends could.

In the exact same way, when Christ looks at you, He doesn't see you as others do... or even as you do. He sees you for who you can be... He sees your full potential. Isn't that encouraging?

You know what the problem is, though? A lot of Christians aren't letting God propel them to their full potential. The reasons for this are numerous, but the most common reason is because most people are afraid to venture out of their comfort zones. Can you relate?

In order for you to reach your full potential as a follower of Christ, you're going to be called out of your comfort zone... probably a lot more than you'd like to be! But here's the great thing about God's call: He doesn't ask you to do anything He doesn't give you the power to accomplish!

When you face trials or times of uncertainty, it can be hard to trust God. But if you just keep following after Him and trusting Him with every step, you will be amazed at how your faith and character will grow.

You will be able to handle much more than you think through God's strength. You'll be able to forgive when you thought you couldn't... you'll be able to wait patiently when you thought you couldn't wait any longer... and you'll have hope when everything around you seems to crumble!

WHEN CHRIST LOOKS AT YOU, HE DOESN'T SEE YOU AS OTHERS DO... OR EVEN AS YOU DO. HE SEES YOU FOR WHO YOU CAN BE... HE SEES YOUR FULL POTENTIAL.

Day 86

And we know that for those who love God all things work together for good, for those who are called according to his purpose.

—Romans 8:28

We all like to be in control… in control of what we wear, what we eat, how successful we are, where we live, how much money we make and so on. And most of us like to think we know it all too! Yet this kind of attitude can hinder what God wants to do in our lives.

As much as we want to be in control of everything, there are some things we just can't control… things like sickness, death, natural disasters, car accidents. So many things really are outside our control! And it's when we come to a place where we realize how limited our control is that we begin to depend on God.

The wonderful thing about God is that He can see the big picture. Don't forget that. As today's verse promises us, "…for those who love God all things work together for good, for those who are called according to his purpose."

Sometimes the Lord reveals why certain trials happen to you. But other times, He doesn't. One thing is for certain, though: God is in control and you can rest in that!

When you begin to hand over control to God, you will experience amazing freedom. No longer will you try to live up to the world's expectations of what you should be, which you can never truly meet anyway.

This world is full of lies telling you that you're never good enough. But God is good enough! And letting God be in control is where true happiness and contentment really are.

IT'S WHEN WE COME TO A PLACE WHERE WE REALIZE HOW LIMITED OUR CONTROL IS THAT WE BEGIN TO DEPEND ON GOD.

Day 87

Therefore, since we are surrounded by so great a cloud of witnesses, let us also lay aside every weight, and sin which clings so closely, and let us run with endurance the race that is set before us, looking to Jesus, the founder and perfecter of our faith, who for the joy that was set before him endured the cross, despising the shame, and is seated at the right hand of the throne of God.

—Hebrews 12:1-2

The key to successfully running the race of life is found in today's verses. And the first step to running the race of life in victory is to run the race with everything you've got!

I don't need to run your race and you don't need to run my race. We've all been given a race and a lane to run in, and we're to run with all our hearts. And to run in your lane well, you just need to give God the best of your time, your talents, your service, and yes, even your tithes.

Secondly, running the race of life well means you say "no" to the sin of compromise. Allowing the sin of compromise to creep into your life is the fastest way to get derailed!

And last, the third step to running the race of life well is to rely completely on God and His Word.... always looking forward, never turning back. Sure, the devil will try to convince you how great your old way of life was. But don't fall for it! Keep your eyes on Jesus... during the good times and the bad.

So as you look back on 2007, let me ask you: Did you run the race with all your heart? Did you keep the sin of compromise out of your life? And did you rely totally and completely on God and His Word?

If you can't say that you did, remember, God promises to give you the desire and power to accomplish all three of these things. So I pray that you'll take Him up on His offer today so you can run the race of life in true victory in 2008!

WE'VE ALL BEEN GIVEN A RACE AND A LANE TO RUN IN, AND WE'RE TO RUN WITH ALL OUR HEARTS.

"Take my yoke upon you, and learn from me, for I am gentle and lowly in heart, and you will find rest for your souls. For my yoke is easy, and my burden is light."

—Matthew 11:29-30

L ife is a journey. And the great thing about this journey is that there is Someone who wants to take it with you. His name is Jesus.

Not only does Jesus want to join you in the journey of life, He wants to bear your burdens along the way. He wants to be there with you and for you when life gets hard… just as we see in today's verses.

There's no doubt that life is hard. But God never intended for you to carry your burdens, anxieties, and fears all on your own shoulders! He wants to help you.

Do you want to find rest for your soul today? Do you want Someone to lighten your heavy load of guilt, shame, or fear? Do you want to come into a personal relationship with God through Jesus Christ and invite Him to join you in your journey of life?

Following Jesus Christ doesn't mean your life will become easier… but it does mean that you'll have Someone to bear your burdens 24 hours of every day.

So rejoice! If you've just become a member of God's eternal family, He will always be there for you along life's often difficult journey!

**THE GREAT THING ABOUT THIS JOURNEY
IS THAT THERE IS SOMEONE WHO WANTS TO TAKE
IT WITH YOU. HIS NAME IS JESUS.**

"And behold, I [Jesus] am with you always, to the end of the age."

—Matthew 28:20

It seems like people are more lonely than ever today… despite all the ways we now have to communicate with each other.

In fact, in a recent study, we learned that the suicide rate among Americans ages 45 through 54 has reached its highest point in at least 25 years. What a tragedy!

This is especially startling when we live in a world where we have instant access to each other through email, text messaging, Skype… I mean, we can be connected to people 24 hours a day, 7 days a week!

Yet the fact remains that many, many people struggle with feelings of loneliness.

You know, whenever I've faced times of sadness, disappointment, or discouragement in life, it's always so comforting to know that a friend or family member is there… that they are a phone call, email, or a car ride away.

I think this is the reason why God reassures us so many times in the Scripture that He is there as well. In fact, this is His most-mentioned promise. Over and over again in the Bible God tells us, "I am with you," "I am with you," "I am with you."

When you accept Jesus Christ as your personal Lord and Savior, a wonderful thing happens. The Holy Spirit begins to live within you… yes, Jesus' living presence lives within your heart. And because of this, you can never be alone!

You can be driving, working, eating, or doing pretty much anything else, and He will always be there for you. In your darkest moments, you can run to Him for comfort… and in your most joyous moments, you can sing His praises for the blessings in your life.

I want to encourage you today that as a believer in Jesus Christ… you are not alone. Take full advantage of the fact that you have a wonderful friend who wants to talk to you. He wants to hear your thoughts, your fears, your insecurities, and your secrets. And He wants to guide you every step of the way!

WHEN YOU ACCEPT JESUS CHRIST AS YOUR PERSONAL LORD AND SAVIOR, A WONDERFUL THING HAPPENS: JESUS' LIVING PRESENCE BEGINS TO LIVE WITHIN YOUR HEART.

Day 90

Blessed be the God and Father of our Lord Jesus Christ, the Father of mercies and God of all comfort, who comforts us in all our affliction, so that we may be able to comfort those who are in any affliction, with the comfort with which we ourselves are comforted by God.

—2 Corinthians 1:3-4

O ne of the most important things to remember in the midst of hard times is that God is deeply concerned about your pain. Jesus came to this earth as a man in order to share in your humanity… to identify with your sufferings… and to provide a way for you to have healing and hope.

And no matter what has happened to you in the past… or what you are going through now… Jesus is right there, as your Friend and Comforter. His desire is to come alongside the wounded heart and to bring restoration and a new beginning.

You see, God is able to turn around any situation… and heal every kind of wound… especially yours.

So today, why don't you bring your broken heart to Jesus? Why not give Him your burdens and fears… and all the wounded places of your heart? As you offer these areas to Jesus, He will begin to bring healing, peace, and restoration to your life again.

And when He does, don't be surprised when God lets you share the comfort you've received from Him with someone else who's going through a trying situation.

Jesus is the friend of the wounded heart. So let Him work in your life today!

NO MATTER WHAT HAS HAPPENED TO YOU IN THE PAST, OR WHAT YOU ARE GOING THROUGH NOW… JESUS IS RIGHT THERE, AS YOUR FRIEND AND COMFORTER.

For we do not have a high priest who is unable to sympathize with our weaknesses, but one who in every respect has been tempted as we are, yet without sin.

—Hebrews 4:15

No one is immune to temptation… including you!

Everyone struggles with temptation at different times. And many of our desires are natural, God-given desires. The problem comes when we try to fulfill those desires in the devil's way—or our own way—and not in God's way.

It is not a sin to be tempted… it's only a sin when we yield to temptation! But God has given us a powerful key to overcoming temptation. It's His Word.

And one of the greatest examples of someone who used the Scripture to defeat temptation is Jesus Christ Himself!

You know, a lot of people I meet really aren't sure that Jesus was tempted like you and I are tempted. Yet He was! The writer of Hebrews confirms this for us in today's verse.

Yes, Jesus Himself was tempted. And He defeated the enemy by using the very same tool that we have available to us—the Word of God. But remember, Jesus didn't just quote the Scripture like some magical hocus-pocus. He submitted His life to the Word of God. And because of this, Jesus was absolutely dependent on God. That's why the devil couldn't succeed at making Jesus fall into temptation!

Let me encourage you today… if you are feeling tempted to sin, talk to God about it. He knows what you're thinking and feeling anyway, so why not be honest with Him about your struggles? I truly believe that God appreciates that kind of honesty.

Take your struggles to the Lord, and at the same time immerse yourself in God's Word. Let the Scripture remind you of God's love for you, and that you can trust Him to bring about His plans for your life!

God is able to satisfy the desires of your heart… in ways that are good and pleasing to Him. Ask Him to help you with the areas where you struggle, and He will make you a victor over sin!

**JESUS DEFEATED THE ENEMY BY USING
THE VERY SAME TOOL THAT WE HAVE AVAILABLE
TO US—THE WORD OF GOD.**

Day 92

And Jesus said to them, "Follow me, and I will make you become fishers of men."

—Mark 1:17

To live like true disciples of Jesus Christ, you and I must do three things.

Just like the first disciples of Jesus, we must believe. To believe in the words and promises of Jesus... to believe that the Father hears when you pray to Him... to believe that He can use you to share the gospel with others.

You don't have to be qualified in any way. Just believe with simple faith like a child!

The second thing that distinguishes a true disciple of Jesus is obedience. By laying down your own agenda and following the ways and instructions of Jesus, you are living as a true disciple of Jesus Christ.

But the ultimate aim of a disciple, of course, is to become a witness for Jesus.

I think a lot of Christians read today's verse and think, "That's great for the disciples, but this doesn't really apply to me." And as a result, sharing the Good News about Jesus Christ isn't a priority for many followers of Christ. For some reason, evangelism has become something separate from their personal relationship with God!

And what about you? Is sharing the gospel with others a priority in your life? If not, why not? Are you afraid to speak about your faith? Do you feel ill-equipped?

There are many reasons why believers shy away from sharing their faith. But let me encourage you today... the more time you spend in the presence of Jesus, the more you will want to tell others about Him.

And if you still struggle with fear about sharing your faith, ask Him to help you. He has promised to "make you become a fisher of men." So allow Him to work in this area of your life, and you will be amazed how He will use you to reach others with the gospel!

**THE MORE TIME YOU SPEND IN
THE PRESENCE OF JESUS, THE MORE YOU WILL
WANT TO TELL OTHERS ABOUT HIM.**

Day 93

And when he returned to Capernaum after some days, it was reported that he was at home. And many were gathered together, so that there was no more room, not even at the door. And he was preaching the word to them. And they came, bringing to him a paralytic carried by four men. And when they could not get near him because of the crowd, they removed the roof above him, and when they had made an opening, they let down the bed on which the paralytic lay. And when Jesus saw their faith, he said to the paralytic, "Son, your sins are forgiven."

—Mark 1:17

There are several things you and I need to do to become more effective in our witness to our friends and relatives.

First, it's important for you to love God with all your heart, mind, soul and strength. When you have a real, daily relationship with Jesus, it will flow out of your life and touch the people around you in a very natural — and powerful — way.

But what is equally important is to be intentional about sharing the Good News with others. We ought to be praying for opportunities… and looking for opportunities… to share our faith with those around us.

It doesn't always have to be as dramatic as busting someone through a roof like the four men did in today's verses! But we need to start making evangelism a part of our lifestyle… not just something we do on rare occasions.

God has done an incredible miracle in our lives by forgiving our sins. Sometimes we can forget how significant that is… how liberating it feels to be cleansed of our sin and to have the confidence knowing that God loves us and accepts us.

But not everybody feels that way. We need to help people around us… our friends, relatives, and our neighbors… to understand that that incredible miracle — the forgiveness of sins — is available for them too.

You don't have to be a theologian to share your faith. Just be who you are and share what you know about Jesus. When you start talking about your own experience… the joy of being forgiven… the peace you feel as you worship… the answers you receive when you pray… the guidance you find in God's Word… your testimony will have an impact. And you will be amazed at how God will use you to draw people closer to Him!

So let me encourage you today, pray for opportunities to share your faith, and to do all you can to bring those around you to Jesus. He wants to minister to the needs of every person… and He wants to work through you to do it!

WHEN YOU HAVE A REAL, DAILY RELATIONSHIP WITH JESUS, IT WILL FLOW OUT OF YOUR LIFE AND TOUCH THE PEOPLE AROUND YOU IN A VERY NATURAL — AND POWERFUL — WAY.

Day 94

And as he reclined at table in his house, many tax collectors and sinners were reclining with Jesus and his disciples, for there were many who followed him. And the scribes of the Pharisees, when they saw that he was eating with sinners and tax collectors, said to his disciples, "Why does he eat with tax collectors and sinners?" And when Jesus heard it, he said to them, "Those who are well have no need of a physician, but those who are sick. I came not to call the righteous, but sinners."

— Mark 2:15-17

As we can see in today's verses, the fact that Jesus would be seen with tax collectors and prostitutes — much less attend the same party as them — was scandalous in His day. No one, especially a religious person, would have dared spend time with those kinds of people!

Yet Jesus often spent time with outsiders. He often went out of His way to embrace those whom society deemed as "riffraff." Why did He do this?

The answer is right there in Mark 2:17 when Jesus says, "Those who are well have no need of a physician, but those who are sick. I came not to call the righteous, but sinners."

There were people who were sick with sin in Jesus' day just like there are people who are sick with sin in our day. Yet so often, we're so offended by other peoples' sin that we isolate ourselves from them. But this isn't something Jesus modeled when He was here on earth!

As believers in the Lord Jesus Christ, you and I ought to be going out of our way to befriend those who are sick with sin. Does this mean engaging in their sin so that we can have an audience with them? Absolutely not. Does it mean condoning their sin so that they might listen to us? Not at all!

What it does mean is that you and I should be willing to meet people where they are in their sin and then introduce them to the only One who can heal them... Jesus Christ, the Great Physician!

Let me ask you, is there someone in your life right now whose sin is so great that you're avoiding contact with them? Maybe it's the guy in your office who's cheating on his wife. Or maybe it's the lady next door to you who constantly yells at her kids.

Whoever it is, you and I should be willing to get out of our comfort zone to befriend those who aren't walking with Christ.

This is what Jesus did... and I pray it's something you and I will do every day!

AS BELIEVERS IN THE LORD JESUS CHRIST, YOU AND I OUGHT TO BE GOING OUT OF OUR WAY TO BEFRIEND THOSE WHO ARE SICK WITH SIN.

"Truly, I say to you, all sins will be forgiven the children of man, and whatever blasphemies they utter, but whoever blasphemes against the Holy Spirit never has forgiveness, but is guilty of an eternal sin...."

—Mark 3:28-29

Time and time again in the Bible we're introduced to a caring, compassionate, loving God who says, "You matter to Me! You matter so much that I come to you at the point of your need, even your sin. I died on the cross for your sin."

The very reason Jesus came was so that, by His cross, He might forgive us of our sin. And the blood of Jesus Christ cleanses from every sin! Not some sins, every sin!

So the Scripture tells us that any sin and every sin can be forgiven. Except one. And Jesus told us about this particular sin. This sin which is unpardonable, this sin which is unforgivable according to Jesus Christ.

It's not the sin of murder... or perversion... or adultery. It's the sin we read about in today's verses: whoever blasphemes against the Holy Spirit never has forgiveness, but is guilty of an eternal sin. And what does it mean to blaspheme against the Holy Spirit?

It means saying NO to Christ, NO to God, and NO to the Holy Spirit enough times for God to give up on you.

This sin is a sin that takes place invisibly, sometimes imperceptibly; in the heart of an individual. It's not something a man says, it's not something a woman does... it is the unpardonable sin to reject one last time the salvation provided through Jesus Christ.

Please don't get the idea that a person can come to Christ and be saved anytime he or she chooses. The Bible tells us that no man can come to Christ unless the Holy Spirit draws that individual to come. And there can come a place in a person's life wherein they have said no to the wooing and the winning of the Holy Spirit in their lives so many times that they say no for the last time.

It's my prayer today... if you've never said YES to Christ... that you will accept the free gift of eternal life!

THE VERY REASON JESUS CAME WAS SO THAT, BY HIS CROSS, HE MIGHT FORGIVE US OF OUR SIN!

*Be patient, therefore, brothers, until the coming of the Lord.
See how the farmer waits for the precious fruit of the earth, being
patient about it, until it receives the early and the late rains.*
—James 5:7

Each follower of Christ has a specific calling of God on their life. But there is one call that's the same for each of us: Every believer in Jesus Christ has the responsibility to be a spiritual farmer.

What I mean by this is that every Christian is called by God to share the life-saving message of Jesus Christ with others!

And there are certain qualities that spiritual farmers exhibit. As we review these, ask yourself how well these qualities reflect you personally.

One, spiritual farmers sow seed with personal concern. They put the Word out there with a burden and water it with their tears. They are personally invested in witnessing to others! So the first characteristic of a spiritual farmer is that they care deeply about the lost.

Two, spiritual farmers realize the importance of partnership. They realize that it's going to take more than just a few of us to broadcast the Good News around the world.

Three, being a spiritual farmer requires patience, as we see in today's verse. James 5:7 is telling us that we need to be sowing seeds at all times… regardless of whether or not we think that seed is taking root!

Today, it's my prayer that God will burn on your heart an even greater passion to share the Good News with others. And as He does, I hope you will be encouraged in knowing that you are answering God's ultimate call on your life!

**EVERY CHRISTIAN IS CALLED BY GOD
TO SHARE THE LIFE-SAVING MESSAGE OF JESUS
CHRIST WITH OTHERS!**

Day 97

And when he got into the boat, his disciples followed him. And behold, there arose a great storm on the sea, so that the boat was being swamped by the waves; but he was asleep. And they went and woke him, saying, "Save us, Lord; we are perishing."

—Matthew 8:23-25

Maybe today you feel like the disciples did when they saw Jesus sleeping in the midst of the storm.

Perhaps you're thinking, "God, don't you care about me? Can't you see that I'm hurting here?" This is a natural, human reaction when it seems that God is distant or unconcerned in the midst of our pain and struggle.

But the fact is… if you're a child of God… He is there in the boat with you. And He will eventually still the storm in your life.

But until that storm is stilled, remember that trusting God produces questions you won't be able to answer. I think that's worth repeating: Trusting God produces questions you won't be able to answer.

I mean, disbelief is pretty easy. Anyone can not believe! Don't get the idea that someone who chooses not to believe is academically or intellectually superior.

Because choosing to trust in God and believe in His promises in spite of your questions… in spite of your problems… that's the real challenge! To suffer and hurt and not know why… but to keep believing and hoping… that's difficult.

So… no matter what you may be going through today… remember this: Jesus is present in the midst of your storms even though He may seem absent. And remember that in God's own time and in His own way… if you will wait on Him and trust in Him… He will calm your storm!

The One who has power over demons, the One who has power over disease, and the One who has power over death also has power over despair and the disturbances in your life. Jesus is your peace in the middle of the storm. So cling to Him today!

**TRUSTING GOD PRODUCES QUESTIONS
YOU WON'T BE ABLE TO ANSWER.**

And he awoke and rebuked the wind and said to the sea, "Peace! Be still!" And the wind ceased, and there was a great calm. He said to them, "Why are you so afraid? Have you still no faith?" And they were filled with great fear and said to one another, "Who then is this, that even the wind and the sea obey him?"

—Mark 4:39-41

D id you know that the Jesus who calmed the storm is the same Jesus who wants to work a miracle in your life today? It's true! As His child, Jesus wants to powerfully touch your life today.

Now, you may be thinking, "Pastor Graham, miracles are reserved for other people... people more religious than me. You don't understand what a mess I've gotten my life into."

You know what? I bet the apostle Paul thought something along those lines when Jesus saved him. I mean, he was an accomplice to the murder of Christians! And Simon Peter? I imagine he probably thought any kind of miracle in his life was a complete impossibility after he denied Christ three times!

Yet Christ touched both of these men's lives... He redeemed them... and He accomplished the "impossible" through them!

Jesus can do the impossible. In fact, He said it Himself in Luke 1:37, "For nothing will be impossible with God."

Christian, if you feel like your sin has taken you further than the powerful touch of Jesus can reach, you are mistaken! Paul says it best in Romans 8:38, "Neither death nor life, nor angels nor rulers, nor things present nor things to come, nor powers, nor height nor depth, nor anything else in all creation, will be able to separate us from the love of God in Christ Jesus our Lord."

Nothing can separate you from the powerful touch of Jesus. All it takes is the simplest act of faith... just a prayer saying, "Jesus, I want to turn from my sin. I need to know the power of your touch in my life today."

No matter what you're facing today, I encourage you to seek out the powerful touch of Christ. Because He's waiting to meet you where you are!

YOUR SIN CAN NEVER TAKE YOU FURTHER THAN THE POWERFUL TOUCH OF JESUS CAN REACH.

Day 99

Therefore you shall keep his statutes and his commandments, which I command you today, that it may go well with you and with your children after you...

—Deuteronomy 4:40

How's your family life? Do you have a strong family?

There's a lot of attention paid today to what's wrong with our families. But in one study at the University of Nebraska, researchers looked at the strengths of successful homes and families. They found six common qualities that identify strong families:

- Strong families are committed to the family.
- Strong families spend time together.
- Strong families have good family communication.
- Strong families express appreciation to one another.
- Strong families have a spiritual commitment.
- Strong families are able to work together to solve problems in a crisis.

As I look at this list, I believe the key to each ingredient is parenting. Successful families have parents who take the lead in each of these vital areas.

So, what about you? Are there any areas above that you could work on as a parent?

Do you have a spiritual commitment so that your family has a spiritual commitment? Do you express appreciation to your spouse and children? Do you foster open communication? Is spending time together important to you?

I want to challenge you today, as a parent, to go through this list and see how you check out. Then, determine to take the lead as a mom or dad in each of these vital areas!

PICK ONE CHARACTERISTIC OF SUCCESSFUL FAMILIES TO FOCUS ON AS A MOM OR DAD THIS WEEK.

Day 100

When his mother Mary had been betrothed to Joseph, before they came together she was found to be with child from the Holy Spirit. And her husband Joseph, being a just man and unwilling to put her to shame, resolved to divorce her quietly. But as he considered these things, behold, an angel of the Lord appeared to him in a dream, saying, "Joseph, son of David, do not fear to take Mary as your wife, for that which is conceived in her is from the Holy Spirit. She will bear a son, and you shall call his name Jesus, for he will save his people from their sins."

—Matthew 1:18-21

Most people, at some point in their life, have suffered the loss of a dream. And it can be an incredibly painful experience.

But one of the most powerful things we can learn from a man like Joseph is the example he set for you and me in the midst of heartache, confusion, disappointment, and shame. Through all this, Joseph remained open to what God wanted to do in his life.

And when God gave Joseph a new dream—a dream that was bigger than he ever could have imagined—Joseph was willing to say yes to God. Despite his fear and uncertainty and regardless of what people thought, Joseph was willing to trust and obey God. And as a result, Joseph lived one of the most significant lives in history as the man who raised and nurtured the Son of God!

You know, sometimes it's easy to look at ourselves and think we could never do something significant for God. But as the Scripture says in 1 Samuel 16:7, "For the LORD sees not as man sees: man looks on the outward appearance, but the LORD looks on the heart."

If God can use ordinary people in the Bible like Joseph and Moses and David and Peter, He can absolutely use you!

Lives of significance are not made by fame or fortune or personality or talent… but by godly character and obedience to the Lord. And those are qualities that every person can attain.

So let me ask you… have you asked God to show you His dream for your life? Have you dared to imagine that He can take you—with the personality and gifts and desires that you have now—and use you for His glory?

As you remain faithful in living out your faith in everyday obedience—just like Joseph did—you will find that God will use you to make an impact that is far greater than you could ever imagine!

LIVES OF SIGNIFICANCE ARE NOT MADE BY FAME OR FORTUNE OR PERSONALITY OR TALENT… BUT BY GODLY CHARACTER AND OBEDIENCE TO THE LORD.

Toward the scorners he is scornful, but to the humble he gives favor.

—Proverbs 3:34

It's important for you and me to remember that throughout history, God identifies with... and reveals Himself to... the humble.

When Jesus came to earth to deliver us from our sins, He was born as a vulnerable child to a teenage couple in a stable. And the first people to hear of His birth were shepherds, the social outcasts of their day! Jesus made His home with the most humble people He could find.

Later on in His life, Jesus spent His time seeking out and caring for the needy and soft-hearted. When He found them, He healed their sicknesses and shared a message of hope with them. He just loved everyday people!

That's encouraging for people like you and me, because Jesus is still like that today. He still wants to identify with, and reveal Himself to, men and women who will humbly come to Him. He will never turn away someone who asks for His forgiveness and help.

So if you need to ask God for His help... or His forgiveness... remember what the writer of Hebrews says: "Let us then with confidence draw near to the throne of grace, that we may receive mercy and find grace to help in time of need" (4:16).

JESUS WILL NEVER TURN AWAY SOMEONE WHO ASKS FOR HIS FORGIVENESS AND HELP.

Day 102

And the Word became flesh and dwelt among us, and we have seen his glory, glory as of the only Son from the Father, full of grace and truth.

—John 1:14

It's pretty astounding when you think about the impact Jesus Christ has had on the world given where He came from and how short of a time He lived.

Jesus was raised as a commoner from a poor family in an out-of-the-way little town called Nazareth. He was an apprentice in a carpenter's shop. He was from a minority race of people. He only lived 33 years before He was executed. And most of what we know about Him is limited to accounts of His birth and early childhood and the last three years of His life.

Yet today, our calendar is based on His birth… billions of people know His name… and millions worship Him! Jesus of Nazareth is without a doubt the most influential person who's ever walked the face of the earth. He has changed the world.

But the question I want to ask you today is, is He changing your world?

Every year, we're surrounded by reminders of Jesus' birth at Christmas, and we're reminded of His death and resurrection at Easter. The truth of who He is is all around us!

So I want to ask you, are you letting the truth of who Christ is and what He did for you affect how you live each day? If not, why not?

Today, I encourage you to allow the truth of Jesus to impact how you think and how you live!

ARE YOU LETTING THE TRUTH OF WHO CHRIST IS AND WHAT HE DID FOR YOU AFFECT HOW YOU LIVE EACH DAY?

Day 103

"Let not your hearts be troubled, neither let them be afraid."

—John 14:27

One of the greatest themes that we find in the story of Jesus' birth and life is "do not fear." We see it when the angel spoke to Joseph and we see it when the angels speak to the shepherds the night Jesus was born. "Do… not… fear."

Do these words from God have special meaning for you today?

Maybe you're experiencing pain and suffering in your life right now, and you don't understand why. Maybe you're struggling with terrible troubles or disease or difficulties. And maybe this has you wondering where God is in the midst of it all!

If so, remember that as a child of God, He is with you. He will never leave or forsake you. This means you're never alone!

And remember, God didn't just speak with words. He came. He came to restore a broken relationship. He came in love and devotion and He sacrificed His life and His love… not with words or platitudes or clichés… but with a cross and with a promise to love you forever.

If you haven't done so in a while, I'd like to encourage you to take a couple of minutes today and thank God that He came to earth… and that He's given you, through His Son, a way to escape fear and worry.

And then, claim today's verse, which says, "Peace I leave with you; my peace I give to you. Not as the world gives do I give to you. Let not your hearts be troubled, neither let them be afraid."

REMEMBER THAT AS HIS CHILD, JESUS WILL NEVER LEAVE YOU OR FORSAKE YOU!

Day 104

But God shows His love for us in that while we were still sinners, Christ died for us.

—Romans 5:8

O nce there was a red bird at my house that kept flying into our window. Over and over again, it flew right into the glass... until it eventually killed itself.

It didn't matter what I did to try to get that cardinal not to keep ramming its head into our window! Nothing I did... no shooing or swatting or yelling could stop that bird from doing what it thought it should be doing. And in the end, that bird paid the price for its ignorance with its life.

Isn't that how it is for so many people today? We try to live life on our terms, doing things the way we think they should be done... not realizing that our repeated attempts at finding meaning or security always end in vain.

But that is what's so great about our God. He saw us in our ignorance... in our sin... and He knew the only way to speak to us... to save us... was to become one of us.

God didn't just see our plight, our need, and our impending death and walk away and give up. He came all this way to live in our hearts, to reconcile us unto Himself! As the apostle Paul tells us in 2 Corinthians 5:18, "All this is from God, who reconciled us to himself...."

So let me ask you, have you been living life like that little red bird? Have you been repeatedly trying in vain to live life your own reckless way... ignoring the warning signs from God and those around you?

If so, it's my prayer that you will be reconciled to God. Turn to Him... and live in the freedom He wants to give you!

TURN TO JESUS TODAY... AND LIVE IN THE FREEDOM HE WANTS TO GIVE YOU!

Day 105

For at one time you were darkness, but now you are light in the Lord. Walk as children of light.

—Ephesians 5:8

A ny light is dependent on its source for power. And the same is true for you and me as followers of Christ. The more dependent we are on Jesus… the one and only true source of our power… the more we'll be able to be bright and shining lights for Him.

So let me ask you, how plugged into that source of power are you? The apostle Paul tells us in Ephesians 5:18, "Do not get drunk with wine, for that is debauchery, but be filled with the Spirit." What Paul is telling us here is that we shouldn't be filled to excess with anything in our lives except the Lord Jesus Christ.

What are you filled to excess with today? Or to put it another way, who… or what… do you worship? It could be that your career ambitions take center stage in your life. Or maybe being well-liked is your god. It could be that relationships… or the search for a relationship… is really where all your attention and energy are focused.

Our world is filled with darkness, and there are people all around us who are living in that darkness. That's why it's so important that, as a follower of Christ, you stay plugged into Him so that you can "let your light shine before others, so that they may see your good works and give glory to your Father who is in heaven," as the Scripture says in Matthew 5:16.

As a believer, Jesus, the light of the world, lives in you. So let your light shine! Show and tell people about the hope you have in Christ.

THE MORE DEPENDENT YOU ARE ON JESUS, THE MORE YOU'LL BE A BRIGHT AND SHINING LIGHT FOR HIM.

Day 106

And it is my prayer that your love may abound more and more,
with knowledge and all discernment, so that you may approve what
is excellent, and so be pure and blameless for the day of Christ...

—Philippians 1:9-10

The Scripture speaks directly to many different issues we're faced with in everyday life. But there are some issues... some debatable issues... where we have to use the principles of Scripture to make good, wise decisions.

These four questions can help you determine God's will when you're making a decision.

Question #1: Is it constructive?
In 1 Corinthians 6:12, Paul says, "'All things are lawful for me,' but not all things are helpful." Paul is emphasizing that you and I need to focus our decisions on things that will help us grow in our Christian life and honor Christ.

Question #2: Is it controlling?
In the second part of 1 Corinthians 6:12, Paul says, "'All things are lawful for me,' but I will not be enslaved by anything." If anything might control you, stay away from it.

Question #3: Is it compassionate?
This is a "me" generation and we often make decisions based upon what "I need"... what "I want." But love says we're to make decisions based on what others need. If there's anything in my life that would somehow cause a little one or weak one to fail or fall, I need to make my decision based on my compassion and care for them.

Finally, question #4: Is it consistent?

Is what you're about to do consistent with your testimony to the world? As believers, you and I are to be passionate about seeing others come to faith in Jesus Christ, and we shouldn't do anything to hinder someone from coming to Christ!

Hopefully these four questions will help you make godly decisions in your life, no matter what you may be facing!

GOD'S WORD HELPS US DISCERN HIS WILL FOR EVERY
SITUATION THAT WE FACE.

*Do not be conformed to this world, but be transformed by the
renewal of your mind, that by testing you may discern what is the
will of God, what is good and acceptable and perfect.*

—Romans 12:2

There are two kinds of people in our world today... those who
live hopeless, aimless, despairing lives, and those who live
hope-filled, certain, and joyful lives.

The difference in these two types of people is how they think about
God.

You see, some people never think about God. And as a result,
their lives are empty. Other people think about God, but they think
wrong things about Him. They live lives of confusion, deception,
and frustration.

Still some other people actually do think right things about God, but
it never touches where they live. They don't let the truth of who God
is transform them... which means they're never capable of making
any lasting changes... and that leads to lives full of discouragement
and defeat.

What about you? Do you think and believe right thoughts about
God... and in turn, have a life that is full of hope, certainty, and joy?

Our culture spouts lies about God every day. That's why I want to
encourage you to really get to know Him by reading His Word.

The Bible will help you think right thoughts about God!

**LEARN TO THINK RIGHT THOUGHTS ABOUT GOD
BY READING HIS WORD EVERY DAY.**

Day 108

And these words that I command you today shall be on your heart. You shall teach them diligently to your children...

—Deuteronomy 6:6-7

Do you know the difference between knowledge and wisdom? As a parent, it is important to teach your children with discernment, understanding, and wisdom.

Knowledge is the accumulation of facts. And, yes, we need an education and we need to be able to assess facts and figures. But Proverbs 24:3 says, "By wisdom a house is built, and by understanding it is established."

Why? Because simple knowledge isn't enough. God teaches us to go a step further. Wisdom is the practical and spiritual application of knowledge. Parents who make a difference teach their children how to put the facts to life and to work. And they also understand that school is not the primary source of a child's education.

A successful child is never fully educated until he or she knows the ways of God from His Word.

I'm sure you're aware of the anti-Christian bias in our schools today. It's a war for the minds of our children! Secular humanists want to remove all mention of God from our textbooks and teachings, which eliminates wisdom from education and leaves just simple knowledge.

So who will teach our children wisdom? Who will teach them about the Word of God and things like truth, purity, integrity, morality, and honesty? Parents.

As parents, it is your responsibility and mine to impart the wisdom of God at home. If we don't teach them diligently the truth about God, about Jesus, and about God's Word, who will?

We must commit to being mothers and fathers who make a difference by imparting wisdom into the lives of our children.

AS PARENTS, IT IS YOUR RESPONSIBILITY AND MINE TO IMPART THE WISDOM OF GOD AT HOME.

And these words that I command you today shall be on your heart.
You shall teach them diligently to your children, and shall talk of
them when you sit in your house, and when you walk by the way,
and when you lie down, and when you rise.

—Deuteronomy 6:6-7

Don't just say it… show it!

This old adage is never more important than it is in parenting.

You know, children can spot a phony from miles away, even if that phony happens to be their parent. They know if we're simply saying something, or if we really believe what we say.

Maybe you know all the right things to say. You've read all the books and manuals on how to raise your children. Today, we can all be "experts."

But, let me tell you, my parents never read a book on how to be a parent. I don't think they ever attended a seminar. And my dad had an eighth grade education. But they made an incredible difference in my life and my brother's life.

How? Because they didn't just tell me what they believed. They showed me! Do your children know it because you show it?

Do you tell them to stay away from alcohol and then grab a beer out of the refrigerator? Do you warn them against immorality and watch immoral television shows and movies?

Your children are watching you, so be their hero. Be a model of virtue and purity. You can be the kind of person your child can trust and respect as a role model.

So start showing them what you believe today!

ASK GOD TO HELP YOU WALK THE TALK AND BE AN
EXAMPLE OF CHRIST FOR YOUR CHILDREN.

Day 110

Fathers, do not provoke your children, lest they become discouraged.
—**Colossians 3:21**

When it comes to disciplining your children, do you ever find yourself majoring in minors?

Parents have to be very careful not to break a child's spirit by constantly finding fault, nagging, and criticizing. In discipline, you and I are to be reasonable, right, respectful, and real.

Now I'm not saying that you should be lacking in discipline. Yes, you should establish firm, age-appropriate guidelines for your children. And sometimes correction and consequences are a part of parenting.

But, many kids are hassled and provoked because parents worry about things that don't mean anything. Some parents are more interested in pushing their kids to the top of the success ladder at school or in athletics than seeing them succeed spiritually. Are you guilty?

According to our verse today, we are not to "provoke" our children. Don't worry so much about the things that have little impact on eternity, on their moral character, or on their spiritual strength. We shouldn't push our children to succeed because of our own failures. Nor should we use our children to compete against others.

Today I want to ask you to take inventory. When it comes to parenting, are you majoring on the minors… or majoring on what's most important?

**TAKE INVENTORY OF THE PRIORITIES YOU
HAVE FOR YOUR CHILDREN. IS THEIR SPIRITUAL
CHARACTER ON THE LIST?**

Day 111

But as for me and my house, we will serve the LORD.

—Joshua 24:15

If you are a parent who wants to pass your faith on to the next generation, I have some advice for you—KEEP IT REAL!

If you and I are going to instill a strong, unshakable faith in our children, we must be transparent, authentic, and real. Exercising your faith at home must be part of your everyday life!

Now you certainly don't have to dress up for it or put a face on for it. Real faith works in a suit or in blue jeans. Make faith a normal, comfortable part of your everyday life and your children will see faith in action.

I love today's verse when Joshua said, "But as for me and my house, we will serve the LORD." He took the lead and made the decision that his household would live for God. You can make the same decision for your family today!

If your heart and soul longs to know Christ, real faith will permeate your life as a parent, whether you are worshipping or working, praying or playing, going to church or fishing. When you rise and when you go to bed at night, be real!

Make God's Word part of your daily walk. Talk the truth, model the truth, and live the truth.

According to Proverbs 22:6, "Train up a child in the way he should go; even when he is old he will not depart from it."

Training your child in the ways of the Lord is a 24/7 job, but you can do it with God's help.

MAKE FAITH A NORMAL, COMFORTABLE PART OF YOUR EVERYDAY LIFE AND YOUR CHILDREN WILL SEE FAITH IN ACTION.

Day 112

Fathers, do not provoke your children to anger, but bring them up in the discipline and instruction of the Lord.

—Ephesians 6:4

America is in danger of losing an entire generation of young people. Why? I believe it's because of a lack of male leadership in the home.

There is a war against the family with high stakes. And the key to winning this war is leadership. We need men to enlist in the war on the family.

Now, if you are a dad, I know you're probably willing to lay down your life for your children.

But my question to you is this: Are you willing to live for your family? Are you willing to sacrifice your life now for your children?

What our children need today is men of spiritual quality who are devoted to their families… real men who raise their children both with strength and sensitivity, and who are in tune with their children's needs.

Here are a few ways to do this…

• Give your child enough freedom to enjoy life without being overprotective.
• Don't show favoritism or compare your children to each other.
• Offer encouragement, not discouragement.
• Don't force your child to be something he or she is not.
• Spend time with your children. Show them you love them.
• Never, ever be cruel.
• Raise your children with strong spiritual direction. That means we're to provide protection, correction, and instruction.

As dads, you and I should have a passion for excellence in parenting. We have the responsibility to bring our children up with the training and admonition of the Lord. They need to know about rewards and consequences. But we also need to nourish them and provide tender care.

Children need dads who are kind, who show appreciation and affirmation, who are sensitive to feelings, and who are not afraid to say, "I'm sorry." They need dads who will teach them the rules, regulations, and provide a moral compass.

Dad, are you the leader of your house? Are you God's man in your home?

DADS, ARE YOU WILLING TO LIVE FOR YOUR FAMILY? ARE YOU WILLING TO SACRIFICE YOUR LIFE NOW FOR YOUR CHILDREN?

"And if I go and prepare a place for you, I will come again and will take you to myself, that where I am you may be also."

—John 14:3

D id you know that God has prepared an eternal home for you? If you've accepted Christ as your Savior, you probably do.

Jesus came to earth, died on the cross, and rose again so that you and I might go to heaven, our eternal home.

As He said in John 14:1-3, "Let not your hearts be troubled. Believe in God; believe also in me. In my Father's house are many rooms. If it were not so, would I have told you that I go to prepare a place for you? And if I go and prepare a place for you, I will come again and will take you to myself, that where I am you may be also."

But God also created a spiritual home on earth for you and me—your church.

Jesus said, "And I tell you, you are Peter, and on this rock I will build my church, and the gates of hell shall not prevail against it" (Matt. 16:18). You and I need to know and experience the fellowship of faith in the family of God known as His Church.

Maybe you come from a broken home. Or maybe you have a large extended family. Whatever your personal family is like, you can still find strength, love, and encouragement in your local church.

FIND A CHURCH HOME AND GET INVOLVED!

Day 114

Behold, children are a heritage from the LORD, the fruit of the womb a reward.

—Psalm 127:3

Do your children know that you love them unconditionally? Do they believe that no matter what they face, no matter how they fail, you love them without question?

As parents, you and I have to look into our children's eyes and tell them that, yes, there are rules and standards in the home, but nothing they do can stop you from loving them. Your children must know that you love them absolutely and unconditionally.

Why? Because that's how much God loves us. He loves us not based on our performance or appearance. By His grace He accepts us as we are… warts and all. And when you love your child as God loves you, it will impact your child for life.

You and I need to tell our children we love them, but we also have to show them!

How do you show love? First, with acceptance. A child needs at least one place on earth where he or she is accepted. Now, I'm not suggesting you lower your morals or your values.

But if your son or daughter gets into trouble, are you going to love them through it? Can your child come to you and share their hurt, brokenness, and sin and find forgiveness, love, and acceptance?

Love is not only expressed in acceptance, but also in affection. Your home needs to be filled with love and affection. And one of the best ways you can show your child acceptance and affection is through your time.

You also show love through affirmation. Are you constantly finding fault in your child? Or do you find things to be proud about? Learn to encourage your child by finding something good that they are doing and telling them about it.

Keep this in mind:
- If you express your love by acceptance, it will produce significance in your child's life.
- If you express your life by affection, it will produce security in a child's life.
- And if you give your child love by affirmation, it will produce self-esteem in your child's life.

**NO MATTER HOW OLD YOUR CHILDREN ARE,
TELL THEM YOU LOVE THEM TODAY!**

Day 115

Train up a child in the way that he should go, and when he is old he will not depart from it.

—**Proverbs 22:6**

One of the most important things you can teach your children is respect.

Because unless a child learns respect, they learn rebellion. Children need to be taught respect for God, for parents, for school authorities, and for church leaders.

The reason is because we are each born with the inclination to rebel and disobey. As Proverbs 22:15 says, "Folly is bound up in the heart of a child, but the rod of discipline drives it far from him."

Now, I know that the "rod of discipline" is a controversial subject in today's society. But regardless of where you stand on spanking your children, every child needs discipline.

So how do you know when you should discipline your child?

• You should discipline your child when he or she willfully disobeys, not matter what their age.

• You should discipline your child when he or she steps out of bounds. Make sure your children know what the boundaries are and correct them when they break the rules.

Make the rules fair and reasonable—don't major in the minors—but enforce the boundaries. When you teach and discipline your children on those things that are precious, valuable, and eternal, you'll give them something to live by. And you'll help grow them into the men and women God created them to be.

ARE YOU MODELING RESPECT FOR GOD, PARENTS, SCHOOL AUTHORITIES, AND CHURCH LEADERS IN YOUR HOME?

Day 116

Like arrows in the hand of a warrior are the children of one's youth.
—Psalm 127:4

How can you make sure your children head in the right direction in life? By leading them there!

Parent, your children are looking to you for an example. All the limits and rules in the world can equal a big zero without leadership. You and I must set an example for our children through our personal habits, our work ethics, our worship life, our church involvement, and much more.

Consider the story of Jotham in 2 Chronicles 27 and 28. Jotham was angry because his father, King Uzziah, was chastised and corrected in the temple. So, when Jotham became king, he refused to attend worship services. But Jotham paid a terrible price for it. When his son became king, he became an idol worshipper and even sacrificed his own children, Jotham's grandchildren!

I want my children to know what I believe. Don't you? If you want them to share your faith and follow in your footsteps, you first have to make footprints. You and I have to walk the talk!

Your leadership will make an eternal difference in the life of your child. You can give them love and limits. And most importantly, you can give your children the Lord.

You do this by talking about your faith with them, by being open about what you believe, and by sharing your love of God in your daily life.

Don't be afraid to admit your mistakes and ask for God's help in front of your children. Tell them Bible stories. Have family devotional time. Pray with your children.

Like the arrows in our Scripture verse, you have the power to point your children in the right direction. Start leading your children into an authentic experience with Jesus Christ today!

START LEADING YOUR CHILDREN INTO AN AUTHENTIC EXPERIENCE WITH JESUS CHRIST BY PRAYING WITH THEM TONIGHT.

Day 117

Now concerning the matters about which you wrote: It is good for a man not to have sexual relations with a woman.

—1 Corinthians 7:1

Are you single? If so, the Bible has some words of affirmation for you.

In our Scripture verse for today, Paul is responding to questions that many of the Corinthian Christians were asking.

Regarding the question of whether it was better to be single or married, Paul responds by saying that it is good when a Christian can, by the call of God, live a celibate, pure Christian life. He is not saying that those who are married are less spiritual.

So the message from the Scripture is clear. If you sense that it is God's plan that you remain single, don't think you're missing out on fulfillment in life. And if you are married, you must be careful not to put down those who choose to remain single.

There are many things that are worse than living a single life. And one of those is to be married to the wrong person!

Remember, if you are single today, God affirms your lifestyle as good. Do not be discouraged. He has a purpose and a plan for your life that can be fulfilling and full of joy!

THERE ARE MANY THINGS THAT ARE WORSE THAN LIVING A SINGLE LIFE. AND ONE OF THOSE IS TO BE MARRIED TO THE WRONG PERSON!

I want you to be free from anxieties. The unmarried man is anxious about the things of the Lord, how to please the Lord.
—1 Corinthians 7:32

Today I want to speak specifically to those who are not married. Why would God choose to cause you to live a single life? Because God may give you a special ability to serve Christ without the responsibility of marriage and family life.

The apostle Paul, who was single himself, said that because of the distressful nature of the times and because times are urgent, single life allows you to serve God without distraction. What potential there is in the single life lived for Jesus Christ! Single adults can be placed into the heart and life of the church.

Some of the greatest Christians who ever lived have been single adults, starting with Paul. Then think about some of the greatest modern disciples who impacted entire nations—David Brainard, missionary to the Indians of North America; Lottie Moon, missionary to China; and Bertha Smith, who also served the people of China. There are so many more!

And don't forget that our Lord Jesus Christ was single. He is the model of what it means to be committed to our heavenly Father's plan. As a single person, you have a unique opportunity to give yourself unreservedly, completely, and totally to the service of Jesus Christ.

THINK ABOUT THE POSSIBLITIES FOR SERVICE IN GOD'S KINGDOM AS A SINGLE ADULT!

Day 119

To the married I give this charge (not I, but the Lord): the wife should not be separate from her husband (but if she does, she should remain unmarried or else be reconciled to her husband), and the husband should not divorce his wife.

—1 Corinthians 7:10-11

Is it okay for a believer to divorce an unbeliever? In 1 Corinthians 7:10, Paul deals specifically with the issue of a believer and an unbeliever being married.

In the New Testament church of Corinth, divorce was one of the issues new believers were questioning. Some who had come to Christ were wondering if they should leave their unbelieving mates.

Maybe you or someone you know is faced with this same question. If you came to know Christ after being married and your spouse has not yet made a decision to share your faith, what should you do?

According to our verse today, Paul discourages divorce for that reason. As a new believer, you should try to be a light for your spouse. Pray for them daily. If you love them, then you will want them to experience the same grace and joy you have found.

However, there are certain Scriptural grounds for divorce. If you are struggling in your marriage, I want to encourage you to discuss your situation with a godly friend or pastor. Go deeper into the Word for your answer.

IF YOU ARE STRUGGLING WITH THE ISSUE OF DIVORCE, PLEASE SEE A TRAINED CHRISTIAN COUNSELOR OR YOUR PASTOR.

Day 120

Finally brothers, whatever is true, whatever is honorable, whatever is just, whatever is pure, whatever is lovely, whatever is commendable, if there is any excellence, if there is anything worthy of praise, think about these things.

—Philippians 4:8

If you are single... and your desire is to be married... I have some biblically-based guidelines for you today.

First, make sure that you are fully committed to Jesus Christ as your Lord and Savior. If you're going to find the right person, you must become the right person.

Second, set the highest possible standards in your relationships. Don't cheat yourself. Don't jump into relationships and end up taking less than the best. You deserve God's very best!

This includes making sure that any person you consider for marriage is a believer in Jesus Christ. No question about it. The Bible says do not be unequally yoked together with unbelievers.

Third, if you are considering marriage to someone, be sure that you sincerely love that person. Ensure that you're not taking the relationship further for what you can get out of it, but what you can give to it.

Fourth, stay pure! Moral purity is a non-negotiable in Scripture. So flee from temptation. You can live a holy and pure life with God's help and the help of Christian friends around you.

IF YOU ARE SINGLE, ARE THERE ANY AREAS ABOVE THAT YOU NEED TO WORK ON? IF SO, TALK TO GOD ABOUT THEM.

Day 121

Likewise, wives, be subject to your own husbands, so that even if some do not obey the word, they may be won without a word by the conduct of their wives, when they see your respectful and pure conduct.

—1 Peter 3:1-2

If you want to understand your mate and create a good, fulfilling marriage, you have to understand your responsibilities as a spouse.

God planned the marriage to be an unconditional commitment with devotion and service to each other. With that comes responsibilities for both the spouses.

Let's look at the wife's responsibilities according to 1 Peter 3:1. There are two major responsibilities for the wife:

1. To have a giving spirit. "Likewise, you wives, be subject to your own husbands" (1 Peter 3:1). Now, for some, "subject" is an ugly word. But it means to rank under authority. All Christians are called to subject ourselves to God and to the body of Christ. And wives are instructed to do the same for their husbands.

However, this doesn't imply any inferiority. Jesus submitted Himself to His heavenly Father and we know that God and Christ are co-equal. It is simply a chain of command or responsibility. Wives are to give themselves voluntarily. Not by coercion or force, but out of love, devotion, and appreciation for God's gift. When you give like that, you can't help but gain!

2. Secondly, wives should have a gentle spirit. "Do not let your adorning be external—the braiding of hair and the putting on of gold jewelry, or the clothing you wear—but let your adorning be the hidden person of the heart with the imperishable beauty of a gentle and quiet spirit, which in God's sight is very precious" (1 Peter 3:3-4).

A gentle spirit does not mean that you're a doormat, but it means serenity, the peacefulness of a quiet, gentle spirit. It refers to the cultivation of inner beauty in the character of Christ.

Wives, Scripture says that if you have a giving and gentle spirit, your husbands will be won without a single word! Your godly life and the beauty of your testimony will reveal Christ to your husband.

JESUS DEFEATED THE ENEMY BY USING THE VERY SAME TOOL THAT WE HAVE AVAILABLE TO US—THE WORD OF GOD.

Likewise, husbands, live with your wives in an understanding way, showing honor to the woman as the weaker vessel, since they are heirs with you of the grace of life, so that your prayers may not be hindered.

—1 Peter 3:7

According to God's plan for marriage, the husband has two major responsibilities.

First, according to today's verse, the husband must understand his wife. Now, to understand our wives means to honor them.

What a vivid description of love—to honor. If you are wondering how to show honor, think of it like this. To honor your wife means to see her as a treasure, to hold her dear, and to cherish her as a precious gift.

Husbands, do you love your wife like that? Do you see her as a gift from God?

This verse also refers to understanding your wife's needs. Gary Smalley, a noted Christian counselor and marriage expert, lists these nine specific needs.

A wife:
- Needs to feel that she is first place in her husband's life.
- Needs to feel that her husband is willing to share an intimate moment of comfort without demanding explanation or giving lectures.
- Needs constant communication.
- Longs to be praised so she can feel valuable.
- Wants to feel free to correct her husband without fear of retaliation or anger.
- Needs to know that her husband will defend and protect her.
- Wants to know that her opinion is so valuable that her husband will discuss decisions with her, evaluate her advice, and then act upon it.
- Needs to share her life with her husband in every area—home, family, and outside interests.
- Wants her husband to be the kind of man her son can follow and her daughter would want to marry.

Secondly, a husband is to undergird his wife with emotional, spiritual and physical support. Why? Because we share the love and grace of God, hand in hand. And we should see each other through the eyes of grace… as God sees us.

TRY VIEWING YOUR SPOUSE TODAY WITH GOD'S EYES. YOU'LL SEE A PRECIOUS TREASURE!

Day 123

"Therefore a man shall leave his father and mother and hold fast to his wife, and the two shall become one flesh'. So they are no longer two but one flesh. What therefore God has joined together, let not man separate."

—Mark 10:7-9

Do you remember the first Rocky movie?

I love the line when someone asks Rocky what he and Adrian saw in each other. He says, "I got gaps; Adrian's got gaps. We fill in one another's gaps."

What a great description of marriage! We fill in one another's gaps!

Have you ever noticed how in many marriages, the weaknesses of one spouse are offset by the strengths of the other? Working together, we are stronger than we could ever be separately.

In marriage, when we can affirm our diversity and accept our responsibilities, then we can rejoice in our unity. In God's miracle mathematics of marriage, one plus one equals one.

How do we achieve that unity? Through the example of Jesus Christ who died for you upon the cross. He is the supreme example of love. Therefore His love is our standard.

Maybe you've never had the right kind of model for your marriage. If you came out of a broken home, maybe you feel doomed to repeat the mistakes of your parents or your own past life. But you don't have to!

Begin today. Start afresh and ask Jesus Christ to help you. I want to encourage you today to follow Christ's example of love and sacrifice in your marriage.

You do this by affirming your diversity, accepting your responsibilities, and rejoicing in your unity as a man and woman who have received God's grace and hope for eternal life.

When you do, you can begin to "become one."

PRAY TOGETHER AND ASK GOD TO HELP YOU "BECOME ONE."

Day 124

For we know that the whole creation has been groaning together in the pains of childbirth until now.

—Romans 8:22

You can't turn on the television or read the newspaper without being reminded about the problems of the environment, wars, and failing economies. But is planet earth really in trouble?

According to our Scripture verse for today, "the whole creation has been groaning." Whether it is the polluted seas, global warming, or deforestation, this is an age of suffering. And creation itself is suffering. You can hear the moaning of creation when the seas are in turbulence or the wind rages.

And the suffering includes all of creation. As believers in Jesus Christ, we are not exempt. Christians face personal tragedy, bad reports from the doctor, and other serious problems.

Maybe you are groaning from pain and tragedy. Are you drowning in a sea of doubts because of suffering in your life? You and I must understand that we live in a world that is affected and infected with a terrible disease—SIN!

When Paul wrote about groaning and suffering, he spoke from experience. He knew about great suffering. Paul was stoned and left for dead, beaten, imprisoned, thrown overboard.

Yes, we live in a broken, bruised, battered, and groaning world.

But Paul also tells us in 2 Corinthians 4 that our affliction "is just for a moment." And despite the pain and suffering, Paul says our hurts are dimmed by the glory that is to come!

IF YOU ARE SUFFERING AS A FOLLOWER OF CHRIST TODAY, REMEMBER IT "IS JUST FOR A MOMENT."

Day 125

For the creation was subjected to futility, not willingly, but because of him who subjected it, in hope that the creation itself will be set free from its bondage to corruption and obtain the freedom of the glory of the children of God.

—Romans 8:20-21

What has happened to this world? God created a perfect paradise and man was placed to rule over it all. Now the earth is cursed with plagues, pollution, greed, destruction, and more.

Again, what happened? Sin. The world was cursed and plunged into corruption by sin and rebellion. When Adam and Eve disobeyed God in rebellion, they placed all of creation into "the bondage of corruption." And now man lives in fear, failure, and frustration.

But did you know that pain can actually be a good thing? How can pain and suffering be good? It's a warning signal to tell us that something is wrong.

How do you know to pull your hand out of the fire unless you feel the searing pain of the heat?

All the groaning, crying, and moaning of this age is God's effort to get our attention. Yes, He cares about you and me. And, yes, He is all-powerful. God has a plan beyond our human understanding. And as Paul wrote, He is preparing His family for a future glory that cannot even be compared to the sufferings and hurt of today.

How do you overcome despite the suffering? Look with expectation for what God has prepared for those who belong to Jesus Christ.

HOW DO YOU KNOW TO PULL YOUR HAND OUT OF THE FIRE UNLESS YOU FEEL THE SEARING PAIN OF THE HEAT?

Day 126

For the creation waits with eager longing for the revealing of the sons of God.

—Romans 8:19

You and I have a promise for a better day. There is a perfect day coming, and all of creation is waiting for the revealing of the Son of God and those who belong to Jesus Christ.

It doesn't matter what man does, all of creation waits for Jesus' return. Mankind cannot save the earth by ecology, social engineering, or political manipulation.

Any man-made solution is inadequate and incomplete. The earth will not be saved until there is a rebirth of planet earth when Jesus comes again. There will never be ecological balance, peace on this earth, or prosperity until Jesus Christ returns.

So how does that make your life better today?

If you can get a glimpse of the glory, the freedom from suffering, and the perfection you will experience upon Christ's return, you'll have the strength you need to weather the groanings of this day and age.

When Jesus Christ ushers in the new age, a new heaven, and a new earth, the curse of creation will be removed. And all of heaven and earth shall celebrate the glory of God.

God has a plan for planet earth. It will not live in futility and vanity much longer. You and I will soon be finally and fully redeemed. We'll have a healthy new body in a perfect environment.

And so, during days of groaning and suffering, look forward to the future. Be strengthened by the glory that is soon to come. Jesus is coming again!

IF YOU CAN GET A GLIMPSE OF THE GLORY, THE FREEDOM FROM SUFFERING, AND THE PERFECTION YOU WILL EXPERIENCE UPON CHRIST'S RETURN, YOU'LL HAVE THE STRENGTH YOU NEED TO WEATHER THE GROANINGS OF THIS DAY AND AGE.

Day 127

For we know that the whole creation has been groaning together in the pains of childbirth until now. And not only the creation, but we ourselves, who have the firstfruits of the Spirit, groan inwardly as we wait eagerly for adoption as sons, the redemption of our bodies.

—Romans 8:22-23

Here's an understatement—we live in a world in pain because of sin. There is plenty of evidence that as Romans 8:22 says "creation has been groaning."

Stress, violence, hatred, wars, disease, and tragedies are all over the news. So, is there any hope for a world like this?

Even Christians groan according to our Scripture verse today! Why? You and I are still members of a fallen race, living in a fallen place!

But today, maybe you're not thinking about the hopelessness of the world. Maybe you're wondering, "Is there any hope for me?"

If you are suffering and hurting, God has a prescription for your pain. He has a medicine of hope! You and I may not have any hope in our world today. But we can find hope in the world to come.

We have hope because of the promise that Jesus has given us. You and I have the hope of the redemption of our body and of living in God's presence forever in joy and peace.

YOU AND I MAY NOT HAVE ANY HOPE IN OUR WORLD TODAY. BUT WE CAN FIND HOPE IN THE WORLD *TO COME*.

Day 128

For in this hope we were saved. Now hope that is seen is not hope.
For who hopes for what he sees?

—Romans 8:24

D id you know that you need hope? We all do.

Swiss theologian M.L. Bruner said, "What oxygen is to the lungs, such is hope to the meaning of human life." Just as our physical bodies would die without oxygen, our spirit will suffocate without hope!

In our culture, we hear a lot about love. We even hear a lot about faith. But we don't hear that much about hope.

Yet from the very beginning, God provided hope. After Adam and Eve sinned and plunged the planet into pain, God gave a promise for a redeemer, a savior. That hope is Jesus Christ!

"For unto you is born this day in the city of David a Savior, who is Christ the Lord" (Luke 2:11).

What do you need hope for today? Physical pain? Disease? Addiction? Depression? Bad habits? A broken heart? Whatever your need, God's plan is to give you a future and a hope.

Jesus Christ was sent to conquer pain and death, and to give hope. He is your Redeemer… your hope. But just like the air you breathe, hope is an unseen promise.

FIND YOUR HOPE IN JESUS CHRIST TODAY.

Day 129

O Israel, hope in the LORD! For with the LORD there is steadfast love, and with him is plentiful redemption.

—Psalm 130:7

What is hope? What does it mean for your life right now?

Hope is far more than positive thinking, wishful thinking or human optimism.

The Bible describes our hope as a living hope, a hope to live by. The hope you and I have in Jesus Christ is the hope of heaven, but it is not just for the next life. It is hope for the NOW life.

Biblical hope is a confidence based upon promises that are guaranteed by God. You and I can have hope right now:

• **That God answers prayer.** "And this is the confidence that we have toward him, that if we ask anything according to his will he hears us" (1 John 5:14).

• **For a new beginning.** No matter how you and I fail in this life, there's always hope for another chance. There is hope for your home, for your marriage, and for your life.

• **That God will turn your suffering into victory.** No matter what the circumstance or situation, God has a plan for your benefit.

• **Over the fear of death.** With Jesus Christ there is hope that we will never die.

Hope is not flimsy or futile. Hope is strong. And hope can build strength and confidence in your life!

BIBLICAL HOPE IS A CONFIDENCE BASED UPON PROMISES THAT ARE GUARANTEED BY GOD.

Day 130

And now, O Lord, for what do I wait? My hope is in you.

—Psalm 39:7

Ｈow can you be confident in your future?

If you have accepted Jesus Christ as your Savior, you have a hope that is grounded in God. And there is nothing stronger, truer, surer, more reliable, more just, or more powerful than Him!

So how is this confident hope made real in your own life?

Hope is made real through the Scriptures. If you want to increase your hope, study the Scriptures. "In his word I hope" (Psalm 130:5). God, who cannot lie, has given us a guarantee, a sure promise in His Word. The revelation of His word is that you and I have a future and a hope.

Hope is also made real by the resurrection. Because Jesus Christ lives, we shall live also. Because He conquered sin, the grave, death, and hell, we are conquerors through Him (Romans 8:37).

And hope is made real by faith. Faith and hope are inseparably linked. Faith is the root, hope is the fruit. Faith produces hope! "For through the Spirit, by faith, we ourselves eagerly wait for the hope of righteousness" (Galatians 5:5).

MAKE YOUR HOPE REAL BY BUILDING YOUR LIFE UPON THE WORD OF GOD.

Day 131

We shall be like Him, for we shall see Him as He is.

—1 John 3:2

Who do you trust when you are in pain or uncertain about life?

Now, there are many people who can help us when we hurt. There are pastors, counselors, friends, and others. We need people to hold us up and give us hope.

But too often, we put our complete confidence in men and what other people tell us when there is no substitute for the truth of hope in Jesus Christ!

Have you lost sight of the fact that our greatest and only everlasting hope is from God? I want to remind you that Jesus is sufficient for your needs and mine. He provides a hiding place in the storms of life.

He is a Father to the fatherless. He is the Great Physician to those who are wounded and sick. He is the Beginning and the End to those who face uncertainty. He is the Resurrection and the Life. And He is your Eternal and Living Hope!

If your hope is in Jesus Christ, there is coming a day when all your physical pain will be no more. You and I will have a new body and a new life in Christ and we will live with Him forever. That's the blessed hope of eternity.

No matter what you're going through today, no matter how much you hurt, persevere. Hold onto your hope.

TURN *TO JESUS* TODAY. TELL HIM
ABOUT YOUR STRUGGLES.

Day 132

Likewise the Spirit helps us in our weaknesses.

—Romans 8:26

Go ahead, you can admit it… prayer is hard work. There is a weakness within us that makes prayer difficult. It is our humanity, our "flesh."

When I start to pray, I can think of about ten other things I could be doing. Does that happen to you? I go over all my responsibilities or my mind wanders. Other times, I just don't feel like praying.

But it doesn't have to be that way! You and I can have effective, fulfilling prayer. What's the key? Praying in the Spirit.

There are two ways to pray. You can pray in the flesh or you can pray in the Spirit. What's the difference? Scripture says, "The Spirit is willing but the flesh is weak."

So if you pray in the flesh, you pray in weakness. Prayer through our own efforts alone and for our own purposes does not get through to God. But if you pray in the Spirit, you pray with strength.

Wouldn't you like to pray with power? Wouldn't you like to know that your prayers are getting through? You can if you partner with the Spirit in prayer.

I want to encourage you to depend upon the Holy Spirit in prayer just as you depend upon the Holy Spirit for witnessing, for teaching others, and more.

Because He is our Comforter and our Help!

PRAYER THROUGH OUR OWN EFFORTS AND FOR OUR OWN PURPOSES DOES NOT GET THROUGH TO GOD. BUT IF YOU PRAY IN THE SPIRIT, YOU PRAY WITH STRENGTH.

Day 133

For we do not know what to pray for as we ought, but the Spirit himself intercedes for us with groanings too deep for words.
—John 14:27

I f I were to title this devotion, I would call it "The Problems with Prayer."

As believers, you and I know that we are commanded and called to prayer. Ephesians 6:18 tells us that we should pray "at all times in the Spirit."

But because of our flesh, there are several "problems" that stand in the way of effective and empowering prayer... problems that the Holy Spirit can help us overcome if we but ask.

First, we lack concern. As humans, lethargy and even laziness battle our desire to pray. We don't feel the need or urgency to pray. The flesh really doesn't want to pray. But the Spirit gives us the concern and prompts us to pray.

Second, we perceive distance between God and ourselves. Many people don't pray because they feel like they're either talking to themselves or to someone who is absent. They cannot sense the presence of God in prayer. That's where the Holy Spirit comes in. We have access by the Holy Spirit to the Father.

According to Galatians 4:6, "Because you are sons, God has sent the Spirit of His Son into our hearts, crying, Abba! Father!"

We have the Spirit of God living within us to make God real and to make God ever present. The Holy Spirit helps us connect with God the Father.

THE HOLY SPIRIT WILL HELP YOU OVERCOME THE "PROBLEMS WITH PRAYER" IF YOU WILL BUT ASK.

Day 134

And he who searches hearts knows what is the mind of the Spirit, because the Spirit intercedes for the saints according to the will of God.
—Romans 8:27

God is looking for people like you and me who will connect with Him in prayer so that He can unleash His power through us.

But where do you start?

First of all, prayer is not just a long list of your needs and wants. Effective, empowering prayer is not even always talking… it also includes listening.

When you and I begin to listen to God, He communicates His will.

How does that work? Through the Holy Spirit. The Spirit teaches us what to pray and interprets the will of God.

Maybe you're struggling with the will of God for your life. You may be looking at your future and need answers from God.

When you can focus on Him, delight in Him, and love and worship Him through prayer, you will be able to pray through the Spirit. And the Comforter will implant God's desire into our hearts and lives.

God will give you His desires and teach you His will… if you take time to listen.

BE STILL AND LISTEN TO GOD'S VOICE TODAY.

Day 135

"But when you pray, go into your room and shut the door and pray to your Father who is in secret. And your Father who sees in secret will reward you."

—Matthew 6:6

If obligations and a busy schedule have exhausted the energy in your spiritual tank, maybe you need to refuel!

Whether you spend your day rushing to meetings, escorting children to school functions and sports events, or ministering to others, life can be exhausting!

So if you feel drained of energy and strength, I want to share how you can be empowered.

The Spirit of God can energize you through your prayer life. And when you worship God in the Spirit, you'll be invigorated.

Personally, when I'm physically tired and begin to worship God, my spirit becomes energized, revived, and revitalized. The same thing can happen to you!

I believe one of the secrets to empowering prayer is committing to private prayer time. Jesus says in Matthew 6:6: "But when you pray, go into your room and shut the door and pray to your Father who is in secret."

Private prayer is that time alone with God when you and I draw near to Him through the Spirit to know Him, to talk with Him. And every Christian who wants to be refueled with the power of prayer must find a place to pray privately.

Do you have a secret place? Do you have a quiet time dedicated to the Lord? Matthew 6:6 continues, "And your Father who sees in secret will reward you."

When we join God in the secret place, His Spirit fills the space and we can truly converse and commune with God. That's prayer that empowers you for living!

**GET ALONE WITH GOD TODAY TO
REFUEL YOUR SPIRIT!**

Day 136

First of all, then, I urge that supplications, prayers, intercessions, and thanksgivings be made for all people.

—1 Timothy 2:1

You have an opportunity for powerful, life-changing ministry without ever leaving your home. It's through the power of prayer.

Prayer is a powerful tool for change in the lives of others. The Spirit of God wants to touch and reach others through your prayers. So, whom should you pray for?

In 1 Timothy chapter 2, Paul tells us to pray for—

• Backsliders. Who do you know who is absent from the worship and service of God? Maybe they've been hurt. Or maybe they've been deceived by their own desires. They need your prayers.

• Public officials. Do you pray for our national and state leaders? The best thing you and I can do for our country is pray for our leaders.

• Those who don't know Jesus Christ. 1 Timothy 2:3-4 says that God "desires all people to be saved." You and I must petition for the souls of the unsaved.

• Our spiritual leaders. Your pastor needs your prayers. Many preachers in America are discouraged and hurting. Please pray for pastors, missionaries, church staff members, and other spiritual leaders.

• The sick. Scripture says, "Is anyone among you sick? Let him call for the elders of the church, and let them pray over him, anointing him with oil in the name of the Lord."

PRAY FOR SOMEONE IN THE LIST ABOVE TODAY.

Day 137

For those whom he foreknew he also predestined to be conformed to the image of his Son, in order that he might be the firstborn among many brothers.

—Romans 8:29

If your life seems out of control today, you're not alone. We all have problems!

What the old adage says is true: You are either going into a problem, coming out of a problem, or right in the middle of a problem. Where are you?

But the good news is that Jesus has promised peace in the midst of our problems.

So how can you find confidence in the midst of trouble?

Realize that the circumstances of your life—both the good and the bad—are part of God's plan for your life.

If you have accepted Jesus Christ as your Savior, you belong to God. He is committed to you and has established a purpose for your life. Because of that, you can be confident that God is putting everything together piece by piece.

And, remember that there are no accidents! God is using the circumstances of your life to conform and change your inner character to be more Christ-like.

So you may not be able to change the circumstances of your life, but you can change how you view them. Don't see them as enemies, obstacles, or barriers. And don't let your circumstances devour you!

See your problems as opportunities to experience God's love and power in a greater way than ever before.

IF YOU HAVE ACCEPTED JESUS CHRIST AS YOUR SAVIOR, YOU BELONG TO GOD. HE IS COMMITTED TO YOU AND HAS ESTABLISHED A PURPOSE FOR YOUR LIFE.

And those whom he predestined he also called, and those whom he called he also justified, and those whom he justified he also glorified.

—Romans 8:30

From where you sit today, the future may look a little bit scary.

Are you facing a major career choice, a decision that will impact your family? Are you wondering where you'll be in 5 or 10 years... or even 20?

Maybe you don't know where you want to go, and you wouldn't know how to get there if you did.

If so, I want to give you a word of encouragement today: God knows where you're going and He knows how to get you there!

In fact, He already considers it a done deal. In God's plan, your purpose is already determined. He is just waiting on the right timing.

If you noticed, our verse for today is in the past tense. In God's mind, He has already called and prepared you for the great purpose of your life. It's already a certainty because God is eternal.

God inhabits eternity. So time means nothing to God... but timing is everything. God has an eternal plan for your life that is complete and perfect. He knows the future and has orchestrated every step along the way.

You are just walking out the plan. That's why you don't need to fear the future.

Every circumstance is part of God's great eternal plan for your life. Just trust Him and be confident that He is preparing and positioning you for His purposes.

TAKE A DEEP BREATH! GOD IS IN CONTROL!

And we know that for those who love God all things work together for good, for those who are called according to his purpose.

—Romans 8:28

If you are going through a problem today, how do you overcome it?

I want to give you a few practical steps to help you weather the storms of your life.

First, trust God. I love what the great preacher Charles Spurgeon used to say, "God is too good to be unkind, too wise to make a mistake. And when you can't trace His hand, you can always trust His heart."

God is committed to bringing glory to Himself and good to your life by making you more like Jesus. He does that through the circumstances of your life.

Be confident in what Scripture says: "And we know that for those who love God all things work together for good, for those who are called according to his purpose."

Secondly, give thanks in all things. You may not understand your circumstances, but you can know that God is using them to make you more like Jesus and move you closer to your purpose in His plan.

The apostle Paul was shipwrecked, beaten, and imprisoned. Yet, in Ephesians 5:20, he challenges us to give thanks "always and for everything to God the Father in the name of our Lord Jesus Christ."

Paul knew how to overcome problems in life—by trusting God and giving thanks to Him in every circumstance.

Why not do the same today?!

GOD IS COMMITTED TO BRINGING GLORY TO HIMSELF AND GOOD TO YOUR LIFE BY MAKING YOU MORE LIKE JESUS.

Day 140

What then shall we say to these things? If God is for us, who can be against us?

—Romans 8:31

Many people are not very happy with America these days.

Whether you're watching the news on television, listening to the radio or reading news and magazine reports, this generation is questioning the future of America.

But I believe the answer lies in our Scripture verse for today: "What then shall we say to these things? If God is for us, who can be against us?"

What made America great was the favor of Almighty God! God gave birth to this nation. He established and blessed it. And He will continue to bless America IF we place our trust in Him.

We do not exist because of our military might, our ingenuity, or our financial power. We exist because of God's hand of protection.

America was founded in the name of freedom for men and women seeking to live their faith. Our nation was established on Christian foundations and principles. The framers of the Constitution implanted the ethics, morality, values, and beliefs of the Old and New Testaments into our government.

The soul of America belongs to God. But we are in danger of losing that soul today. The day that America decides that we don't need God is the day that America begins to die.

Because the opposite of Romans 8:31 is also true. If God be against us, who can be for us? Ultimately, it's not a question of whether or not God is on our side. The question is who is on the Lord's side?

AMERICA DOES NOT EXIST BECAUSE OF OUR MILITARY MIGHT, OUR INGENUITY, OR OUR FINANCIAL POWER. WE EXIST BECAUSE OF GOD'S HAND OF PROTECTION.

Day 141

For you were called to freedom, brothers. Only do not use your freedom as an opportunity for the flesh....

—Galatians 5:13

I want to dispel a modern myth today about the separation of church and state.

In our culture, too many people have bought into the misinformation that our founding fathers were seeking freedom from faith in government.

The architects of the Constitution did not want to establish a secular state, but rather one that would not be dominated by any one church. The separation of church and state DOES NOT mean the separation of God and government!

Regardless of how some revisionists are trying to rewrite our history, 50 of the 55 framers of the Constitution considered themselves to be born-again believers.

One of those, James Madison, our fourth president, said, "We have staked the whole future of American civilization not upon the power of government... upon the capacity of each and all of us to govern ourselves... to sustain ourselves according to the Ten Commandments of God."

In a 1783 circular to the states, George Washington, our first president, wrote, "I now make it my earnest prayer, that God would have you, and the State over which you preside, in his holy protection... to do Justice, to love mercy, and to demean ourselves with that Charity, humility and pacific temper of mind, which were the Characteristics of the Divine Author of our blessed Religion, and without an humble imitation... we can never hope to be a happy Nation."

You and I must stand up for the freedom for faith by praying for our leaders and our nation, teaching our children and grandchildren about America's foundation of religious freedom, and by living a life that reveals the true freedom found in Christ!

LIVE BOLDLY FOR CHRIST AS A LIGHT TO AMERICA!

But God's firm foundation stands, bearing this seal: "The Lord knows those who are his."

—2 Timothy 2:19

There's a lot of talk about American values today. But have you ever wondered what that means?

Let me give you a quick look at some of the biblical principles our nation was founded upon.

Sanctity of life. America was built upon the value of a person and the dignity of the human life. If we believe that all men are created equal by God, then when God gives life, we should treat it with sanctity.

Home and family. The biblical model of a family is where a mother and father are committed to one another, love their children, and serve God.

Common decency. There used to be a time when you could walk down the street without hearing obscenities and vulgarities. Now pornography is a $4 billion business and what used to slink down the back alleys of our cities now struts down Main Street.

Work ethic. The Bible is clear about the dignity and value of work. Any welfare system that strips an individual of the value and fulfillment of work is wrong.

God-centered education. God has been cut out of our education system. Creation is out and condoms are in. Prayer has been abandoned and the Bible run off campuses.

Church. God established the Church. And as the Church goes, so goes the nation. I don't think there is much wrong in America that couldn't be settled in the churches if we had men and women who would stand as salt and light in this generation.

Let us pray that America will return to the biblical values it was established upon!

HOW CAN YOU GET INVOLVED IN YOUR COMMUNITY TO HELP RESTORE BIBLICAL VALUES IN OUR COUNTRY?

Day 143

He who did not spare His own Son but delivered him up for us all,
how will he not also with him graciously give us all things?
—Romans 8:32

What does the word *freedom* bring to your mind?

Maybe you imagine the celebrations of the Fourth of July, or see images of soldiers in battle. Possibly you think of the American flag. Or you might think about your freedom to worship and exercise your faith.

But there is a greater freedom for you than even our national freedom.

It is the freedom of your soul and mine, bought and paid in full by the blood of Jesus Christ. He gave the ultimate price for your freedom, He poured out His blood so you can be free!

Think about this, if God would not even spare His only Son, don't you know He will freely give you all things in Him?

Our Scripture verse today says, "He who did not spare His own Son but delivered him up for us all, how will he not also with him graciously give us all things?"

You can be free from addictions, from sin, and from death. You can experience liberty, joy, victory, and peace. All you have to do is accept Jesus Christ as your deliverer today.

IF YOU NEVER HAVE, ASK GOD TO FORGIVE YOU
OF YOUR SINS TODAY.

Day 144

No, in all these things we are more than conquerors through him who loved us.

—Romans 8:37

As a Christian, is it wrong to want to succeed? Is it wrong to be competitive?

Not at all! As a believer, God can take your drive to succeed, your passion for success, and your competitive edge and refocus it for His glory.

Our Scripture verse says "We are more than conquerors through him who loved us." God wants us to live in super, abundant victory.

We are in this race of life to win. Paul puts it this way in Corinthians, "Therefore, run to win." Don't just finish, win!

Now there are accusers and opponents that try to keep Christians from winning. The devil is our adversary. He is called the accuser of the brother in the Bible. The devil is constantly trying to discourage us, defeat us, and defame our testimony.

But I want to warn you against focusing on the devil today. Don't let the devil distract you from the victory you have in Jesus Christ. Don't be on the defense in life. Play offense. And run to win!

WHEN YOU KNOW JESUS, HE WILL TAKE YOUR DRIVE TO SUCCEED, YOUR PASSION FOR SUCCESS, AND YOUR COMPETITIVE EDGE AND REFOCUS IT FOR HIS GLORY.

Day 145

For I am sure that neither death nor life, nor angels nor rulers, nor things present, nor things to come, nor powers, nor height nor depth, nor anything else in all creation, will be able to separate us from the love of God in Christ Jesus our Lord.

—Romans 8:38-39

In the game of life, you can sometimes be your own worst enemy. And your conscience can attack you.

Do you feel badly about your past? Are you haunted by the ghost of guilt? Sometimes, do you just feel like a loser? It's pretty easy to get down on yourself when you focus on your own failures, frustrations, and inadequacies.

But if you spend your life looking at past defeats and mistakes, you won't be able to live today. When you are constantly looking at instant replay, you can't enjoy the victory that you can have in Jesus Christ for today and tomorrow.

Of course, the devil loves to bring up your past and dig up dirt on you. He wants to put a wedge of separation between you and God. But your conscience doesn't have to keep you down.

If you have asked for God's cleansing grace, trust in His forgiveness. Trust in His faithfulness. Focus on Him. Get past the past and move on for Christ!

As a Christian, you have the righteousness of Jesus Christ. When Christ died on the cross for you, He took your sin, your faults, your failure, and your defeat. Instead, He gave you His righteousness, His perfection, and His victory.

Nothing in your past can change that. And most importantly, nothing in your past or present can separate you from the love of God.

PUT YOUR PAST IN THE PAST!

Day 146

*I am speaking the truth in Christ—I am not lying; my conscience
bears me witness in the Holy Spirit—that I have great sorrow and
unceasing anguish in my heart.*

—Romans 9:1-2

You and I have an awesome job! We have the greatest mission
known to man. Jesus said, "You shall be My witnesses."

But how can we be most effective in our mission? Let's look at the
apostle Paul as an example. According to our Scripture verse for today,
he had a sincere concern for souls.

Paul lived this concern every day. Do you have a sincere, genuine
concern for people who do not know Jesus Christ?

You know, your zeal will never be greater than your convictions. Your
compassion for people will never be greater than your commitment to
the Word of God. I've noticed that the people who believe the Bible
the most are the ones who share it the most.

Paul was a courageous Christian who boldly shared his faith. What
made him so bold? His sincere concern. Paul was heartbroken over
people who did not know Jesus.

Christ also wept for individuals. He was broken over the city of
Jerusalem. When Jesus saw great crowds, He was moved with
compassion.

How long has it been since you've been devastated by those who are
spiritually lost? When was the last time you wept over someone dying
without Christ? Sincere concern is the key to a great witness.

**FOCUS ON SOMEONE YOU KNOW WHO IS LOST
AND PRAY FOR THEM.**

Day 147

Go therefore and make disciples of all the nations, baptizing them in the name of the Father and of the Son and of the Holy Spirit.

—Matthew 28:19

Do you remember when you first found Jesus Christ?

The fire, the passion, and the excitement were overwhelming. Didn't you want to tell everyone about the joy you found?

But what about now? Over time, we can get comfortable. We can lose the urgency. Maybe life crowds in and you lose the passion.

But the apostle Paul kept the fires burning in his spirit. He kept the desire to share Christ with others. How did he do it?

Through prayer. That is where the fire is lit for sharing Christ with others. When you get serious about prayer, you find yourself getting serious about bringing people to Christ.

I know it's true in my life. And I believe it can be true in your life, too.

In God's Word, prayer and evangelism are inseparably linked. Jesus told His disciples to pray for the mission field in Matthew 9:37-38: "Then he said to his disciples, 'The harvest is plentiful, but the laborers are few; therefore pray earnestly to the Lord of the harvest to send out laborers into his harvest.'"

Consistent prayer encourages and equips us to carry out the mission of evangelism. Prayer enlarges our heart with compassion for people and reignites our fire to share Christ with them.

So I challenge you to get serious about prayer today!

WHEN YOU GET SERIOUS ABOUT PRAYER, YOU FIND YOURSELF GETTING SERIOUS ABOUT BRINGING PEOPLE TO CHRIST.

Day 148

For I could wish that I myself were accursed and cut off from Christ for the sake of my brothers, my kinsmen according to the flesh.

—Romans 9:3

Y ou probably have someone in your life who doesn't know Jesus Christ. We all do. Do you have a plan to share the gospel with them?

Matthew, one of Jesus' disciples, had a simple plan. He was a former tax collector who wanted some of his old friends to meet Jesus. So, he threw a party. They met Jesus and He changed their lives.

The apostle Paul took an even bolder approach. He was willing to do anything to save his fellow Jews from hell.

According to Romans 9:3, he seemed to be willing to even trade places with them in eternity!

That's commitment! That's compassion! But I don't believe your plan has to go that far. God is just asking you to be willing to introduce Jesus to others. The Lord will do the rest.

Christian, God is looking for someone just like you. And the only requirement is to care. The greatest ability is availability. So make willingness part of your plan to introduce others to Jesus.

THINK ABOUT HOW YOU MIGHT SHARE YOUR TESTIMONY WITH SOMEONE.

Day 149

"I will have mercy on whom I have mercy, and I will have compassion on whom I have compassion." So then it depends not on human will or exertion, but on God, who has mercy.

—Romans 9:15-16

D id you know that God chose you?

Sometimes, we get caught up in our decision to accept Christ and forget that, as Scripture says, "We loved Him because He first loved us."

It's not by natural birth or human descent that we are placed into the family of God. But it is by new birth and that new birth takes place by the choice of God in our lives.

Why are we chosen? Why are we blessed? I don't know. And neither do you. We need to learn to let God be God. God chose us before we were born. And that is not an unjust choice.

Paul said in Romans 9:14, "What shall we say then? Is there injustice on God's part? By no means!"

We cannot begin to understand God. When you imagine all His attributes—His love, power, omnipotence, omnipresence, eternal being, holiness, and so much more—it is unfathomable to try to put God in a box.

But there is a balance between God's plans and man's responsibility. The sovereign choice of God and the moral responsibility of man run side by side. You and I are not saved because of our own goodness or righteousness.

As Christians, God chose you and me in Jesus Christ and offered His grace and love for us.

I GIVE GOD THANKS TODAY FOR CHOOSING YOU!

Day 150

But who are you, O man, to answer back to God? Will what is molded say to its molder, "Why have you made me like this?"
—Romans 9:20

Maybe you have some questions for God today. Questions like, Why did you make me like this? Why was I born into this family? Why do I have this limitation? Why did this happen to me?

Well, according to Scripture, when we question God, it's like a piece of clay questioning the master potter. God is sovereign. He chooses, forms, and has a plan. Life is God's potter's wheel.

But life is not simply turning in circles. God knows and understands every turn of the wheel. What a potter can do with a lump of clay on the wheel, God can do in your life!

God has a master plan for you that is beautiful and wonderful. He knows your name and even the number of hairs on your head! He is working creatively and progressively in your life.

But, like a lump of clay, we are nothing apart from the work of God. You and I can never be made complete without the touch of the Master's hand.

I want to encourage you today to yield to the Master's hand. He sees the future and knows how to form you into the perfect vessel!

GIVE THANKS TO GOD TODAY FOR THE THINGS THAT MAKE YOU UNIQUE.

Day 151

And the vessel he was making of clay was spoiled in the potter's hand, and he reworked it into another vessel, as it seemed good to the potter to do.

—Jeremiah 18:4

Are you a broken vessel today?

As clay in the potter's hands, we can get marred because of impurities in our lives. On the potter's wheel, any foreign object in the clay can cause a fracture in the vessel.

Sometimes the potter must stop and remove the impurities before going on. Do you feel resistance in your life today? Maybe there is an impurity or reluctance that is keeping God from creating His masterpiece in you.

And maybe you've already been fractured. If you are a broken vessel today, you may be wondering, is it too late for me? Absolutely not!

If you will give God the broken pieces of your life, He'll put you back together. But you must be willing to turn loose of the impurity or resistance.

When you do, today's Scripture says the potter can make the vessel again. I'm so glad God is a God of a second chance, third chance, a tenth chance, and even a one-hundredth chance!

He gave Jacob another chance, Jonah another chance, Sampson another chance, Peter another chance… and He'll give you another chance, too.

God can take you in your broken condition and make you over again!

GIVE GOD THE BROKEN PIECES OF YOUR LIFE SO THAT HE CAN REMAKE YOU IN THE VESSEL HE WANTS YOU TO BE.

Day 152

"Thus says the LORD of hosts, the God of Israel, behold, I am bringing upon this city and upon all its towns all the disaster that I have pronounced against it, because they have stiffened their neck, refusing to hear my words."

—Jeremiah 19:15

How many chances do you get in life?

You and I were born in sin. We started out in a rebellious state. But the sad truth is that some people live in that place of resistance.

In our Scripture verse for today, God hardens the heart of some who continue to reject and refuse Him.

You see, God offers His love, grace and mercy over and over again. But there comes a time—if you continue to say no to Christ and to God's love—that you cross God's deadline and your heart hardens.

It is possible to reject the love of Jesus Christ so much that you pass the point of no return.

The Bible says, "My Spirit shall not abide in man forever" (Genesis 6:3). When Jesus looked out across the city of Jerusalem that was broken and ruined, he wept over the city. He said, "O Jerusalem, Jerusalem, the city that kills the prophets and stones those who are sent to it! How often would I have gathered your children together as a hen gathers her brood under her wings, and you would not!" (Luke 13:34).

What a frightening thought! Don't let that happen to you.

**IF YOU HAVEN'T, ACCEPT GOD'S GRACE
BEFORE IT'S TOO LATE!**

Day 153

But now, O LORD, you are our Father; we are the clay, and you are our potter; we are all the work of your hand.

—**Isaiah 64:8**

According to today's Scripture, you and I are like clay vessels made by God, the Master Potter.

And there are four kinds of people, or vessels. Which category do you fall into?

A vessel being formed. God is making and developing you. He's creating something beautiful, according to His plan and purpose for your life. And as you cooperate and yield to His hands, you are being formed into a beautiful, purposeful creation.

A vessel fractured. Maybe your life seems to be out of control. Has your heart been broken? If you are a fractured, broken vessel, God can put the pieces back together. If you turn your life and struggles over to Him, He will put you back on the potter's wheel and put your life back together again.

A vessel fixed. If you've experienced pain, but God has brought you through and restored your life, then you are a vessel fixed. You know the power of the Master Potter to restore, refresh, and renew because He's done it for you!

A vessel finished. This is the most frightening condition. If you and I say no to God's grace too many times, we can become hardened. Don't let that happen to you! Accept God's love and grace. Ask for His forgiveness!

TAKE A LOOK AT YOUR LIFE. WHAT KIND OF VESSEL ARE YOU?

Day 154

Elijah was a man with a nature like ours.

—James 5:17

Have you ever felt depressed? Everyone experiences some form of depression, whether it's just the moody blues, a complete chemical or clinical depression, or something in between.

It might surprise you to know that some very important people in the Bible dealt with depression. Moses, Jonah, and the prophet Elijah all experienced severe disappointment, disillusionment, and even depression.

In the book of Numbers, you can read how Moses, in a fit of depression, prayed that he would die. Elijah did the same.

Even great people and people who are spiritually strong can deal with emotional problems. James 5:17 tells us Elijah had the same feelings and emotions that we all do.

So if you are experiencing emotional problems like depression, don't think that you are alone. Don't believe the lie that you aren't fit to be God's child. God wants to help you with your emotional struggles. And His Word will give you the strength and power to deal with it.

**READ ABOUT MOSES, ELIJAH, OR JONAH
AND DISCOVER HOW GOD CAN USE PEOPLE WITH
EMOTIONAL STRUGGLES.**

Day 155

And he asked that he might die, saying, "It is enough; now, O LORD, take away my life, for I am no better than my fathers."
—1 Kings 19:4

Maybe you feel like Elijah today. In our Scripture verse above, he was so depressed and distraught that he actually prayed that God would take his life!

What set Elijah up for such depression? What sets you up for emotional turmoil?

Depression can set in after a great spiritual high. Depression hit Elijah after the mountaintop experience recorded in 1 Kings 18, when he stood against the prophets of Baal.

Right after he did this, the bottom fell out! Elijah fell off his spiritual perch because like you and me, he was most vulnerable after great victory.

That's why the Bible says, "Be sober-minded; be watchful. Your adversary the devil prowls around like a roaring lion, seeking someone to devour" (1 Peter 5:8).

After the spiritual victory, Elijah was physically, emotionally, and spiritually drained. So when word came that Jezebel the queen wanted him dead, he ran for his life.

And here's the key: Elijah took his eyes off God. Nowhere in Scripture does it say that God told him to run. Elijah took off on his own.

Don't take your eyes off of God for a second. Maybe you've experienced spiritual victory time and time again. Don't let your guard down and begin acting on your own. Trust God every step of the way.

IF YOU'VE EXPERIENCED A SPIRITUAL HIGH, REMEMBER THAT YOU'RE A TARGET FOR SATAN.

Day 156

The LORD is my rock and my fortress and my deliverer, my God, my rock, in whom I take refuge, my shield, and the horn of my salvation, my stronghold.

—**Psalm 18:2**

What are the causes of depression?

If you look at Elijah's bout with depression in 1 Kings 19, you'll discover that depression is fueled by:

• **Fear**. Elijah heard that Jezebel was after him and was afraid. According to Zig Ziglar, FEAR equals False Evidence Appearing Real. The way to avoid fear is to walk in the truth of the Word of God and not according to the false evidence that is all around us.

• **Unbelief**. Elijah had seen the mighty miracles and works of God, but still allowed feelings of unbelief to creep in. He didn't trust God to handle the situation.

• **Impatience**. Elijah ran ahead of God. He was trying to live and die on his own schedule, rather than trusting God to give him life, strength, and health.

• **Pride**. As Elijah sat under the juniper tree, he cried out, "I'm no better than my fathers!" Where did he get the idea that he was better than his fathers to begin with?

• **Self-pity.** Elijah was feeling sorry for himself. He looked at his problems and just wanted to give up.

Here's the formula for depression: insult + anger x self-pity = depression. If you see yourself going down that road, put on the brakes!

Then put your trust in God. When you do, as the psalmist says in our Scripture today, He will be your deliverer, your refuge, your shield, your stronghold, and your salvation.

IF YOU'RE FEELING DEPRESSED, TAKE INVENTORY OF YOUR ATTITUDE LATELY. ARE THERE SIGNS OF FEAR, UNBELIEF, IMPATIENCE, PRIDE, OR SELF-PITY?

Day 157

But they who wait for the LORD shall renew their strength; they shall mount up with wings like eagles; they shall run and not be weary; they shall walk and not faint.

—Isaiah 40:31

If you are feeling low today, God has a plan to help you defeat your depression!

First, God can refresh you. When Elijah was exhausted and emotionally drained, God provided refreshment. "And he looked, and behold, there was at his head a cake baked on hot stones and a jar of water. And he ate and drank and lay down again" (1 Kings 19:6).

God took care of Elijah's physical needs—food and rest. Sometimes you need to withdraw physically, emotionally, and spiritually and be encouraged in the Lord.

Secondly, God rebuked Elijah. In verse 9, God asks, "What are you doing here, Elijah?" Yes, God sent the earthquake and the fire. But in the end, God spoke to Elijah in "low whisper" (1 Kings 19:12).

You and I often want God to speak to us with spectacular events and situations. But God most often speaks in the still small voice of His Word.

And thirdly, God recommissioned Elijah. "And the LORD said to him, 'Go, return on your way to the wilderness of Damascus. And when you arrive, you shall anoint Hazael to be king over Syria'" (1 Kings 19:15). God told Elijah that it was time to get back in the game!

ALLOW GOD TO REFRESH YOU, AND THEN REACH OUT TO SOMEONE ELSE!

"You shall love the Lord your God with all your heart and with all your soul and with all your strength and with all your mind, and your neighbor as yourself."

—Luke 10:27

I know you want your family to be successful. Whether you're a parent or grandparent, you want your children to be healthy, successful, and productive.

But what is true success? Jesus addressed this in Luke 10 when he was confronted by a lawyer asking, "What shall I do to inherit eternal life?"

Jesus replied with a question, "What is written in the Law?" The answer is our verse today: "You shall love the Lord your God with all your heart and with all your soul and with all your strength and with all your mind, and your neighbor as yourself."

Jesus said, "Do this, and you will live" (Luke 10:28). If you want your children to really live, a successful life comes from a strong faith.

You may be asking, "So how do I instill that faith into my children?"

It's not as hard as society likes to pretend. You see, God wants your children to know and love Him even more than you do.

That is why He has provided you with an instruction manual, His Word. If you and I simply apply the Scriptures to our lives and homes, we will raise godly children!

IF YOU'RE STRUGGLING IN A PARTICULAR AREA AT HOME, SEE WHAT GOD'S WORD HAS TO SAY ABOUT IT.

Day 159

His offspring will be mighty in the land; the generation of the upright will be blessed.

—Psalm 112:2

What do your children need and want more than anything? YOU!

The cry of "generation next" is for their parents. God has placed your children in your hands, not just to provide for, but to shape and mold. And that takes your time, energy, and presence.

You and I have a responsibility too great to waste the moments, days, and years we have as parents. We must take every opportunity to teach, train, nourish, nurture, love, and prepare them for the world.

I remember reading an article in *Newsweek* about the next generation. One 17-year-old was quoted, "There's a lot of anger in my generation. You can hear it in the music. Kids are angry for a lot of reasons. But mostly because parents aren't around."

Your children need your attention, because the time really is fleeting. I can't believe how quickly the time has passed since my children were born. Now, they are grown. So, I want to urge you today to make every moment count.

Now, none of us are expected to be perfect parents. And that's good because none of us are, myself included!

But God does expect you and me to be priority parents. Parenting is a full-time responsibility and we are called to put our children and our families first in our lives.

When you do, Psalm 112:2 says this generation will be blessed.

**SPEND SOME ONE-ON-ONE TIME WITH YOUR
CHILDREN THIS WEEK.**

"And these words that I command you today shall be on your heart."

—Deuteronomy 6:6

What are your children exposed to in their daily lives? Children mimic what they see. They become what they are taught face-to-face, heart-to-heart, and life-to-life.

According to Scripture, we should teach our children values, faith, and biblical truths personally. Unfortunately, many parents leave the teaching to television, music, peers, schools, or even church.

While Sunday school, Christian school, and church activities are all great tools to help instill faith, none are meant to be a substitute for you.

So I want to encourage you today to live every day loving God, fearing God, and obeying God. There's no "time out" for parenting. Every day, every hour, and every moment is important. Why? Because you can't plan the best teaching moments.

Have you ever noticed that the best family moments are when you're hanging out, talking, and just being together? You can't put your children on hold while you fulfill your own life. You must be engaged.

Today's families need moms and dads who will step in and personally teach faith and values.

ACCORDING TO SCRIPTURE, WE SHOULD TEACH OUR CHILDREN VALUES, FAITH, AND BIBLICAL TRUTHS PERSONALLY.

Day 161

"You shall teach them diligently to your children."

—Deuteronomy 6:7

How can you raise children who love and obey God? With passion and persistence.

In our verse today, the Hebrew word *diligently* means to penetrate, like the cutting of a knife. As a parent, your teaching must be strong enough that it penetrates.

Why is this so critical? As a parent, you must be passionate about what you believe because you are competing against messages from movies, music, friends, peers, marketing campaigns, and so much more.

Is it the passion of your life to see your children grow up to share your faith? You must do everything you can to teach them with conviction so that it's credible and believable. You and I must be persistent and consistent as believers.

In fact, the impact of your passionate teaching will last beyond your children.

Deuteronomy 6:2 says, "That you may fear the LORD your God, you and your son and your son's son, by keeping all his statues and his commandments, which I command you, all the days of your life...."

You and I are responsible, not only for this generation, but for the next and those that follow. Your legacy will live far beyond you and your children. Be passionate about what that legacy will be.

AS A PARENT, YOU MUST BE PASSIONATE ABOUT WHAT YOU BELIEVE BECAUSE YOU ARE COMPETING AGAINST SO MANY OTHER MESSAGES!

Day 162

"When your son asks you in time to come, 'What is the meaning of the testimonies and the statutes and the rules that the LORD our God has commanded you?'"

—Deuteronomy 6:20

I love the old adage, "The best kind of teaching is as much caught as it is taught." That's certainly true with parenting. The most effective lessons can happen during the simple routines of life.

Sometimes, those priceless moments of sharing come while you're watching television together, driving home after a baseball game, or struggling through a homework project.

Remember those unexpected times when your children are responsive and open? In those quiet moments together, you have the opportunity to teach them right and wrong based upon what's actually happening in their life. That's practical teaching.

If you, as mom or dad, are serious about your relationship with God, no matter what the situation or circumstance, your child will see faith as a reality. And if you are committed to living what you believe day in and day out, your children can see faith as practical.

Deuteronomy 6:7 says the practical teaching of God's Word should be a part of your everyday life. "You shall teach them diligently to your children, and shall talk of them when you sit in your house, and when you walk by the way, and when you lie down, and when you rise."

Let your children see you obeying God's commands and applying them to your life daily.

**PRAY FOR GOD'S WISDOM AS YOU DAILY
INFLUENCE YOUR CHILDREN.**

Day 163

Fathers, do not provoke your children to anger...

—**Ephesians 6:4**

If you are a parent, you have been given a great responsibility—to give your children roots. God has commanded you to ground them in faith so that in the future, they may take wings and fly.

In Ephesians 6:4 the apostle Paul offers some ways you and I can do this. One is to BUILD YOUR CHILD UP.

Be a positive parent, not a negative one. Encourage rather than exasperate your children. We provoke our children when we neglect them or when we compare them to each other or to other kids.

You have the power to tear down or build up your child. Every child is potentially a winner. But to succeed, your child needs you cheering him or her on. Your child needs constant affirmation to build confidence.

I've heard it described as "emotional nutrition." Encouragement is to the soul and spirit like food is to the body.

Now, I'm also talking about building your child up in a home environment in which your child can know Christ as soon as possible. You are the best evangelist for your own children!

When you build your home on the foundation that is in Jesus Christ, you set your children up for success.

WHAT ONE WORD OF ENCOURAGEMENT CAN YOU GIVE YOUR CHILDREN TODAY?

Day 164

But bring them up in the discipline and instruction of the Lord.

—**Ephesians 6:4**

As parents, not only are you and I to encourage our children when they do something good, we are also supposed to discourage them from doing wrong. God's Word tells us to discipline and train our children.

If you are a parent, it is your responsibility to set parameters for your child and, if necessary, discipline them when they go out of bounds. Kids tend to run out of bounds and in the wrong direction without someone to "redirect."

You and I are to set them on the right path and prepare them for the real world. Discipline is part of that preparation. And if we fail, it's a sin against God.

Remember Eli in the Old Testament? God judged him along with his entire household. "And I declare to him that I am about to punish his house forever, for the iniquity that he knew, because his sons were blaspheming God, and he did not restrain them" (1 Samuel 3:13).

To discipline your child means to bring them under submission. Here are a couple of challenges from God's Word for parents:

• Discipline your children out of love. The purpose of discipline is to prepare your child for success. Never discipline out of anger. Follow God's example. "For the Lord disciplines the one he loves" (Hebrews 12:6).
• Start early. The earlier you begin training, the less discipline you will have to enforce later. "Whoever spares the rod hates his son, but he who loves him is diligent to discipline him" (Proverbs 13:24).

Training your child is so critical that Scripture says when you discipline your child, "you will save his soul" (Proverbs 23:14).

DISCIPLINE SETS YOUR KIDS ON THE RIGHT PATH AND PREPARES THEM FOR THE REAL WORLD.

Day 165

And Jesus increased in wisdom and stature and in favor with God and man.

—Luke 2:52

Would you like to bring up your children like Jesus? We have a great model for giving our children instruction from Luke 2:52.

If you look at our verse today, you will see four critical components of fully developing a child through Jesus' example.
And Jesus increased in wisdom... —Jesus grew intellectually.
and stature... —Jesus grew physically. *and in favor with God* —Jesus grew spiritually. *and man.* —Jesus grew socially.

These are the four areas that we as parents should give our attention in instructing our children. In each area, we should teach them from God's perspective and make sure they know the fundamentals of faith.

If you're not sure about the fundamentals, here are the non-negotiable beliefs of the Christian faith:
• The divine authority and inerrancy of the Word of God.
• The depravity or fall of man causing a need for salvation.
• Salvation by grace through faith in Jesus Christ alone because of what He did for us on the cross and through the resurrection.
• Knowledge that every life has a destiny with God, either separated from God forever or in the presence of God forever in heaven.

If you are a parent or grandparent, you must instill these beliefs in your children before anything else.

THINK ABOUT YOUR CHILDREN. ARE YOU HELPING THEM GROW MENTALLY, SOCIALLY, AND SPIRITUALLY?

Day 166

Therefore take up the whole armor of God, that you may be able to withstand in the evil day, and having done all, to stand firm.

—Ephesians 6:13

D° you love your family enough to protect it? You're probably thinking, "Of course I do!" But do you know how?

We live in a world of possibilities and opportunities. But we also live in a world of frightening vulnerabilities—the internet and its predators, violence, immorality, and more.

As a parent, it is your job to discern the dangers of our time and protect and prepare your children for the real world.

One of the most disturbing tragedies of our times is school shootings. Children who are deeply disturbed have committed unforeseen acts of violence against their peers and adults.

Here are some lessons we've learned from living through these violent times:
- Children need adult role models and guidance.
- We must do everything we can to check evil.
- It is important to teach young people respect for adults and people in authority.
- Parents must set boundaries.

And finally, as parents we must love our families enough to be a filter between them and the world. We must provide a spiritual filter between our children and the messages of immorality and sinfulness.

To do that, we must be willing to make hard decisions in order to protect our children. We must be willing to get involved in the lives of our children.

HOW WELL DO YOU KNOW YOUR CHILDREN'S FRIENDS?

Day 167

In the fear of the LORD one has strong confidence, and his children will have a refuge.

—Proverbs 14:26

Does your family have a healthy fear of God? They should.

The first line of defense against the dangers of this world is an understanding of the greatness and power of God.

According to Proverbs 1:7, "The fear of the LORD is the beginning of knowledge." And in our verse today, "In the fear of the LORD one has strong confidence, and his children will have a refuge."

The fear of God is a filter, a fence built around your family to protect it. Now I'm not talking about an unhealthy or phobic fear, but a godly fear.

It is a reverence for God. It recognizes that God is holy and lives in majesty and pleasure. When you live in fear of God, you live in obedience to God.

And when you face temptation, obedience depends upon knowing the two great truths of God:

God's love. If you truly understand how deeply God loves you and the sacrifices Jesus made for you, you realize that to break His commandments is a betrayal.

We readily teach our children about God's love. They sing about it from the time they can speak. But many of us are only telling our children half the story.

On one hand is the love of God and on the other is God's law. Children need to understand that God is holy and righteous and that there are consequences for disobeying His laws.

DOES YOUR FAMILY HAVE A HEALTHY FEAR OF GOD?

Finally, be strong in the Lord and in the strength of his might.

—Ephesians 6:10

If you are a parent or grandparent today, I've got a message for you: Be strong!

As your children grow, the pressure to conform is incredible. So how can you teach them to be strong and live a life without compromise? Be strong yourself and grounded in God's Word.

And here are four ways I believe you can instill that strength of spirit and character in your children:

Teach them the importance of choices. Instruct your children on how to say "yes" to the things that are right and "no" to those that are wrong. Every time you make the right choice, you are strengthened. And each wrong choice weakens you.

Teach them the importance of convictions. Before you can make the right decision, you must know what you believe and why you believe it. If you instill values and biblical principles in your children from a young age, they won't flinch when they face a tough decision.

Teach them the importance of conscience. Foster a sensitivity to sin in your children. They need to know about consequences. Their conscience should be conditioned by the Word of God and by the teaching of the family.

Teach them the importance of companions. You need to know your children's friends and monitor them. Mentor your children on how to choose the right kind of companions.

GROUND YOURSELF IN GOD'S WORD SO YOU CAN BE STRONG FOR YOUR CHILDREN.

Day 169

For we do not wrestle against flesh and blood, but against the rulers, against the authorities, against the cosmic powers over this present darkness, against the spiritual forces of evil in the heavenly places.

—**Ephesians 6:12**

Prayer is the most powerful weapon of protection for your family that you have.

Remember, we are in a spiritual battle in this world. There is a great battle for the soul of America and for the soul of our families. And prayer is your most powerful line of defense.

Pray together as a family. But I also want to encourage you to make prayer for your children and grandchildren a very personal and consistent part of your life. Pray for their salvation, for their safety, for their peers, for their mate, for their character, for God's will in their life.

And the great thing about prayer is that there is no time limit! When your babies outgrow the Bible stories and the bedtime prayers, you can still pray for them.

When your children begin driving and go off to college, you can still pray for them. When they start their first job and get married, you can still pray for them. And when they have their own children and grandchildren, you can still pray for them!

Wherever your children live and whatever their situation, you can always pray for them. Your children need your prayers.

**MAKE PRAYER FOR YOUR CHILDREN
A REGULAR PART OF YOUR DAY.**

Day 170

Forgetting what lies behind and straining forward to what lies ahead, I press on toward the goal for the prize of the upward call of God in Christ Jesus.

—Philippians 3:13-14

Are you looking forward or back?

I want to encourage you today to live in view of eternity.

Consider Hebrews 12:1-2, "Let us also lay aside every weight, and sin which clings so closely, and let us run with endurance the race that is set before us, looking to Jesus, the founder and perfecter of our faith, who for the joy that was set before him endured the cross, despising the shame, and is seated at the right hand of the throne of God."

So, the focus should be onward, upward, and into the future, living with the end in mind. Paul put it this way, "forgetting what lies behind and straining forward to what lies ahead, I press on toward the goal for the prize of the upward call of God in Christ Jesus."

That's living with eternity in view. As believers, you and I should consider every day as an investment in eternity. We should also look forward to the promise and hope of eternity.

Paul said, "My desire is to depart and be with Christ, for that is far better" (Philippians 1:23).

Are you homesick for heaven like Paul was? Most of us are willing to go to heaven, but we want to stay here for now. We live our life focused on here and now. What if you and I turned our daily affections and ambitions toward eternity with Christ?

I believe you would see more passion, excitement, and focus in your life.

AS BELIEVERS, YOU AND I SHOULD CONSIDER EVERY DAY AS AN INVESTMENT IN ETERNITY.

Day 171

Which he commanded our fathers to teach to their children, that the next generation might know them.

—Psalm 78:5-6

What's your job description as a parent or grandparent? According to Psalm 78, we are to teach the next generation to put their faith and trust in God.

I believe the highest occupation in life is to raise godly children, lead them to Christ, and help them discover God's plan and purpose for their lives.

How do you do that? By living a legacy.

Many people talk about leaving a legacy. And that's good. But I prefer to think of my life as a living legacy.

And to live a legacy you need to make sure your children know that you are committed to Jesus Christ and to the upward call upon your life.

Sounds like a big responsibility, doesn't it? But here's how you can get started. You do the right thing today. You live for Jesus today in the power of the Holy Spirit today.

You ask God to help you invest in the lives of your children today with a genuine, authentic faith today.

Paul said this to young Timothy, "I am reminded of your sincere faith, a faith that dwelt first in your grandmother Lois and your mother Eunice and now, I am sure, dwells in you as well" (2 Timothy 1:5).

Sincere faith is not always perfect, but it is one that is rooted in Jesus Christ. And it is a faith that is lived out moment by moment, hour by hour, day by day… starting with today.

MAKE AN EFFORT TO LIVE OUT YOUR FAITH IN JESUS CHRIST TODAY.

Day 172

Let us also lay aside every weight, and sin which clings so closely.

—Hebrews 12:1

I want to challenge you today to live without limits. Remove anything and everything in your life that would keep you from achieving God's best.

Sometimes, we are slowed down in life by trivial things. What distractions are bogging you down?

You see, some decisions in life are not just between good and evil, but between good, best, and better. When you get passionate about something that is trivial, it's easy to lose interest in what really matters.

Living without limits is not only setting aside all hindrances, but it is also knowing that victory is yours!

Times may be tough and there are always challenges, but our victory is in Jesus Christ. Paul says, "Do you not know that in a race all the runners run, but only one receives the prize? So run that you may obtain it" (1 Corinthians 9:24).

And according to Romans 8:37, "in all these things we are more than conquerors through him who loved us."

Live a dynamic faith of confidence and freedom, knowing that you are more than a conqueror in Jesus!

WHAT ARE THE TRIVIAL THINGS THAT ARE HOLDING YOU BACK IN LIFE?

And he arose and came to his father. But while he was still a long way off, his father saw him and felt compassion, and ran and embraced him and kissed him.

—**Luke 15:20**

Are you a broken-hearted parent today because of the choices your child has made? If so, I want to give you a message of encouragement, comfort, and counsel.

Maybe you've done your very best as a parent and yet your children are not walking in truth. God gives every person a will of his own and you can't force feed your faith to your children.

Every person has a choice and we are not just victims of our culture or families. We choose to rebel because of the rebellious nature of the human heart.

Now I know there is no greater pain than for a parent to see a child fail or fall. But don't be eaten up with guilt or questions. You can't change the past. All you can do is pledge to be the kind of parent God has called you to be today.

I want to comfort you as well with the knowledge that God wants your child to return to Him even more than you do.

The unconditional grace and love of God is illustrated In the parable of the prodigal son. When the lost son returns, the father runs to meet him, kisses him, and has a party in his honor. According to Luke 15:10, "There is joy before the angels of God over one sinner who repents."

Here's the bottom line. Parent, Jesus loves you and God is faithful. The Holy Spirit is working whether your see it or not. So, keep reading God's Word, keep praying, and don't give up.

What your children need to see is that you are consistent in your faith and faithful in your prayers.

DESPITE ANY PAST FAILURES, COMMIT TO BEING THE KIND OF PARENT GOD HAS CALLED YOU TO BE TODAY.

Day 174

For this reason I bow my knees before the Father, from whom every family in heaven and on earth is named. So that Christ may dwell in your hearts through faith.

—Ephesians 3:14-15, 17

No one really wants to give up control of their life. Do you?

Because if you do, your life will spin out of control, right? And if you're like most people, you constantly worry about how to keep the lid on your life. You want to be in charge of your life and control your own destiny.

As Christians, you and I are commanded to give ourselves unconditionally to the leadership of the Holy Spirit and the lordship of Jesus Christ in our lives. As our verse today says, Jesus wants to "dwell" in your heart.

He doesn't want you to live a divided life—one secular and one spiritual. Christ wants to consume and control your very being all the time. Every choice and every circumstance ought to be for God's glory.

But I want to make one thing very clear. When you give up your life to Christ, you're not giving up. When you allow Christ to guide your life, you gain productivity, sweet rest, overflowing joy, and power!

Today, I want to challenge you to give up every part of your life to Jesus in exchange for His. You're getting the better deal!

ARE YOU ALLOWING THE LORD TO DWELL IN EVERY AREA OF YOUR LIFE? IF NOT, PRAY FOR THE COURAGE TO GIVE CHRIST COMPLETE CONTROL.

Trust in the LORD with all your heart, and do not lean on your own understanding. In all your ways acknowledge him, and he will make straight your paths.

—Proverbs 3:5-6

The Christian life is really a matter of the heart. That's what God is really interested in. What this means is that you and I are really supposed to live "inside out."

Our verse today has a promise you can live by. The promise is that God has a will for your life, which is His best for you.

How do you say yes to God's best? Trust Him. When you trust God, you look to Him, count on Him, and have confidence in Him. When we accept Jesus Christ as our Savior, that's trust. But it's only the beginning.

Because trust is not only an act, it's an attitude. Trust is an activity that we live every day of our lives. It's both a point and a process. It's knowing that God is for you and that He is working with your best interest at heart.

According to 2 Chronicles 16:9, "For the eyes of the LORD run to and fro throughout the whole earth, to give strong support to those whose heart is blameless toward him."

When you trust God, you begin an exciting adventure. When you surrender and give Him control of your life, that's when you can start to see God's best for you.

TRUST IS NOT ONLY AN ACT, IT'S AN ATTITUDE.

Day 176

In all your ways acknowledge him, and he will make straight your paths.

—Proverbs 3:6

God has a perfect plan and will for your life. So how do you make sure you're on the right path?

Make a daily appointment with God. Take time on a regular basis to seek and listen to Him. Give the very best part of your day to God and open His Word.

Expect peace and joy. When you trust and believe in God, you'll find peace and joy.

Be willing to wait. If in doubt, you and I should wait on God. We may not be ready to move on. God may be preparing us for what's ahead.

Keep moving forward. (And that's not a contradiction to #4!) I'm talking about keep doing the will of God. So much of the will of God we already know. And God will not take us one step further until we obey what He has already commanded us to do.

Seek wise counsel. Find someone who knows and loves you... and who knows and loves God. Turn to a minister, pastor, family member, or friend.

Be bold. Take some risks. If you step out in faith and believe God, He will direct your steps.

WHAT AREAS ABOVE NEED YOUR FOCUS TODAY?

Day 177

Rejoice in the Lord always; again I will say, Rejoice. Let your reasonableness be known to everyone. The Lord is at hand; do not be anxious about anything, but in everything by prayer and supplication with thanksgiving let your requests be made known to God.

—Philippians 4:4-6

Do you need a little peace in your life?

The apostle Paul wrote some practical help for you in Philippians 4:4-9. Now keep in mind, he was in prison when he wrote it. So, Paul knew what he was talking about!

First, rejoice in all things. Paul knew how to keep from becoming calloused by life's troubles. His life was full of God's joy. Paul knew the importance of rejoicing and laughter.

Don't worry. Trust God. Worry wastes your time and accomplishes nothing. Instead of being gripped by fear, worry, and stress, be gripped by the grace of God. Rest and relax in Him. He has promised to deliver you from all your fears.

Pray about everything. Really converse with God on a daily basis. Pray with an attitude of devotion and trust. That's when prayer accomplishes something. When you pray, you won't be immune from the problems of life, but you will be in touch with the Redeemer.

So I challenge you to get serious about prayer today!

TALK TO GOD ABOUT YOUR WORRIES TODAY.

Day 178

With thanksgiving let your requests be made known to God. And the peace of God, which surpasses all understanding, will guard your hearts and minds in Christ Jesus.

—Philippians 4:6-7

Are you worried or stressed today?

As believers in Christ, we know we will have eternal peace when we get to heaven. But Philippians 4:4-9 offers some practical tips to help you cope with your anxieties and fears today.

Be thankful for everything. Don't just thank God for the good things, thank Him for all things. Genuine gratitude and praise produce peace because God inhabits the praises of His people. God draws near when we praise Him.

Think on the right things. It's nearly impossible to think two thoughts at once. So if you are thinking on the right and good things, you can't think of the wrong things.

Do the right thing. One cure for worry is work. I've known a lot of people who have died of worry, but I've known very few who died of work. Put your faith to practice, get involved in life. Give yourself to meaningful ministry and live out the Christian life.

ARE YOUR THOUGHTS MORE POSITIVE OR MORE NEGATIVE? IF THEY'RE MORE NEGATIVE, PRAY THAT GOD WILL HELP YOU THINK ABOUT THE BLESSINGS IN YOUR LIFE INSTEAD OF THE WORRIES!

Day 179

Keep your heart with all vigilance, for from it flow the springs of life.

—Proverbs 4:23

The Bible says you should guard, or watch, your heart. Why? Because your heart is your core being. It's your character. And out of your heart the rest of your life's story will unfold.

So, guard your heart. Protect it. Here's how according to Scripture.

Purpose to live a pure life. Don't live by preferences, but by convictions.

Prepare for ambush. Expect and detect temptation. Know your vulnerabilities and your weaknesses. Be honest with yourself and guard your eyes. Run from temptation.

Practice spiritual disciplines. Strengthen your heart with the Word of God. Keep a vital prayer life.

Ponder the consequences. Think about the effect on your life if you don't guard your heart. If you don't guard your heart, you can lose your spiritual influence and the right to lead your family.

Partner with other believers. Become accountable. Partner with another believer or group of believers who you trust and who can hold you up in prayer. Find someone who will listen to you and with whom you can be transparent.

WHAT CAN YOU DO TO GUARD YOUR HEART TODAY?

Jesus stood up and cried out, "If anyone thirsts, let him come to me and drink. Whoever believes in me, as the Scripture has said, 'Out of his heart will flow rivers of living water.'"

—John 7:37-38

Are you going with the flow? Once you begin living in the flow of the Spirit of God, I believe your life will explode with spiritual power!

You'll begin to break the habits that are binding you. Your prayer life will take on new power. You'll share Jesus with others more than ever before. You will literally be set free by the Spirit of God in you.

That flow begins with a miracle—the miracle of Jesus Christ dwelling in you. To become a Christian is to drink of Christ, to take Him in. By the greatest miracle of all, Jesus enters the human heart by His Spirit.

And that's when He begins to live His life through you. Jesus promises to dwell in you. And His Spirit lives in you.

If you have a thirst and a passion for the flow of Christ in your life, you can receive it. You can be filled with His Spirit through desire, trust, and faith.

According to John 7:38, "Whoever believes in me, as the Scripture said." You and I don't' have to rely on emotions. We can be filled if we thirst because the Scripture says we can.

So, let me ask you. Do you thirst for Him? Do you have a passion for spiritual life? Do you ask the Spirit of God to guide, lead, and work through you? That is what Jesus said is abiding in Him... being thirsty.

ASK GOD'S SPIRIT TO FILL YOU TODAY.

Day 181

And I will give you a new heart, and a new spirit I will put within you.

— **Ezekiel 36:26**

You and I need a miracle… the miracle of transformation that comes from accepting Jesus Christ.

Maybe you've experienced that miracle by accepting Jesus Christ as your Lord and Savior. If so, you know just how amazing the transformation is.

First it is a **changing experience.** "Therefore, if anyone is in Christ, he is a new creation. The old has passed away; behold, the new has come" (2 Corinthians 5:17). When you repent, God gives you a new heart and changes you inside and out.

It is also a **cleansing experience.** "I will sprinkle clean water on you, and you shall be clean from all your uncleanness, and from all your idols I will cleanse you" (Ezekiel 36:25). Every sin, stain, and blemish from your past, present, and future is forgiven because Jesus bore your sin and guilt when He died upon the cross.

And finally, it is a **continual experience.** "I will put My Spirit within you and cause you to walk in my statues" (Ezekiel 36:27). Jesus promised that when His Spirit lives inside of you, you have a dramatic, dynamic connection with God.

If you've experienced the miracle of salvation, I encourage you to share your story with someone who needs to hear it this week.

THANK GOD TODAY FOR THE MIRACLE OF TRANSFORMATION THAT COMES FROM SALVATION IN CHRIST.

Day 182

They said to each other, "Did not our hearts burn within us while he talked to us on the road, while He opened to us the Scriptures?"

—Luke 24:32

A re you burned out? Running on empty?

If so, here are four ways to rediscover and rekindle your spiritual passion in life.

Revelation. You and I need to get a new recognition and revelation of who Jesus really is. It is in the Word of God that you can meet the risen Christ. Learn the reality of Jesus Christ by reading about Him in the Bible.

Relationships. Develop relationships with other believers who will spark your faith and who will encourage you. Don't stick around people who drain you spiritually, but find someone whose heart can beat with yours in spiritual passion.

Resurrection. If you've been to the cross for pardon, don't forget the empty tomb for power. Allow the living Christ to fill your life! Abide in Christ, listen to His voice, and live in His victory.

Realignment. If you and I are to have passion for life, there needs to be a mission that's bigger than ourselves. That's the Kingdom of God. Your passion, your purpose, and your mission are to be a living testimony of the reality of Jesus Christ.

READ ABOUT JESUS IN GOD'S WORD TODAY AND BE ENCOURAGED.

Day 183

Your Word is a lamp to my feet and a light to my path.

—Psalm 119:105

Life is a series of decisions. Where you are today is the result of decisions you have made in the past. Where you will be tomorrow is determined by the choices you make today.

In fact, where you will be in eternity is determined by the decisions and choices you make today. Sadly, there is an anti-God and anti-Christian bias in the world. It's easy to be sucked into making wrong decisions if you listen to the world instead of the Word.

So, if you are going to make decisions based out of your convictions, you must hide the Word of God in your heart.

If you devour the Word of God, you won't be ruled by emotions, feelings, or popular thinking. You'll live by the principles of the Word of God.

According to Psalm 119:97-100, "Oh, how I love Your law! It is my meditation all the day. Your commandment makes me wiser than my enemies, for it is ever with me. I have more understanding than all my teachers, for your testimonies are my meditation. I understand more than the aged, for I keep your precepts."

DO YOU TEST EVERY MAJOR DECISION IN YOUR LIFE AGAINST GOD'S WORD?

Day 184

But Daniel resolved that he would not defile himself.

— **Daniel 1:8**

Are you determined to live for God? If so, you have to decide now, before temptation comes.

Like Daniel did in our verse today, you must purpose in your heart to follow your convictions before the pressure is on. Determine in your heart that no pleasure is worth sacrificing your relationship and fellowship with God.

The reality is that your faith will be tested. It's a certainty, according to Scripture. A faith that can't be tested can't be trusted!

So you must make the purposeful decision to be true to the Lord and to live for Him now. There will be peer pressure and cultural force. And it will seem like everyone else is compromising.

You see, many of the spiritual decisions that we make demand sacrifice and commitment. It may cost you friends to follow Jesus Christ. It may cost you a promotion at work.

But if you make those tough decisions, God will honor your convictions. So set your limits now. Make the decision to build up your relationship with God, rather than tear it down. When you do that, God will bless your decision.

**DETERMINE IN YOUR HEART THAT NO
PLEASURE IS WORTH SACRIFICING YOUR
RELATIONSHIP AND FELLOWSHIP WITH GOD.**

Day 185

I have great sorrow and unceasing anguish in my heart.

—Romans 9:2

The greatest investment in life you can make is in another soul. If you are a believer, you are charged with sharing the message of Jesus Christ with passion and compassion.

The apostle Paul is a great example for us to follow. As you can see in today's verse, his heart was broken for those who did not know Jesus Christ.

As a result of this, Paul moved beyond his borders to share Jesus. Paul was actually grief stricken by the possibility that someone would spend eternity separated from God. You and I are called by God to reach out to others with that same compassion.

The fact is that if we don't have a compassion for telling others about Jesus Christ, our own spirit is in serious condition. You and I should never become casual about soul-winning. We can never get comfortable in our pew, our classroom, and our lifestyle.

So often in the book of Acts, Paul begins sharing his faith by telling his personal testimony. He begins with his own experience of grace in the Lord Jesus Christ. Paul never got over his salvation. He couldn't believe that God would love him so much and spent the rest of his days telling others what Jesus had done for him.

Are you overwhelmed by the love of Christ in your life? Do you really comprehend what Jesus did for you? If so, you will want to share with others your experience.

THINK ABOUT WHERE JESUS HAS BROUGHT YOU FROM, AND SHARE IT WITH ANOTHER PERSON THIS WEEK.

Day 186

For I could wish that I myself were accursed and cut off from Christ for the sake of my brothers, my kinsmen according to the flesh.

—Romans 9:3

If you are a follower of Christ, people are watching you. They want to know if you care about others. The way they know this is if you have a "yes" face or a "no" face.

Here's what I mean by that...

Grace is God's "yes" to us. And once we have experienced God's grace, it changes our countenance and attitude, and gives us a "yes" face for all to see!

Jesus had a "yes" face. And our calling as His followers is to say "yes" to those who are hurting. Every Christian should have a compassionate heart that shows up in our lives, our actions, and our attitudes.

Yet some people have a "no" face. They shut others off. Too many churches are known more for what they are against than what they're for. They push people away with "no" faces and attitudes.

Your mission and mine... as people who have experienced God's grace... is to say to those around us, "Yes, God loves you. Yes, we care about you. Yes, you can find His grace, compassion, and love."

TELL SOMEONE "YES" BY SHOWING THEM LOVE AND COMPASSION IN AN UNEXPECTED WAY.

Day 187

For I am sure that neither death nor life, nor angels nor rulers, nor things present nor things to come, nor powers, nor height nor depth, nor anything else in all creation, will be able to separate us from the love of God in Christ Jesus our Lord.

—Romans 8:38-39

The greatest sentence ever uttered was spoken by Jesus Christ in John 3:16 when He said, "For God so loved the world, that he gave his only Son, that whoever believes in him should not perish but have eternal life." These life-giving words were spoken to a man named Nicodemus.

Nicodemus was like a lot of people in the church today. He knew a lot about God—he pursued God, he championed God, and he pleased God in a lot of ways. Yet Nicodemus had a longing for a relationship with God. This is what led him to engage Jesus in conversation.

And Nicodemus reacted to Jesus in a way that a lot of people react to Jesus. He thought it sounded too good to be true!

Have you ever had that same thought yourself?

When it comes to accepting Jesus Christ's love and acceptance of you, the devil wants to make you believe that you're too far gone... that your sin is too great for God to really ever love you... or that you've committed the same sin too many times for God to accept you again.

But nothing could be further from the truth! You're never too far gone for God to love you.

When you accepted Jesus Christ as your personal Lord and Savior, your sins—past, present, and future—were taken care of at the cross. So please don't let Satan weigh you down with guilt about your sins and failures.

Yes, your sins have consequences. But God loving you isn't one of them!

**GOD LOVES YOU AND ACCEPTS YOU
IN SPITE OF WHAT YOU'VE DONE.**

Day 188

If you confess with your mouth that Jesus is Lord and believe in your heart that God raised him from the dead, you will be saved.
—Romans 10:9

There are three things that go hand-in-hand with becoming a follower of Jesus Christ. But these three things don't add to your salvation as a believer in Christ. They accompany your decision to follow Christ. Or to put it another way, they are three responsibilities you have that go along with your salvation.

The first responsibility you have as a believer is to make sure you have a profession that's public.

There's no such thing as a secret disciple of Jesus Christ! In fact, it was Jesus Himself who said in Luke 12:8-9, "Everyone who acknowledges me before men, the Son of Man also will acknowledge before the angels of God, but the one who denies me before men will be denied before the angels of God."

The second responsibility you have as a Christ-follower is to make sure you have a baptism that is biblical.

I think there's a lot of confusion out there about the ordinance of baptism. Remember, baptism itself cannot save you. It expresses your faith in the Lord Jesus... and it's an act of obedience that God blesses!

Finally, the third responsibility you have as a Christian is to make sure you belong to a fellowship that is faithful.

The reason we belong to and commit to a local church is because godly character isn't only taught, it's caught! The Scripture even reminds us in Proverbs 13:20 that "whoever walks with the wise becomes wise."

It's my prayer that you will follow Christ in obedience in these areas today!

**AFTER YOU ACCEPT CHRIST, GOD ASKS YOU
TO FOLLOW AND OBEY HIM.**

Day 189

This is the day that the LORD has made; let us rejoice and be glad in it.

—Psalm 118:24

One of the keys to making every day count as a follower of the Lord Jesus Christ is found in the words He spoke in Matthew 6:34: "Therefore do not be anxious about tomorrow, for tomorrow will be anxious for itself. Sufficient for the day is its own trouble."

A lot of people can't do this because they're too focused on yesterday… tomorrow… or themselves!

Some people just think about yesterday… the past. Just like you're going to have an accident if you drive your car looking in the rear-view mirror, you're going to have an accident in life when all you do is live life looking over your shoulder!

Yet other people can't live for the Lord today because they're too busy focusing on themselves… and in the meantime they're sort of just getting by in life.

Still other people only focus on the future. They worry about everything that's going to happen next. They are so busy planning tomorrow or the next big thing that they never live today!

But today… I want to challenge you to be the kind of person who lives today for today. I challenge you to commit today's verse to memory: "This is the day that the LORD has made; let us rejoice and be glad in it."

Just as John Maxwell says, "Today is the most important day of my life. Yesterday with its successes and victories, struggles and failures, is gone forever. The past is past. Done! Finished! I cannot relive it. I cannot go back and change it. But I will learn from it and improve my today. Today, this moment, now! It is God's gift to me and it is all that I have."

MAKE TODAY… AND EVERY DAY… COUNT FOR CHRIST!

Day 190

*Now the angel of the LORD came and sat under the terebinth at Ophrah,
which belonged to Joash the Abiezrite, while his son Gideon was beating
out wheat in the winepress to hide it from the Midianites. And the angel
of the LORD appeared to him and said to him, "The LORD is with you, O
mighty man of valor." And Gideon said to him, "Please, sir, if the LORD
is with us, why then has all this happened to us? And where are all his
wonderful deeds that our fathers recounted to us, saying, 'Did not the
LORD bring us up from Egypt?' But now the LORD has forsaken us and
given us into the hand of Midian."*

—**Judges 6:11-13**

In today's passage, we see Gideon described as a "mighty man of valor."
Yet Gideon was anything but a champion when God called him!

Gideon was beaten down. He was hopeless. He had lost his faith! Can you
imagine God using someone like that? Nevertheless, God spoke to Gideon
through an angel and said, "The LORD is with you, O mighty man of
valor."

This is another example in Scripture when we see that God doesn't call
the equipped. He equips the called!

Christian, the evil one wants to discourage you. He does his best to convince you you'll never change… that your marriage will never improve…
that your kids will never come back to the Lord… that you'll always be
sick… that you'll never conquer fear. And you know what? Far too often
we believe the lies that Satan tells us!

But you know what's great about our Lord? He doesn't see us like we see
ourselves. As a believer, the Lord Jesus sees your potential… just like He
saw Gideon's potential. In addition to that, Paul tells us in Romans 8:37
that "we are more than conquerors through him who loved us."

If you are a follower of Christ, you need to stop believing the defeating
lies of Satan and start believing again who you are in Christ! Start trusting
in the God who can do the impossible in your life!

Yes, your enemy is mighty, but God is almighty. That means there's no
problem, difficulty, danger, darkness, fight, or struggle you face in life that
you and God can't handle together.

So stand on this promise today!

**GOD DOESN'T SEE YOU AS YOU SEE YOURSELF.
AS A BELIEVER, HE SEES YOUR POTENTIAL.**

Day 191

...looking to Jesus, the founder and perfecter of our faith, who for the joy that was set before him endured the cross, despising the shame, and is seated at the right hand of the throne of God.

—Hebrews 12:2

Today, I'd like to challenge you with this thought: When life starts to get you down, you need to look up!

Verse after verse in Scripture reminds us of the Lord Jesus' presence in our lives. Yet so often how we forget what God's Word says!

- In 2 Chronicles 20:12, Jehoshaphat prays, "We do not know what to do, but our eyes are on you."

- In Psalm 16:8, David says, "I have set the LORD always before me; because he is at my right hand, I shall not be shaken."

- And the writer of Hebrews reminds us in today's verse to look "to Jesus, the founder and perfecter of our faith, who for the joy that was set before him endured the cross, despising the shame, and is seated at the right hand of the throne of God."

If you're feeling down and out today, lift your spirit by looking up to Jesus!

**WHEN LIFE STARTS TO GET YOU DOWN,
YOU NEED TO LOOK UP!**

Then Mordecai told them to reply to Esther, "Do not think to yourself that in the king's palace you will escape any more than all the other Jews. For if you keep silent at this time, relief and deliverance will rise for the Jews from another place, but you and your father's house will perish. And who knows whether you have not come to the kingdom for such a time as this?" Then Esther told them to reply to Mordecai, "Go, gather all the Jews to be found in Susa, and hold a fast on my behalf, and do not eat or drink for three days, night or day. I and my young women will also fast as you do. Then I will go to the king, though it is against the law, and if I perish, I perish."

—Esther 4:13-16

Have you ever thought about how your choices can either help you fulfill God's plan for your life… or keep you from it?

Esther's life teaches us that God is deeply interested in our character… not our appearance, our money, or our talent. He is seeking people with godly character to fulfill His purposes on the earth.

Character is something that is built and proven over time. And the way we develop character in our lives is by consistently making choices to follow God's way—not our own way—each and every day.

That's what set Esther apart. She made a choice to make the lives of others more important than her own… which, of course, is what Jesus commands us to do also. And by making that choice, God used her to save an entire nation from genocide!

Now, not everyone will be called to save a nation. But you just don't know what kind of impact your choices and daily obedience to Christ will have on the lives of others!

It's exciting to realize that God can use anybody—including you and me—to be a part of His purposes for this earth. And you can live a life of incredible significance right where you are.

You don't have to be famous or beautiful or clever to make a mark on this world. You just need to make right choices, every day, to live in obedience to God… and watch what happens!

Just like Esther, you'll find yourself presented with all kinds of incredible opportunities to impact people's lives for the better… and to bring pleasure and glory to God through your life.

THE WAY TO DEVELOP CHARACTER IS TO CONSISTENTLY MAKE CHOICES TO FOLLOW GOD'S WAY EVERY DAY.

Now the word of the Lord came to Jonah the son of Amittai, saying, "Arise, go to Nineveh, that great city, and call out against it, for their evil has come up before me." But Jonah rose to flee to Tarshish from the presence of the Lord.

—Jonah 1:1-3

Have you ever wondered if God can use you in spite of your mistakes? Today, you can be encouraged by Jonah's story because he was an ordinary person who got off course for a while. Yet he still managed to fulfill God's call on his life!

Jonah had a bad attitude and was willfully disobedient. He made some big mistakes. But the Lord never gave up on him! God still wanted to use Jonah to fulfill the original plan He had for him—which was to go to Ninevah and impact an entire city.

As soon as Jonah made a decision to repent—to stop going his own way and to start obeying God again—the calling that was on his life began to unfold. He was able to get back on track again and fulfill exactly what God wanted him to do!

Remember, you are not disqualified from God's calling just because you have sinned and made mistakes. You might say, "Oh, but you don't know what I've done!" No, I don't know what you've done. But I do know there is forgiveness for you… if you'll ask for it.

First John 1:9 says, "If we confess our sins, He is faithful and just to forgive us our sins and to cleanse us from all unrighteousness." That's what Jonah did… he recognized that he was going the wrong way… and then he cried out to God in repentance. And God heard his prayer and turned the situation around.

The same is true for you and me. All of us can lose our way. Sometimes we're just a little bit off course… sometimes we don't know how we could ever find our way back to the Lord and fulfill His plans for our life.

But God is gracious… and all-powerful… and He can redeem our lives and change our future, even when we think we've messed it up completely. All it takes is for you to come to Him, with a humble heart, and say, "I'm sorry, Lord… please help me to follow You."

If you're not quite where God wants you to be right now, let me encourage you that you can find your way again... just like Jonah did. Being off course doesn't mean it's the end of the journey!

YOU ARE NOT DISQUALIFIED FROM GOD'S CALLING JUST BECAUSE YOU HAVE SINNED AND MADE MISTAKES!

And at the time of the offering of the oblation, Elijah the prophet came near and said, "O LORD, God of Abraham, Isaac, and Israel, let it be known this day that you are God in Israel, and that I am your servant, and that I have done all these things at your word. Answer me, O LORD, answer me, that this people may know that you, O LORD, are God, and that you have turned their hearts back." Then the fire of the LORD fell and consumed the burnt offering and the wood and the stones and the dust, and licked up the water that was in the trench. And when all the people saw it, they fell on their faces and said, "The LORD, he is God; the LORD, he is God."

—1 Kings 18:36-39

We live in a time when there is a great need for spiritual revival… not only in the world, but also in the church. God is looking for men and women to rise up with a passion for Him and with a boldness to declare His Word to this generation!

He wants to use you—with your unique gifts and personality—for this time in history. The life of Elijah lends some specific keys to unleashing the revival fire of God through your own life.

First, live in the Lord's presence every day. If we are going to impact the lives of others, we need to know the reality of the risen Christ ourselves. It's only as we become full of His Spirit that the people around us will see that there is something different about us!

Secondly, praying releases a reviving fire through your life. Elijah spent time alone with the Lord… establishing a very real and personal relationship with Him. And it was this time of private devotion that developed the incredible faith that was later seen in his public ministry.

Lastly, fearlessly proclaim the Word of God. Even though it's controversial and often difficult to talk about Jesus Christ, it's the Word of God that brings spiritual revival to the hearts of men and women. The Lord is seeking people who will courageously declare His Word as the truth!

If you want to be a person who is used by God to bring spiritual revival to those around you, it has to start first with you! Let your own life be completely sold out for God. Be single-minded and passionate about your devotion to Him, just like Elijah was, and the fire of God's Spirit will begin to influence everyone around you!

HOW CAN YOU DECLARE GOD'S WORD
TO SOMEONE YOU KNOW TODAY?

Day 195

That very day two of them were going to a village named Emmaus, about seven miles from Jerusalem, and they were talking with each other about all these things that had happened. While they were talking and discussing together, Jesus himself drew near and went with them. But their eyes were kept from recognizing him.

—Luke 24:13-16

I love this story about the two disciples walking to Emmaus because it's such an honest reflection of how we can often act during difficult times in our lives.

These men had just experienced an overwhelming disappointment in their lives. Jesus, whom they had been following, had been brutally killed. They were shocked... confused... and grieved. They couldn't understand why this had happened. And they didn't know how to respond.

And then unexpectedly, as they went about their everyday lives, a stranger joined them on their journey and began to speak with them. And they didn't even recognize that it was Jesus!

How often we do the same thing! We can be going through an extremely difficult time in our life and feel that all hope is lost. And all along, Jesus is right there with us... and He is trying to help us understand how God is at work, even in times of despair.

Today's verses are a challenging reminder that Jesus really is with us... all the time... even when we don't feel like He is.

In Joshua 1:5, God made this promise, "I will not leave you or forsake you... I am with you." And in the original Hebrew language this verse actually says, "I will never, no never, no never, no never in any way, no never will I leave you or forsake you." The Scripture couldn't have been clearer than that!

This is the great hope we have—of an ever-present Savior—because Jesus is risen! We need to remember... that our Lord is alive today... and is always working in our lives. He has not forgotten you or your situation... He is with you even now.

So, if you are feeling alone, confused or anxious, take a moment to reflect on this promise that the Lord has given you: "I will never leave you or forsake you... I am with you."

JESUS IS WITH YOU *ALL* THE TIME... EVEN WHEN YOU DON'T FEEL LIKE HE IS.

But God shows his love for us in that while we were still sinners,
Christ died for us.

—Romans 5:8

As believers, it should be natural for you and me to share the love and hope we find in today's verse. Yet many Christians never do this!

The fact is, if you know Christ, you will want to make Him known. If you believe He has forgiven all your sins and changed your life and given you a hope and future that is forever with Him, how can you not speak of Him?

Today, if you're a child of God, I want to encourage you to think about the difference Christ has made in your life. What thoughts do you not have now that you used to have? What habits did you use to be slave to that you aren't any more? What peace have you found now that used to elude you?

Now, I want to challenge you to share the ways Christ has changed your life with one person in the next week. It doesn't have to be some forced conversation. It can be something as simple as a short note of encouragement to someone who's hurting. Or it can be a phone call to let someone know you're praying for them.

Whatever God leads you to do, do it! If you're scared or nervous, just ask God to give you the power and boldness—through the name of Jesus Christ—to share Him with someone else.

I truly believe… as you commit to sharing Christ with others… God will give you a measure of boldness you may never have known before. And I believe He will use you to impact lives as you show Christ's love to others!

IF YOU KNOW CHRIST, YOU WILL WANT
TO MAKE HIM KNOWN.

And while staying with them he ordered them not to depart from Jerusalem, but to wait for the promise of the Father, which, he said, "you heard from me; for John baptized with water, but you will be baptized with the Holy Spirit not many days from now."

—**Acts 1:4-5**

You know, I think it's funny that the first thing Jesus said about powering up in life was not to "go," but to "wait." Right here at the beginning of the book of Acts, He said, "What I want you to do is to wait right here in Jerusalem for the coming of the Spirit."

And the Scripture says that's exactly what Jesus' followers did!

They waited and prayed together as one heart and one soul. And as a result, they received the power and the presence of the Holy Spirit in their lives.

So, what about you today? Are you ready to see evidence of the Holy Spirit in your life?

I meet so many followers of Christ who want to see Christ change their life. They want Him to revolutionize their family. They desperately desire for Him to give them the power to overcome temptation.

But what you and I must remember is that the first step in tapping into this power is to do what those first followers of Christ did: wait and pray. Engage with God in prayer and wait on Him!

That's my encouragement to you today, believer. Pray for the power of the Holy Spirit to come upon your life. And just wait to see what He accomplishes in and through you!

**WAIT AND PRAY FOR GOD'S TIMING.
AND JUST WAIT TO SEE WHAT HE ACCOMPLISHES
IN AND THROUGH YOU!**

Day 198

There is therefore now no condemnation for those who are in Christ Jesus. For the law of the Spirit of life has set you free in Christ from the law of sin and death.

—Romans 8:1-2

I'd like to ask you a question today. Which set of words better describe your life today: empty, defeated, and fearful or fulfilled, faithful, and courageous?

Only a life that's being transformed by the power of the Holy Spirit can be described as fulfilled, faithful, and courageous! And if you're anything like me, I know you want your life to be described in these ways.

Yet so often, we get hung up on our past… how we failed God… or how we sinned. I mean, think about Simon Peter! He denied Christ three times the night before our Lord was crucified. He had reason to beat himself up and disqualify himself from God's service!

But Christian, that's not how God operates. God renewed, restored, and used Peter… just like He can renew, restore, and use you today.

So let me ask you—is there something in your past that's keeping you on the bench spiritually? Please think about it for a moment. Maybe it's more than one thing. Maybe it's a hundred things!

Whatever it is, let me assure you, if you are a child of God, your slate is clean. As Paul tells us in today's verse, "There is therefore now no condemnation for those who are in Christ Jesus."

Satan wants you to believe the exact opposite. And oh, how easy it is to believe him at times! But as a follower of Christ, you aren't condemned for your sins, no matter how many they may be. You're never condemned because God loves you and gave His Son's life for you!

Focus on this truth today. And it's my prayer that you will become a fulfilled, faithful, and courageous follower of Christ who God uses in amazing ways!

**REMEMBER HOW MUCH GOD LOVES
AND ACCEPTS YOU TODAY… AND EVERY DAY!**

And Peter said to them, "Repent and be baptized every one of you in the name of Jesus Christ for the forgiveness of your sins, and you will receive the gift of the Holy Spirit. For the promise is for you and for your children and for all who are far off, everyone whom the Lord our God calls to himself." And with many other words he bore witness and continued to exhort them, saying, "Save yourselves from this crooked generation."

—Acts 2:38-40

The apostle Peter was a man well acquainted with fear. The night before Christ was crucified, he had been scared to even be associated with Jesus... and he ended up denying he knew Christ three times!

Yet in Peter's first sermon in Acts chapter 2, we see a completely different side of him! We see a courageous Peter. We see an empowered Peter. We see a bold Peter.

And that same courage, empowerment, and boldness we see in Peter is the same courage, empowerment, and boldness you can have as you share Christ with others. It's true!

First, when Peter shared the Good News of Jesus Christ, he relied on the power of the Holy Spirit... not on his own oratory skills or powers of persuasion. And he aimed primarily at the heart... not at the head.

Secondly, it's important to remember that when Peter shared with people, he was practical. He was down to earth. He proclaimed the facts, and with the force of the gospel, delivered the goods!

Thirdly, when Peter preached, he was personal. He met people where they were and he professed that Jesus was Lord.

Lastly, when Peter spoke about the Lord Jesus, he was persuasive. With passion he proclaimed that everyone, all people, must repent and receive Christ. And many, many people were moved by the Spirit working through Peter, and they were saved!

It's my prayer... as you look at the example of Peter today... that you will realize the tremendous potential you have to impact more and more people around you through the power of the Holy Spirit working through you!

THE SAME COURAGE, EMPOWERMENT, AND BOLDNESS WE SEE IN PETER IS THE SAME COURAGE, EMPOWERMENT, AND BOLDNESS YOU CAN HAVE AS YOU SHARE CHRIST WITH OTHERS!

Day 200

And all who believed were together and had all things in common. And they were selling their possessions and belongings and distributing the proceeds to all, as any had need. And day by day, attending the temple together and breaking bread in their homes, they received their food with glad and generous hearts, praising God and having favor with all the people. And the Lord added to their number day by day those who were being saved.

—Acts 2:44-47

D o you want to be fully engaged and empowered to live the Christian life? More than likely, you do! Yet far too many followers of Christ in our world today are disconnected from one of the main sources of empowerment: the local church!

The reasons for this are many, but the fact is, many, many believers aren't having the impact they could have for Christ because they're trying to live the Christian life in isolation… cut off from a local group of other learning, growing Christians.

What about you? Are you actively involved in a church? Now, please know that I'm not simply asking whether or not you attend church. Because truly being spiritually engaged means so much more than showing up at church every Sunday morning.

It's about whether or not you have plugged into the church of Jesus Christ in order to become a part of transforming our culture.

Just like a balled-up fist has more power than one puny finger, so too do you and I have more power as Christians when we stand in unity under the banner of Christ. A church united truly is a force to be reckoned with in our generation!

In today's passage, we read about people who were fully engaged and committed to each other, and therefore empowered to live the Christian life. And they turned the world upside down!

That was the church of the 1st century… and by God's grace, let it be the church of the 21st century, too!

ARE YOU ACTIVELY INVOLVED IN A LOCAL CHURCH?

Day 201

As he drew near to Jericho, a blind man was sitting by the roadside begging. And hearing a crowd going by, he inquired what this meant. They told him, "Jesus of Nazareth is passing by." And he cried out, "Jesus, Son of David, have mercy on me!" And those who were in front rebuked him, telling him to be silent. But he cried out all the more, "Son of David, have mercy on me!" And Jesus stopped and commanded him to be brought to him. And when he came near, he asked him, "What do you want me to do for you?" He said, "Lord, let me recover my sight." And Jesus said to him, "Recover your sight; your faith has made you well." And immediately he recovered his sight and followed him, glorifying God. And all the people, when they saw it, gave praise to God.

—Luke 18:35-43

The Bible is full of stories like this of people whose lives were radically transformed by Jesus Christ. Their amazing testimonies proved to everyone around them that Jesus was at work, and many people came to know the Lord as a result!

You know what, though? Not everyone has experienced something as dramatic as a healing or miraculous deliverance. And if you don't have a past that reads like a fiction novel, it doesn't mean that your story is any less powerful than those who do!

You see, when you ask God to come into your life, He begins to work, and He continues to work.

Each and every day He is changing you, restoring you, and making you more into the image of Jesus. He is transforming your life… just as powerfully as He transformed the blind man's life. It's just that you can't always see it!

With all of the distractions of daily life, it's easy to overlook the ways that God is answering your prayers, speaking to you through His Word, arranging your circumstances, or encouraging you through other people.

Yet all the while, God is trying to show you how very present He is in your life, and He is giving you your own testimony of His power to share with those around you! Yes, the Lord Jesus is powerful, and He is powerfully at work in you!

So I encourage you to look for the daily evidence of God at work in your life, and tell other people about it!

Don't wait for spectacular demonstrations of God's power to share with others. Share the daily demonstrations of His power—because they're happening all the time!

THE LORD JESUS IS POWERFUL, AND HE IS POWERFULLY AT WORK IN YOU TODAY!

Day 202

Go therefore and make disciples of all nations, baptizing them in the name of the Father and of the Son and of the Holy Spirit, teaching them to observe all that I have commanded you. And behold, I am with you always, to the end of the age.

—Matthew 28:19-20

You know, it would be criminal if you discovered the cure for cancer, but kept it to yourself. Yet at the same time, many Christians have found eternal life in Christ, but never tell others about it!

The fact is, if you know Christ, you will want to make Him known. If you believe He has forgiven all your sins and changed your life and given you a hope and future that is forever with Him, how can you not speak of Him?

Today, if you're a child of God, I want to encourage you to think about the difference Christ has made in your life. What thoughts do you not have now that you used to have? What habits did you use to be slave to that you aren't any more? What peace have you found now that used to elude you?

Then, I'd like to challenge you to share the ways Christ has changed your life with one person this week. It doesn't have to be some forced conversation. It can be something as simple as a short note of encouragement to someone who's hurting. Or it can be a phone call to let someone know you're praying for them.

Whatever God leads you to do, do it! If you're scared or nervous, just ask God to give you the power and boldness—through the name of Jesus Christ—to share Him with someone else.

I truly believe as you commit to sharing Christ with others, God will give you a measure of boldness you may never have known before. And I believe He will use you to impact others for Him!

ASK GOD TO GIVE YOU THE BOLDNESS TO SHARE CHRIST'S LOVE AND TRUTH WITH SOMEONE THIS WEEK!

And when they had prayed, the place in which they were gathered together was shaken, and they were all filled with the Holy Spirit and continued to speak the word of God with boldness.

—Acts 4: 31

How can you engage in a deeper level of prayer, like the early Christians did?

First of all, always remember that when you pray, God moves! As you read about the early Christians... and as you think about incidents in your own life when you've prayed... you can see that God hears and answers prayer.

Secondly, the aim for all believers is for prayer to become a way of life— not just something you do now and then. The Scripture encourages you and me to engage in constant and passionate prayer... about everything!

This doesn't mean you have to give up your daily commitments so you can pray all day long! Apart from praying during your regular times of devotion to the Lord... and while meeting together with other believers... you can incline your heart towards the Lord all through your day. In this way, you can invite His presence and power into every moment!

And finally, as you continually surrender to the Lord in this way, the Holy Spirit will enable you to trust in the Lord more and more... to endure any kind of challenge that comes your way... and to find the courage you need in moments of uncertainty. Just like the early apostles did.

As today's verse tells us, when the early apostles yielded themselves to the Lord in prayer, "the place they were praying was shaken." And when you yield yourself to the Lord in prayer, you also can expect God to reveal Himself and empower you for every situation.

Prayer is one of your most valuable weapons as a follower of Jesus Christ!

Through believing prayer, God's very presence is released, and you and I can grow into the kind of people that the Lord has called us to be... faithful followers of Him.

So let me encourage you today to make prayer a way of life!

REMEMBER THAT WHEN YOU PRAY... GOD MOVES AND ANSWERS PRAYER!

And Stephen, full of grace and power, was doing great wonders and signs among the people. Then some of those who belonged to the synagogue of the Freedmen (as it was called), and of the Cyrenians, and of the Alexandrians, and of those from Cilicia and Asia, rose up and disputed with Stephen. But they could not withstand the wisdom and the Spirit with which he was speaking.

—Acts 6:8-10

A first-century Christian, Stephen was an ordinary person, just like you and me. He faced challenges and fears and times of weakness. But his greatest pursuit was to live a life that was pleasing to God.

It's good to stop and remind yourself every now and then that that is what life is really all about… pleasing God. It's so easy to get distracted by the busyness and pressures of daily life and momentarily lose focus on what is really important. But ultimately, you and I are living for an audience of One—our God in heaven.

Stephen made pleasing God his highest priority. He knew the Word of God… he courageously lived it out… and as a result, he reflected the love and grace of Christ to everyone around him.

As you and I continue to live lives that are dedicated to the Lord, we can expect to become full of faith… full of the Holy Spirit… full of grace… full of power… full of wisdom… and full of the glory of God! That is a very full life!

And that, I believe, is what is so remarkable about Stephen, and what you and I can learn from his example. In the end, Stephen didn't live a long life, but he lived a full life. His life was full of character… full of courage… and full of Christ. What an inspiration!

Stephen shows us what it really means to live life in full. And it's a life that is available to every person—including you—as you make your number one priority in life to please God in everything you do.

IS YOUR NUMBER ONE PRIORITY TO PLEASE GOD IN EVERYTHING YOU DO?

Day 205

Because I hear of your love and of the faith that you have toward the Lord Jesus and for all the saints, and I pray that the sharing of your faith may become effective for the full knowledge of every good thing that is in us for the sake of Christ. For I have derived much joy and comfort from your love, my brother, because the hearts of the saints have been refreshed through you.

—Philemon 1:5-7

What are some keys to sharing your faith on a daily basis?

The first key to giving your faith away every day is to be **open** to the prompting of the Holy Spirit. God is at work in the lives of men, women and children all around you… and He wants to use you to help them come to know Jesus.

If you are open to the Holy Spirit… and sensitive to His gentle promptings… you will walk into divine opportunities to share your faith every single day.

The second key to giving your faith away is to be **obedient**. Once you have felt the Lord's gentle nudge to make that phone call… to buy that gift… or to visit that person… don't be slow to act! Be sure to obey the Lord right away!

Often the Lord will prompt you at a specific moment so you can deliver a timely word to a person who is in desperate need. For you to delay might cause you to miss that crucial moment.

The third important key to giving your faith away is to be **observant**. Sometimes it is possible to see that God is at work in someone's life and that they are becoming more open to talking about Christ.

So pay attention to what is happening in the lives of those around you. And take every opportunity to speak into situations where you know that people are ready and open to hearing about Jesus!

The Lord is constantly presenting you and me with opportunities to share our faith! The challenge before us—every single day—is to become more open to the Holy Spirit… more obedient to His promptings… and more observant of the opportunities around us!

ARE YOU LOOKING FOR OPPORTUNITIES EVERY DAY TO SHARE YOUR FAITH WITH OTHERS?

Day 206

Trust in the Lord with all your heart, and do not lean on your own understanding. In all your ways acknowledge him, and he will make straight your paths.

—Proverbs 3:5-6

Do you ever wonder if you can really know God's will for your life each and every day?

Well, let me reassure you: You absolutely can! It really is possible to be in sync with the Spirit every single day.

But being in sync with the Holy Spirit is more than responding to a gut feeling or heeding your own human intuition. It comes about as you "abide" or stay connected to Christ every day.

Let me ask you an honest question: How often do you think about the Lord Jesus throughout your day?

I think one of the biggest problems in the Church today is that there are a lot of Christians who "do the God thing" on Sunday morning, and then live the rest of the week without giving Christ or His desires for their life a second thought!

But to live in step and in sync with God, and to know His will for our lives every day, you and I must learn to focus more on Him… every single day!

I know that life is busy, and that there are a thousand distractions each and every day. But I want to challenge you to start giving God more time throughout your week.

When your feet hit the floor in the morning, say a quick prayer, committing your day to Him. When you're about to walk into a meeting at work, ask God to guide your speech. When you lay your head down on your pillow at night, thank God for another day of life!

And, as you begin to focus more and more on God every day, you're going to see how He is leading you each step of the way!

**TO LIVE IN STEP AND IN SYNC WITH GOD,
YOU MUST LEARN TO FOCUS MORE ON HIM…
EVERY SINGLE DAY!**

Day 207

There is therefore now no condemnation for those who are in Christ Jesus. For the law of the Spirit of life has set you free in Christ Jesus from the law of sin and death.

—Romans 8:1-2

D id you know that you have an enemy of your soul?

You may not know it, but as a follower of Christ, you have a very real adversary. His name is Satan. But through the power of God, you can have victory over Satan!

There are two misunderstandings about the devil that a lot of people believe. One is that he's a myth and doesn't matter. The other is that he matters too much and that we have no victory over him.

But the fact is that we have victory in Jesus Christ! And I want to remind you how you can defeat Satan whenever he attacks you.

When Satan tries to dominate you by reminding you of your sinful past, remember what Jesus told us in John 8:32: "You will know the truth, and the truth will set you free." In Christ, you're free from the guilt and shame of sin!

When Satan tries to tempt you, remember what James 4:7 says: "Resist the devil, and he will flee from you." Jesus taught us how to do this when He went into the desert and there with the Word of God in prayer and fasting, He overcame the power of Satan and the temptation of Satan that came at Him again and again!

When Satan tries to accuse you, remember what today's verse says: "There is therefore now no condemnation for those who are in Christ Jesus. For the law of the Spirit of life has set you free in Christ Jesus from the law of sin and death."

And finally, when Satan tries to confront you, remember what Jesus told Simon Peter in Luke 22:31: "Satan demanded to have you, that he might sift you like wheat, but I have prayed for you that your faith may not fail." The only way you will defeat the confrontation of Satan is to pray Jesus' prayer that your faith will not fail!

Christian, I encourage you to commit each of these verses to memory so that you won't be caught off guard the next time Satan targets you.

And it's my prayer that you will be able to defeat Satan's attacks through the power of the Holy Spirit working in your life!

YOU HAVE VICTORY OVER SATAN THROUGH THE POWER OF JESUS CHRIST!

Therefore, since we have been justified by faith, we have peace with God through our Lord Jesus Christ. Through him we have also obtained access by faith into this grace in which we stand, and we rejoice in hope of the glory of God.

—Romans 5:1-2

Are you an optimistic Christian? I'm not speaking of a superficial optimism, but of a genuine outlook on life that is free from self-condemnation.

The book of Romans tells us clearly that our world apart from Jesus is condemned. And if that is all there is to life, there would be no reason to be anything other than a pessimist. But there is great news! We are justified in Christ when we believe and trust in Him.

And because of our justification... which is a legal transaction by God, the ultimate Judge of the universe... we now have a right standing before God. Most people don't understand what justification is and who we are because of it. But when you begin to understand what it means, then you will understand why every Christian should be an optimist!

As a believer, you can have peace in Jesus Christ. And when we realize that our true hope is found in Him, we will learn what it means to be an optimistic Christian, and we will see the positive benefits of being justified through Jesus.

The first benefit is **serenity**. As today's verse tells us, we will experience the peace of God because as believers, we are at peace with God. We need that type of peace with God because we were born into this world of sin separated from Him. And Christ is the One who reconciled us with God. He bridged the gap between us and God so we could have a relationship with Him.

Secondly, we have **stability** as a result of our justification. It was Paul who said, "I know whom I have believed, and I am convinced that he is able to guard until that Day what has been entrusted to me" (2 Timothy 1:12). As Christians, we are not to live in fear because the steps of the righteous man are ordered by the Lord!

And finally, we have **security** through Jesus Christ. We have peace that covers our past, access that takes care of our present, and hope that prepares us for the future.

Now you can understand why every Christian should be an optimist! There's hope today and tomorrow. Jesus is not just a proposition to us. He is our permanent possession!.

There's reason to be optimistic in the Christian life because we know that nothing can "separate us from the love of God in Christ Jesus our Lord" (Romans 8:39).

AS A BELIEVER, YOU CAN EXPERIENCE THE PEACE OF GOD BECAUSE YOU ARE AT PEACE WITH HIM.

What then shall we say to these things? If God is for us, who can be against us? He who did not spare his own Son but gave him up for us all, how will he not also with him graciously give us all things?

—Romans 8:31-32

There is a serious pessimism among people today who ask, "Are we really better off than we were? Are things getting any better?"

I know things aren't perfect in our world, but we need to remember that America has flourished over the years due to God's favor and blessing.

Today's verse tells us, "If God is for us, who can be against us?" And this verse can help us understand the stability we have in God and why this nation was founded upon Christian principles. We exist today in our current state not because of our military strength, our technological ingenuity, or our financial power. We exist because of God's favor.

This nation was founded upon the principles found in both the Old and New Testaments. Our nation's founding fathers shared the same ethics and values, which they integrated into the original documents, that formed our nation and gave us the right to exercise our religion freely.

But we're in danger of losing our soul as a nation. America today is not what it is by chance or destiny. God orchestrated the hearts, minds, and lives of the people who founded this great country. I don't know how long we'll have the freedoms we enjoy so much today, but if we as Christians don't stand for Christ, I believe these freedoms will be ripped from our hands!

The day Americans decide they no longer need God or His principles is the day America will begin to wither away and die. I pray that our deterioration as a country hasn't already begun.

We should be thankful for the freedom paid for by all those who have sacrificed so greatly for our nation. But let me remind you true freedom only comes through the blood of the Lamb.

Today's verse says, "He who did not spare His own Son, but delivered Him up for us all, how shall He not with Him also freely give us all things?" The blood of Jesus bought true freedom!

That is the truest meaning of Paul's great exclamation, "If God is for us, who can be against us?"!

ARE YOU ENJOYING THE FREEDOM THAT CHRIST'S BLOOD BOUGHT YOU?

Day 210

So Jesus said to the Jews who had believed in him, "If you abide in my word, you are truly my disciples, and you will know the truth, and the truth will set you free."

—John 8:31-32

Is there something in your life that you'd like to be set free from? Think about that for a moment.

Did you know that as a follower of Christ, Jesus wants you to be free from that struggle or sin? That's right, He does! And one way you can do this is by claiming your freedom and acting upon it.

The Scripture says, "So you also must consider yourselves dead to sin and alive to God in Christ Jesus." When you die to your sin… when you realize you are no longer a helpless victim constantly under the control of evil… you will be a victor in the Lord!

How do you do this? It starts by understanding that obedience to anything leads to slavery. As Romans 6:16 says, "Do you not know that if you present yourselves to anyone as obedient slaves, you are slaves of the one whom you obey, either of sin, which leads to death, or of obedience, which leads to righteousness?"

Whatever or whomever you obey, you serve. If you are obedient to sin, then you will become a slave to sin. And if you obey righteousness, then you will serve righteousness.

Are you desperate enough to break free from sin that you will yield your life to serve Jesus?

Today, I want to encourage you to make that decision to no longer serve sin. And then plant the seeds of righteousness in your life and water them daily through prayer and the study of God's Word.

Discover a new power to break free from the old life and live victoriously in the new life through complete obedience to Jesus Christ!

**WILL YOU YIELD YOUR LIFE TO JESUS
SO THAT YOU CAN BREAK FREE FROM SIN?**

Day 211

In the beginning, God created the heavens and the earth.

—Genesis 1:1

Most Christians have read today's verse, the first verse in the Bible. But I'm not sure many realize its simple, yet profound, message!

You see, this verse clearly states where mankind began and who created everything. God is the beginning of it all!

Yet Satan knows that if he can attempt to destroy the root of our faith among unbelievers, then he can go as far as trying to destroy the entire legacy of our faith.

This verse in Scripture signifies so many things—beginnings, generations, creation, the origin of man and woman, the family, and so on. The Bible's first sentence is the perfect segue into discovering who God is and how He has chosen to bring us into a relationship with Him.

Genesis 1:1 disperses all the ideas of atheism, polytheism, pantheism, humanism, secularism, and naturalism. The Word of God deals with these theories at the outset.

The Bible says in 2 Timothy 3:16, "All Scripture is breathed out by God and profitable for teaching, for reproof, for correction, and for training in righteousness."

Over the next several days, I want to encourage you to read through the first chapter of Genesis. And as you do, it's my prayer that your love and understanding of God's Word will deepen... that you will be better equipped to share the message of Christ with our post-modern culture... and that you will deepen your biblical world view!

ARE YOU LETTING GOD'S WORD INFORM YOUR VIEW OF THE WORLD?

Day 212

And the free gift is not like the result of that one man's sin. For the judgment following one trespass brought condemnation, but the free gift following many trespasses brought justification. For if, because of one man's trespass, death reigned through that one man, much more will those who receive the abundance of grace and the free gift of righteousness reign in life through the one man Jesus Christ. Therefore, as one trespass led to condemnation for all men, so one act of righteousness leads to justification and life for all men.

—Romans 5:16-18

D o you know you can live like a king in this world? I know it may be hard to imagine when you look around at the sin in our world today, but God offers us redemption and grace that allow us to live like kings through Him.

When you read the news or turn on the television, do you feel bombarded by the evil that has engulfed our world? You probably do! Many people are looking for the answers to why this evil exists and how to overcome it… but often in all the wrong places.

You see, we can only find why the human condition is the way it is in God's Word. What happened in the Garden of Eden started the decline of our world. And because of Adam's sin, we all were born into sin and death reigned over us.

Today's passage tells us that "the judgment following one trespass" … Adam's trespass… "brought condemnation, but the free gift following many trespasses brought justification. For if, because of one man's trespass, death reigned through that one man, much more will those who receive the abundance of grace and the free gift of righteousness reign in life through the one man Jesus Christ."

That's good news, my friend! That's the hope we have! Jesus has made it possible for you to live like a king.

That is the best news you can have in a world filled with sin and death!

If you have accepted Jesus Christ as your Savior, you are no longer ruled by death, but instead you can reign in life through Christ our Lord!

YOU CAN REIGN IN LIFE THROUGH JESUS CHRIST!

Therefore, if anyone is in Christ, he is a new creation. The old has passed away; behold, the new has come.

—2 Corinthians 5:17

I don't know if you've ever thought about it before, but God doesn't need human beings. Before there was man, He had angels to worship Him day after day. He didn't create us because He had a void in His life He wanted to fill. God is completely self-sufficient and always has been. He simply created us for His pleasure and praise!

The purpose for which He created us is so that we would glorify Him… and we do that by putting Him first in our lives, in our families, in our careers, and in our bodies. You see, our God is One of might and miracles and He desires for His power to be revealed through us… to the praise of His glory.

The point is… we are His creation. And unfortunately, we still face a great denial from people on the subject of creation… even though leading scientists of our day are now saying there is at least "intelligent design." In other words, as scientists, they see that there is intelligence behind what they observe in nature.

So what does creation tell us today? It tells us that there is a Creator… and as we witness in God's Word, He is a Creator who loves you and me. He loves us so much that He sent His only Son, Jesus Christ, to give us eternal life!

Without God, the human soul is in darkness… just like the earth was in darkness before God moved in the story of creation. But just as God's Word moved and spoke creation into existence, God's Word can move with power in the heart of the unbeliever and bring that person to faith and salvation.

If you haven't accepted God's free gift of salvation in Jesus Christ, then I urge you to do so today. While God does not need you, He wants you to become His child.

So place your faith in Christ today, and begin to experience life as the child of the Creator!

GOD LOVES YOU SO MUCH THAT HE SENT HIS ONLY SON TO GIVE YOU ETERNAL LIFE!

So God created man in his own image, in the image of God he created him; male and female he created them.

—Genesis 1:27

It's amazing and awesome to think about the making of the body of man. God has done a miracle not only in creation, but in the birth of every human being. Each person is a magnificent and mysterious unit of living complexities that God stitched together in the womb of his or her mother!

God has also performed a miracle in the way He created us to mature. What makes our bodies grow and develop the way they do? It's all part of God's magnificent creation!

Science explains that the body is constantly changing, breaking down, and being built up again. Think about that. That is the marvel of God's handiwork!

And we can't forget God's brilliance in constructing the mental capacity of humans. We are capable of learning so many things… things that animals could never learn. You can see the power of God's creativity when you consider the capabilities of the mind. Words cannot adequately explain the beauty and marvel of this creation.

Finally, it's important to remember that God created in man a spiritual marvel. That's why in Genesis 1 we are told that God created us in His image. It means we have a likeness to God or that we are in His shadow. In our fast-paced life, we don't usually take the time to think of these great wonders.

Remember that each of us have cravings for deity, the capability for dominion, the capacity for dignity, and the comprehension of destiny. The only question that remains is why are you living? What's your purpose? God has made you to fulfill His plan… and to worship Him with your mind, your body, and your soul forever!

ARE YOU FULFILLING GOD'S PLAN FOR YOUR LIFE?

Day 215

"The thief comes only to steal and kill and destroy. I came that they may have life and have it abundantly."

—John 10:10

Genesis 2:7 says that God created man from dust and breathed life into his body. The amazing thing about His creation of mankind is that He made the universe by speaking it into existence, but with man He took the dust of the earth and formed us in His own hands!

In the beginning, man and woman were personally ideal— physically, psychologically, and spiritually. God gave them all things to enjoy and a purpose. In order to establish His authority, the Lord gave man freedom with only one prohibition, and yet both Adam and Eve chose to disobey Him. God warned them of the death, or separation from Him, that would fall upon them if they ate from the tree of forbidden fruit.

When the man and woman violated God's command and ate of the fruit, they died and passed on this death to all humanity. They died in spirit, and now we are all born spiritually dead. But God... out of His great love... also created in man a way to choose to turn away from sin and death to follow Him.

This means that lives of brokenness can be mended, healed, and restored back to wholeness through the acceptance of Jesus Christ.

As we see in today's verse, Christ came to this earth, lived a sinless existence, died on the cross for our sins and rose again that we might have eternal life—a life in paradise.

My prayer for you today is to experience true life as a new creation in Jesus!

LIVES OF BROKENNESS CAN BE MENDED, HEALED, AND RESTORED BACK TO WHOLENESS THROUGH THE ACCEPTANCE OF JESUS CHRIST.

Day 216

Therefore a man shall leave his father and his mother and hold fast to his wife, and they shall become one flesh.
—Genesis 2:24

At the beginning of time, God designed a model for what marriage should be—His way!

The Lord said in Genesis 2:18, "It is not good that the man should be alone; I will make him a helper fit for him." And then the key statement is found in today's verse which says, "Therefore a man shall leave his father and his mother and hold fast to his wife, and they shall become one flesh."

God desired a wife for Adam, so He designed and delivered her. It wasn't an accident of creation, but it was a divine origin of new beginnings and a permanent commitment between this first couple.

God's purpose was that one man and one woman would live together for life. The woman was and is to be her husband's helper for companionship, cooperation, completion, and communication.

God also created Adam and Eve to be transparent, vulnerable, and accepting of one another. They had an intimate love, without fear. God's intention for the marriage between Adam and Eve was to be divine in origin, supreme in relationship, permanent in condition, and filled with a mutual submission. I believe these biblical principles hold true today as well!

Your marriage may be hanging by a thread… or you may think it is good, but could definitely use some improvements. Remember that love is like a garden that must be cultivated and nurtured to grow. It takes time together and unconditional love to make it work.

I challenge you today to build your marriage on the principles I have outlined above. If you do, then when the rains and storms come, your marriage will not be shaken because it is built upon the sure and eternal truth of God's Word!

LOVE IS LIKE A GARDEN THAT MUST BE CULTIVATED AND NURTURED TO GROW.

And God spoke all these words, saying, "I am the LORD your God, who brought you out of the land of Egypt, out of the house of slavery. You shall have no other gods before me."

—Exodus 20:1-3

In today's passage, we see from the first of the Ten Commandments what our number one priority should be as followers of Christ: not to place anything else above God.

In addition to this, there are four others things we need to know when it comes to our view of God and our relationship with Him.

- First is the **reality of God**. God exists. So many people today, perhaps even you, live life as though God doesn't exist. He does! And you can know Him personally. What a powerful truth!

- Second, is the **priority of God**. As we see in the first commandment, God wants you and me to put first things first— Him.

- Then, there is the **liberty of God.** Our God has delivered us just as He did the Israelites. Sin enslaved you and me, but our God has set us free from a life without hope, a life without purpose, a life without peace, a life of loneliness, and ultimately He has set us free from death.

- Finally, the **personality of God.** He is a person you can know intimately through Jesus Christ.

If you want to know God personally, you must come to Him submissively, sincerely, and scripturally. This first commandment is an affirmation and declaration of who God is. It is the most important because it declares He exists… and He wants you to put Him first in your life.

There is a God, and you can know Him personally through His Son, Jesus Christ!

IF YOU WANT TO KNOW GOD PERSONALLY, YOU MUST COME TO HIM SUBMISSIVELY, SINCERELY, AND SCRIPTURALLY.

Day 218

If we confess our sins, he is faithful and just to forgive us our sins and to cleanse us from all unrighteousness.

—1 John 1:9

Many people in our world today have a distorted image of who God really is. And that's a tragedy because how you view God affects how you view yourself, your family, your friends... even your career!

That's why today, I want to ask you to think about what comes to mind when you think about God. Is your God a stern policeman that sits in the shadows just waiting for you to break the law and punish you?

Is your God the mechanic who comes in to fix things in your life when there's an emergency or when things such as health, marriage, or finances are broken?

Or is your God a decrepit, kindly old grandfather with a long white beard sitting on his rocker in heaven that you go and visit every once in a while?

I think many people think of God in one of these three ways. But the truth is that these are all gods of our imagination—false images of the true God! They don't describe the God revealed in the Scripture.

The God of the Bible, the one true God, is a God who knows our weaknesses and sinful nature. Even though He is holy and sinless, He extends grace and forgives us time and time again. He is loving, kind, and gracious!

Never forget that He is the true, living God... a God whose lap you can crawl into when you've failed for the hundreth time... a God you can call Abba Father, or Daddy.

I hope this truth encourages you today!

HOW YOU VIEW GOD AFFECTS HOW YOU VIEW YOURSELF, YOUR FAMILY, YOUR FRIENDS... EVEN YOUR CAREER!

Day 219

"You shall not take the name of the LORD your God in vain, for the LORD will not hold him guiltless who takes his name in vain."

—Exodus 20:7

The third commandment instructs us not to take the name of the Lord in vain. But this verse is talking about more than not using God's name profanely. It speaks of how we shouldn't use it in any way that is irreverent or disrespectful either.

Think about it. You can break this law when you participate in hypocrisy… or when you worship or pray meaninglessly.

God's name stands for His character, reputation, and authority, so His glory is at stake when we use His name. But He promises blessing after blessing when we use His name properly.

So how do you take the name of God seriously?

First, love the name of God. Use it carefully and tenderly as an act of worship. Mean it when you evoke His name.

Second, live the name of God. The Scripture says in 2 Timothy 2:19, "Let everyone who names the name of the Lord depart from iniquity." This verse literally means for people not to involve themselves in wickedness. If you bear the name of Jesus, don't shame His name by your actions and words.

Finally, lean on the name of God. Treat His name with the utmost love and respect. Jesus said in John 14:14, "If you ask me anything in my name, I will do it."

If you find yourself taking the name of the Lord meaninglessly, begin to praise Him. Because you can't praise God and curse Him at the same time!

And remember, if you show respect for the name of God around others, people will show more respect for you.

**GOD PROMISES BLESSING AFTER BLESSING
WHEN WE USE HIS NAME PROPERLY!**

Day 220

"Remember the Sabbath day, to keep it holy. Six days you shall labor, and do all your work, but the seventh day is a Sabbath to the LORD your God. On it you shall not do any work, you, or your son, or your daughter, your male servant, or your female servant, or your livestock, or the sojourner who is within your gates. For in six days the LORD made heaven and earth, the sea, and all that is in them, and rested on the seventh day. Therefore the LORD blessed the Sabbath day and made it holy."
—Exodus 20:8-11

Let's face it. Life is hard. And because God knew that our lives would be hard and demanding, He gave us this commandment to prevent us from burning out!

I think the length of this commandment, when compared to the other nine, emphasizes its importance. Here we have 98 words of the English language that underscore the importance of resting!

God was even an example of this commandment Himself. He created the world in six days and rested on the seventh.

God knows there are going to be some weeks or months that are more hectic for you than others. But He's provided a rest stop in the middle of life's busy highway each week so you can catch your breath and regain your strength.

That's why the Scripture says the Sabbath is a holy day—a day that's different, separate, and set apart for God.

Each of us—mentally, physically, and spiritually—needs a day of rest each week. But we also need that day of rest set apart to worship God as we rejuvenate our spirits and minds.

I want to challenge you today to maintain a healthy balance. Life is more than labor. If you don't take time to worship God and acknowledge the day of rest He's set aside, life will become increasingly difficult for you!

Today, make a commitment to take a break from the marathon of life, catch your breath, praise the Lord for bringing you thus far, and enjoy a time of renewal.

GOD'S PROVIDED YOU A REST STOP IN THE MIDDLE OF LIFE'S BUSY HIGHWAY EACH WEEK SO YOU CAN CATCH YOUR BREATH AND REGAIN YOUR STRENGTH. SO TAKE ADVANTAGE OF IT!

Day 221

"Honor your father and your mother, that your days may be long in the land that the LORD your God is giving you."

—Exodus 20:12

When it comes to being a parent, there are no perfect moms or dads. Period!

Only with God's help are you able to raise children that honor God. That means the best thing you could ever do for your child is to lead them to know and love Jesus Christ. And if they know and love Him, they will honor and respect you!

Now, as a son or daughter, you can honor your parents by respecting them… willingly, lovingly, and with an attitude of genuine esteem.

This is God's plan for every person, regardless of age. As you get older in life, you begin to realize that your parents have some genuine faults as all people do. But you will honor them if you give them the respect they are due.

If you've had a painful relationship with one or both of your parents, the first step to accepting them is to forgive them. You need to affirm your parents—especially those single parents who took on the enormous job alone.

And of course, adult children of older parents should show affirmation by simply staying in touch, making a call every now and then, writing a letter, or being there to visit.

No matter their age, your parents are to be taken care of by you. The Scripture says in 1 Timothy 5:8, "But if anyone does not provide for his relatives, and especially for members of his household, he has denied the faith and is worse than an unbeliever."

Begin today to follow the commandment of honoring and respecting your parents… and teaching your children to do the same!

ARE YOU HONORING YOUR PARENTS BY GIVING THEM THE RESPECT THEY ARE DUE?

Day 222

And this is the testimony, that God gave us eternal life, and this life is in his Son. Whoever has the Son has life; whoever does not have the Son of God does not have life.

—1 John 5:11-12

B elieving that Jesus rose again from the grave to save you and me from our sins has more benefits than just securing your place in heaven!

First John 5:12 says, "Whoever has the Son has life; whoever does not have the Son of God does not have life." What this verse tells us is that eternal life is more than a home in heaven when we die. It means we have life right now… today!

Yet… and this is the sad part… so many people today can't really say that they have life.

Sure, they may do the stuff of life like going to the movies, going to the ball game, reading books, going to the mall, going to church, listening to music. But on the inside, there is a void… a vacancy that they just can't quite ever seem to fill.

Today, think about one person you know who needs to hear about the life that Jesus Christ gives. Now, write their name down.

What can you do this week to share the Good News with them?

YOUR WORLD IS FULL OF PEOPLE WHOSE LIVES ARE EMPTY INSIDE, BUT YOU HAVE THE HOPE THEY NEED. SO SHARE IT!

Day 223

"Go therefore and make disciples of all nations, baptizing them in the name of the Father and of the Son and of the Holy Spirit, teaching them to observe all that I have commanded you."
—Matthew 28:19-20

Do you want to change the world?

As we see in today's verse, Jesus clearly told us to "go therefore and make disciples of all nations...." That means our number one goal as believers should be to bring people to Christ. We're to make disciples by baptizing them into the body of His church. And we are to mature disciples by building them up in faith, hope, and love.

So let me ask you: Are you doing everything you can to change the world for Jesus Christ? Are you bringing people to Christ... and maturing disciples in their faith?

If not, why not?

The promises and commands given to us in the Scripture didn't just apply to Bible times. They're also meant for you and me as believers today!

Jesus gave the same promise to us—the power of the Holy Spirit—that He gave to the small group of Christians who were first given the assignment we read about today in Matthew chapter 28.

And Jesus promised to equip and empower the first Christians despite their faults and weaknesses with the insurmountable, unimaginable power of the Holy Spirit. He promises the same thing to you and me!

So I want to challenge you today to lay claim to the power that's already within you... so that you can change the world for Christ!

**ARE YOU DOING EVERYTHING YOU CAN
TO CHANGE THE WORLD FOR JESUS CHRIST?
IF NOT, WHY NOT?**

"And I will ask the Father, and he will give you another Helper, to be with you forever, even the Spirit of truth, whom the world cannot receive, because it neither sees him nor knows him. You know him, for he dwells with you and will be in you."

—John 14:16-17

Unlike every other founder of world religions who came to teach good things and departed on their own way, Jesus Christ came to stay.

He committed Himself to us as believers when He promised to give us a Helper that would abide within our hearts, and who would never leave or forsake us.

That was the promise of Jesus Christ... and He never breaks His promises!

And what I want to help you understand today is that this Helper, the Holy Spirit, isn't an influential being, a force, or a theological fact. It is the presence of Jesus Christ living inside you! All you have to do as a believer is simply receive Him.

Romans 8:9 says, "You, however, are not in the flesh but in the Spirit, if in fact the Spirit of God dwells in you." We don't have to beg the Holy Spirit to fill us, but instead we must only permit Him to fill us.

On the day of Pentecost, which is recorded in Acts 2, there were three recorded miracles that occurred when the Holy Spirit filled the people there—the miracles of sound, sight, and speech.

And just as those powerful winds did miraculous things, so can amazing things happen when the Spirit of God blows through your life!

**THE HOLY SPIRIT WILL DO AMAZING THINGS
IN YOUR LIFE IF YOU WILL LET HIM!**

Day 225

"And you will know the truth, and the truth will set you free."
—John 8:32

O ur world has a growing dissatisfaction with things such as materialism, secularism, and humanism. And as a result, people are increasingly moving away from these things in search of fulfillment and truth.

Not only that, people are becoming more aware of the dysfunctional family and the proliferation of failed marriages. And people are becoming more disheartened by the violence and crime we see all around us.

Sadly, instead of turning to the Church and the truth only found in Christ, people are turning to New Age philosophies, Eastern mysticism, and other kinds of man-made religions to get the answers they are desperately searching for.

That's why nothing is more urgently needed in our society right now than the contagious ministry of the local church. Not a body of believers stuck on cruise control or living in the past... but those who know the needs of today's culture and those who pray, truly believe, and are passionate about sharing Christ with this generation of people!

More than anything, this generation is searching for people who know the truth and will tell it just like it is.

That's why I want to challenge you today to tell those around you the truth about who Jesus is and the answers people can find in Him. Cut to the heart of the gospel so that others can come to Jesus!

**THIS GENERATION IS SEARCHING
FOR PEOPLE WHO KNOW THE TRUTH AND WILL
TELL IT JUST LIKE IT IS.**

Day 226

And they devoted themselves to the apostles' teaching and the fellow-
ship, to the breaking of bread and the prayers. And awe came upon every
soul, and many wonders and signs were being done through the apostles.
And all who believed were together and had all things in common. And
they were selling their possessions and belongings and distributing the
proceeds to all, as any had need. And day by day, attending the temple
together and breaking bread in their homes, they received their food with
glad and generous hearts, praising God and having favor with all the
people. And the Lord added to their number day by day those who were
being saved.

—Acts 2:42-47

One common question people often ask is, "What do I look for in a church?"

And while there are many reputable, Bible-based churches today, I want to show you what to look for in a church, according to what the Scripture says.

The first and obvious sign of a good church is one that it is filled with people who know and love the Lord Jesus Christ.

In today's passage, we're reminded that the "Lord added to their number day by day those who were being saved." Those who accepted Jesus as their Savior, believed the Word of God, and were then baptized in obedience to Christ, were added to the early church.

What this teaches us is that every follower of Christ should either be in a church or looking for a church that is…

- filled with growing believers in Jesus,
- has a high priority upon the study of God's Word,
- has a corporate worship of Jesus Christ,
- bathes everything they do in prayer, and
- stays on mission by sharing Jesus Christ with the lost and hurting.

If you follow these simple guidelines, I'm confident you will find a dynamic, growing church where God is adding people every day to the family, faith, and fellowship of other believers!

**THE FIRST AND OBVIOUS SIGN OF A GOOD CHURCH
IS ONE THAT IT IS FILLED WITH PEOPLE WHO KNOW
AND LOVE THE LORD JESUS CHRIST.**

Day 227

Now Peter and John were going up to the temple at the hour of prayer, the ninth hour. And a man lame from birth was being carried, whom they laid daily at the gate of the temple that is called the Beautiful Gate to ask alms of those entering the temple. Seeing Peter and John about to go into the temple, he asked to receive alms.

—Acts 3:1-3

Just as the man we read about in today's passage was crippled and had no hope, many people today feel just as helpless. And they act much like he did too—crying out for answers, looking for help… but really going nowhere.

The most beautiful part of this story is the picture we get of Christ in the way Peter and John responded to the crippled man. They paid attention to him… just as Jesus pays attention to the broken people of the world. And they showed him the way to restoration and healing.

Christ came to save those… like the man in today's passage… who are crippled at birth. He came to help those who have been crushed and crippled by the strains and stresses of life.

In Acts 3:8, it says, "And leaping up he stood and began to walk, and entered the temple with them, walking and leaping and praising God." This man went into the temple for the first time leaping, dancing, and praising God because he had been healed!

Jesus is the only One who can put the unbeliever on his or her dancing feet forever. And He's the only One who can put the rhythm back into the steps of the believer who has lost his or her leap.

So I urge you, if you are in need of healing, turn to Jesus Christ today!

**JESUS CAME TO HELP THOSE WHO
HAVE BEEN CRUSHED AND CRIPPLED BY THE
STRAINS AND STRESSES OF LIFE.**

Day 228

I have stored up your word in my heart, that I might not sin against you.

—Psalm 119:11

We live in a society and a world that is tolerant of everything… except those who claim that Jesus is the only way to salvation. And we also live in a culture that defines all truth as relative.

Because of this, living for Christ can be a real challenge… or even a seeming impossibility!

But I'm here to tell you that the one way you can live a life against the odds that are stacked against us as believers is to make God's Word preeminent in your life.

As we see in today's verse, David understood the importance of the truth of God's Word penetrating to the core of his being… and driving all his life. The same is true for you and me!

If you are serious about your faith, commit today to reading, studying, knowing, and living God's Word. If you do, you will have the foundation to stand against all odds as a follower of Jesus Christ in the days ahead.

**THE ONE WAY YOU CAN LIVE
A LIFE AGAINST THE ODDS THAT ARE STACKED
AGAINST US AS BELIEVERS IS TO MAKE GOD'S WORD
PREEMINENT IN YOUR LIFE.**

Day 229

If we confess our sins, he is faithful and just to forgive us our sins and to cleanse us from all unrighteousness.

—1 John 1:9

I have a major concern for the church in America today. And it is simply this: Too many Christians are living lives of defeat, succumbing to the deception of our age.

In a word, too many believers are living a Christian life that is devoid of the power of God!

If you have placed your faith in Jesus Christ for your salvation... if you have accepted his gift of eternal life that He bought through His blood on the cross... then you have been baptized with the Spirit of God, and that very Spirit is resident in you right now.

But too many Christians have quenched the work of the Spirit of God because of sin. They don't experience a fulfilled and satisfied life because they have unplugged the power of God in their lives!

So let me ask you a straightforward question... a challenging question: Are you quenching the Spirit's power in your life through sin and disobedience?

If you are, you will never know the power of God in your life. And you will never know the fulfillment God desires for your life.

So my challenge to you today is to confess that sin and ask God to fully allow His Spirit to empower you for His glory. If you do, you will see God work through your life... and you will know fulfillment far beyond anything you could ever imagine!

ARE YOU QUENCHING THE SPIRIT'S POWER IN YOUR LIFE THROUGH SIN AND DISOBEDIENCE?

Day 230

For though we walk in the flesh, we are not waging war according to the flesh. For the weapons of our warfare are not of the flesh but have divine power to destroy strongholds.

—2 Corinthians 10:3-4

So many Christians, I believe, don't really understand the reality of the evil forces at work to undermine their walk with Christ.

First, we must recognize the reality of the spiritual forces that are at work against us. Friend, you are a target of the enemy forces who want nothing more than to see you fail in your Christian walk!

And you ignore their work in your life to your spiritual peril.

And second, you must live in the victory of Jesus Christ over those forces. His power is in you and me… in the words that we speak and in the message that we declare.

In Matthew 28:18, Jesus says, "All authority in heaven and on earth has been given to me." This means that Jesus has ultimate power over Satan and his demonic forces.

So my challenge to you today is to live in light of the evil spiritual forces at work against you to ruin your life. And as you do this, claim the victory that is yours in Christ Jesus our Lord over those forces!

**AS A BELIEVER, YOU ARE A TARGET OF
THE ENEMY FORCES WHO WANT NOTHING
MORE THAN TO SEE YOU FAIL IN YOUR
CHRISTIAN WALK!**

Day 231

"But you will receive power when the Holy Spirit has come upon you, and you will be my witnesses in Jerusalem and in all Judea and Samaria, and to the end of the earth."

—**Acts 1:8**

The first-century Christians were bold in seeking to capture their city, country, and world for Jesus Christ. And that same boldness can be yours as you share the message of eternal life with others!

The challenge is that the church today has become increasingly distracted from what God has called us to do—to share the message of salvation in Christ with the world. People desperately need the hope that is only found in Jesus… and it is our job to tell them!

If revival is going to come about in our world, then it needs to first begin in your heart and mine. We must become like the early Christians who had a boldness in the face of fierce resistance.

Through that boldness, the gospel spread like wildfire… and it happened without technology, computers, or e-mail!

How did they do that? Well, look at today's verse again. They did it through the power of the Holy Spirit!

Wouldn't you like to see a spiritual awakening in our nation and world? It can happen as you and I are empowered by the Spirit of God to boldly proclaim the gospel wherever God might place us.

And when we're emboldened with His power, we can make a difference in this generation for Jesus!

IF REVIVAL IS GOING TO COME ABOUT IN OUR WORLD, IT NEEDS TO FIRST BEGIN IN YOUR HEART AND MINE.

Day 232

And when they had prayed, the place in which they were gathered together was shaken, and they were all filled with the Holy Spirit and continued to speak the word of God with boldness.

—Acts 4:31

T he secret to experiencing God's power is through prayer. And we see in today's verse, God moved powerfully because of the prayers of the early Church.

In the same way, you and I need to stay connected to God by prayer so that we can allow Him the opportunity to move in our hearts... and open the door for Him to show His power through us.

For example, maybe you're in a situation today where there seems to be no way out. Maybe you're in an impossible predicament that doesn't seem to have an answer.

Whether your marriage is in trouble or your finances are crumbling, there is power, comfort, and wisdom in God through prayer. And as you take your request to God, people will see the work of His power and peace in your life.

As Paul tells us in Philippians 4:6-7, "Do not be anxious about anything, but in everything by prayer and supplication with thanksgiving let your requests be made known to God. And the peace of God, which surpasses all understanding, will guard your hearts and your minds in Christ Jesus."

It's my hope today that you will show off God's power in your life as you submit to Him in prayer... and as His peace and power is seen in you!

**WE NEED TO STAY CONNECTED TO GOD
BY PRAYER SO THAT WE CAN ALLOW HIM
THE OPPORTUNITY TO MOVE IN OUR HEARTS...
AND OPEN THE DOOR FOR HIM TO SHOW
HIS POWER THROUGH US.**

Day 233

... Judge me, O Lord, according to my righteousness and according to the integrity that is in me.

—Psalm 7:8

Integrity is an absolute requirement if we are to be authentic in our faith and be able to impact the lives of others.

And one of the hallmarks of integrity is being more focused on others than on yourself.

In the book of Acts, we see that members of the early Church lived with integrity. And one of the ways it was displayed in their lives was through their generosity. They took care of one another physically, emotionally, spiritually, and financially.

Being concerned for the needs of others and living a life of generosity is one way you can demonstrate integrity to those around you.

Another way you can demonstrate integrity is by living a life of truthfulness.

Part of caring for others is being honest with them. A man or woman of integrity will always maintain a genuine profession... in everything they do. This is only fitting for a follower of Jesus Christ!

Being generous with your possessions, and genuine in your professions, are just two keys to living a life of integrity. And a life of integrity will ultimately influence others!

**INTEGRITY IS THE KEY TO
AUTHENTIC FAITH... AND TO INFLUENCING
THE LIVES OF THOSE AROUND YOU!**

But you will receive power when the Holy Spirit has come upon you,
and you will be my witnesses in Jerusalem and in all Judea and
Samaria and to the end of the earth.

—Acts 1:8

B elievers in the early church had a deep commitment to
bringing others to Christ. They sought to share the gospel
with those who lived nearby in their own city of Jerusalem... and
also with those who lived further away, even in distant nations.

And they were remarkably effective! Despite strong opposition and
persecution, members of the early Church were consistent in sharing
their faith and they made a profound impact for Christ!

So let me ask you today... are you doing all you can to bring others
to Christ?

If you feel that you could do more, I encourage you to get on your
knees before the Lord and ask the Holy Spirit to come upon you and
help you to become a more effective witness for Christ.

After all, it's only the Lord who can change hearts! And you need
to rely on Him to give you the wisdom, boldness, and opportunities
to share the Good News with those around you.

BECOMING A TRULY EFFECTIVE
WITNESS FOR CHRIST BEGINS WITH ASKING
THE HOLY SPIRIT TO HELP YOU!

Day 235

*And Stephen, full of grace and power, was doing great wonders
and signs among the people.*

— **Acts 6:8**

Stephen was a giant of our faith. He was a man of impeccable
character and commitment, and the Bible says that his face
glowed like that of an angel!

What was this man's secret, that he could live an outstanding life
and die a courageous death?

I believe there are several characteristics that helped Stephen to be
the godly man that he was... here are just three that you and I can
imitate:

Integrity: Stephen was a man of "good reputation, full of the Holy
Spirit and wisdom" (Acts 6:3). Although his enemies despised him,
they respected the holy man of God that he was.

Servanthood: Stephen was actively involved in serving widows and
those in need among the Christian community. His compassion was
known to all... and even with his last breath, he was forgiving those
responsible for his death (Acts 7:60).

Tenacity: Stephen boldly preached the gospel and stood firm in
his faith, regardless of the threats, intimidation, or violence of his
persecutors.

If you're like me, then I know you want more than anything
to please the Lord in all you do. But this requires the kind of
impeccable character that Stephen had!

TO LIVE AN OUTSTANDING LIFE
FOR JESUS CHRIST REQUIRES
IMPECCABLE CHARACTER.

Day 236

…Even Satan disguises himself as an angel of light. So it is no surprise if his servants, also, disguise themselves as servants of righteousness….

—2 Corinthians 11:14-15

Many people are clueless when it comes to understanding the manipulation that Satan uses to attack and defeat them. And the primary weapon he uses to do this is deception.

False religion and witchcraft are rampant in our culture. At times they can appear so appealing and even godly… yet their source is from the enemy!

Jesus warned us of the devil's character, saying, "He is a liar and the father of lies" (John 8:44). He will use any scheme to draw people away from the truth.

The challenge for you and me is to be so thoroughly immersed in the Word of God, and to walk so closely with Jesus Christ, that we know His voice. This is essential to being able to recognize, and avoid following, the voice of a stranger (John 10).

So let me encourage you today… be on your guard! There are many voices claiming to be the truth, but keep your eyes fixed on Jesus Christ and you will avoid falling into the trap of deception.

**IMMERSE YOURSELF IN GOD'S WORD
AND HIS PRESENCE AND YOU WILL KNOW THE
VOICE OF TRUTH FROM DECEPTION!**

Day 237

And He said to them, "Go into all the world and proclaim the gospel to the whole creation."

—Mark 16:15

You don't have to be a preacher, missionary, or Bible scholar to be a powerful witness for Christ. You don't even have to have all the answers!

God has empowered you through His Holy Spirit to be a witness for Him. And He will give you the words you need... at just the right moment... that will speak into the heart of the person you are sharing with.

As time goes by, you will become more effective, and more confident, in your Christian witness. You simply need to be willing and available to share the hope that you have experienced in Jesus Christ... and the Lord will do the rest!

If you're a believer, you have a story of how Christ has changed your life. You've experienced times when your prayers were answered, or when a Bible verse gave you direction or comfort at a crucial moment.

That's your story... and that's what the people around you need to hear! So let me challenge you to ask the Lord to give you boldness, and begin to share your faith with others.

You'll be amazed by how God will use you to be a witness for Him!

**YOUR STORY OF HOW GOD IS
AT WORK IN YOUR LIFE IS POWERFUL!
HE WILL ENABLE YOU TO BE A POWERFUL
WITNESS FOR HIM.**

Whoever brings blessing will be enriched, and one who waters will himself be watered.

—**Proverbs 11:25**

You may be successful in your business, in society, or with your finances, but if you are not successful in your relationships, you won't be fulfilled. Life won't be what you— or what God—wants it to be.

If you want to become the person that God wants you to be, you must become a people person. But that doesn't mean you have to be an extrovert!

A people person will respond to others generously... receive others gladly... rejoice with people greatly... and renew people graciously. In short, a people person will refresh others!

Is your life a river of encouragement, acceptance, and love to those who come in contact with you? Or is it a desert?

I encourage you today to be that river of refreshment to those around you. Look for people that you can pick up and encourage along the way and trust that God will equip you to be the people person He wants you to be!

BY BECOMING A PERSON WHO ENCOURAGES OTHERS, YOU WILL REFRESH AND ENRICH YOUR LIFE.

Day 239

"Until now you have asked nothing in My name. Ask, and you will receive, that your joy may be full."

—John 16:24

We are living in challenging days that can cause you to get off track as a Christian and lose your focus. In fact, you may be asking yourself, "Where is my life going? What is my purpose?"

Well, let me ask you… have you truly experienced the power of prayer in your life?

It may be that you aren't focusing on the most important thing as a believer—your own personal relationship with the Lord.

I believe that more than ever, you and I have to spend time on our knees in prayer… not only for the situations in our own lives, but also for those around us.

When you're trying to dig your way through the mess of life, it is prayer that will get you through. Without prayer, you will never know the provision, peace, and power you desperately need!

So let me remind you today that prayer dramatically changes situations. So be sure not to remain silent, but to bring your requests to Him!

AS YOU FACE THE CHALLENGES OF LIFE, REMEMBER THAT PRAYER IS WHAT WILL GET YOU THROUGH.

Day 240

"Go therefore and make disciples of all nations, baptizing them in the name of the Father and of the Son and of the Holy Spirit."

—Matthew 28:19

As a member of God's family, you and I must determine that we are going to advance His Kingdom by obeying His command to share the gospel.

Not because we have to... but because we want to!

There are so many men, women, and children around your life who desperately need to know that they are loved, forgiven, and destined by God to live a life of purpose.

You've discovered for yourself that this is true... so now you can be a messenger!

You don't have to go on a preaching circuit to "make disciples." Just share your life with others. Talk about how God's Word is helping you in your life, or how you are finding new strength as you pray, or as you fellowship with other believers.

Your testimony is powerful! And it's only as you share it, that you will begin to see those around you influenced for Jesus Christ... and eventually grow into true disciples.

Every believer is a powerful tool in the hands of God... and that includes you! I encourage you to ask the Holy Spirit to help you to "make disciples" as you share your faith with those around you.

**ONE OF THE MOST POWERFUL WAYS
YOU CAN MAKE DISCIPLES IS TO TELL OTHERS
WHAT GOD IS DOING IN YOUR LIFE.**

He was despised and rejected by men, a man of sorrows and acquainted with grief...

—**Isaiah 53:3**

The Christian life has always been a high-risk life.

Barnabas and Paul were "men who have risked their lives for the sake of our Lord Jesus Christ" (Acts 15:26). And today in many countries, Christians are still risking their lives by following Jesus.

In our culture, you may not run the risk of being killed for your faith... but you will run the risk of having your faith rejected by others.

Sometimes that is enough to make Christians silent. They are afraid of rejection, so they choose not to reveal their Christian convictions.

I believe we need to be men and women with enough courage to take a stand for our Christian faith—even if that will invite rejection at times. We have to be prepared to take a few knocks for what we believe!

Paul said of his sufferings for the sake of the gospel, "I am not ashamed, because I know whom I have believed..." (2 Timothy 1:12). When you are convinced of what you believe, you can handle the opposition that will inevitably come.

Don't let the fear of rejection silence you. Be prepared to take a risk... to speak up about your faith... even if it does invite rejection!

TO FOLLOW CHRIST, YOU RISK REJECTION.
BUT REMEMBER THAT HE WAS REJECTED TOO...
FOR YOU.

Day 242

Through him then let us continually offer up a sacrifice of praise to God, that is, the fruit of lips that acknowledge his name.

—Hebrews 13:15

Paul and Silas were two shining examples of men who praised the Lord despite their circumstances. Even in prison, they lifted their voices to God in praise (see Acts 16:25)!

While you and I may never be imprisoned for sharing the gospel, the Bible says that we will have hard times in this life.

The question is how will you choose to respond when those hard times come?

Learning to praise the Lord in every circumstance is so important. It doesn't mean that you are happy about the situation… or that you are denying the very real problem you are facing.

It simply means that you are making a choice to remember who God is in the midst of your crisis, and you are lifting Him above the situation. You are declaring that He has power and wisdom in every situation… and that is something to be thankful for!

So the next time you face one of life's storms, remember to lift your voice in praise to God. As you do, you will experience peace and strength that is not your own.

**WHEN YOU FACE PROBLEMS,
REMIND YOURSELF OF WHO GOD IS AND
LIFT YOUR VOICE IN PRAISE TO HIM.**

Day 243

God is our refuge and strength, a very present help in trouble.

—Psalm 46:1

All Christians will face difficulties and struggles. But there is one element that separates those who live a defeated life from those who live a victorious life.

It all has to do with where you find your source of strength.

Perhaps you are facing problems with your health, family, finances, or career. Whatever you are facing, I want to remind you to look to the Lord for His strength.

It might seem like you will never come out from under the weight of despair. But as you call upon Him, and draw strength from His Word and His presence, He will give you the strength you need to persevere.

Be encouraged today by the words of Isaiah 40:29-31:

He gives power to the faint, and to him who has no might he increases strength. Even youths shall faint and be weary, and young men shall fall exhausted; but they who wait for the Lord shall renew their strength; they shall mount up with wings like eagles; they shall run and not be weary; they shall walk and not faint.

The Lord knows your situation, and He is with you to help you through this time.

WHEN YOU FEEL THAT ALL OF YOUR STRENGTH IS GONE, INVITE THE LORD TO RENEW YOU WITH HIS STRENGTH.

Day 244

Trust in the Lord with all your heart, and do not lean on your own understanding.

—Proverbs 3:5

Y ou will encounter rough terrain as you travel the path of life. But when the storm clouds start to roll in, it's so important to put your trust in the Lord.

The apostle Paul was caught in frightening situations time after time. But he always reminded himself of God's character and His promises, and he managed to rise above his circumstances with unwavering trust in God.

If you've been walking with the Lord for a while, you know that there are times when it is very difficult to understand His will... especially when you're in the middle of a crisis.

But let me encourage you. When the skies darken, the thunder booms, and the lightning claps, don't panic! Ask God to help you to look beyond the storm and remember that He is with you in the midst of the storm.

Remember to take your refuge in Him, just as David did in times of crisis:

Be merciful to me, O God, be merciful to me! For my soul trusts in you, and in the shadow of your wings I will make my refuge until these calamities have passed by (Psalm 57:1).

**GOD OFFERS HOPE AND PEACE
FOR THE TERRIFIED TRAVELER WHEN YOU
TRUST HIM AND MAKE HIM YOUR REFUGE.**

Day 245

But in your hearts honor Christ the Lord as holy, always being prepared to make a defense to anyone who asks you for a reason for the hope that is in you....

—1 Peter 3:15

As followers of Jesus Christ, you and I have been called to share the gospel with others. But not everyone finds that an easy task!

If you feel unsure about how to express your faith, or you feel afraid of what people will say, how can you break through that barrier and obey God's command to tell others about Jesus?

First of all, I believe you need to ask the Lord to help you. As you come to Him, admitting your fears, asking Him to give you the desire, courage, and opportunities to share your faith, He will enable you to do it.

There are many things in life that we feel unable to do. It doesn't mean we can't do it... it just means we need the Lord's help!

And secondly, watch for opportunities to let people know that you are a Christian and let the conversations unfold naturally. Almost every week, someone will ask you what you did on the weekend. Tell them you went to church!

There are a thousand ways you can let people know that you believe in Jesus and that He has changed your life. Just make a start and you'll grow in confidence!

AS YOU LET YOUR PRIVATE CHRISTIAN LIFE BECOME PUBLIC, YOU'LL FIND MANY OPPORTUNITIES TO SHARE YOUR FAITH.

Day 246

For to us a child is born, to us a son is given; and the government shall be upon his shoulder, and his name shall be called Wonderful Counselor, Mighty God, Everlasting Father, Prince of Peace.

—Isaiah 9:6

One of the names given to Jesus is "Wonderful Counselor"... and it reveals His desire to counsel and comfort you in your time of need.

Maybe today, your life is a mess and you feel like you're hanging by a thread. Or maybe you are facing big decisions or changes that you need wisdom to handle.

Don't fall into the trap of trying to alleviate the pressure you are feeling by turning to things like drugs, false religions, or even to other people in the hope that they can fix your problem. Ultimately, none of these things will meet your deepest needs.

Jesus, the Wonderful Counselor, can give you the clarity, comfort, and direction you need right now. He can restore your peace in the midst of brokenness and confusion.

Jesus said, "Come to me, all who labor and are heavy laden, and I will give you rest" (Matthew 11:28).

The secret is simply to come to Him... and then you will discover the peace, wisdom, direction, and love that you need. He is the Won-

**TURN TO THE WONDERFUL COUNSELOR
FIRST AND YOU WILL FIND THE COMFORT
AND DIRECTION YOU NEED.**

Day 247

For to us a child is born, to us a son is given; and the government shall be upon his shoulder, and his name shall be called Wonderful Counselor, Mighty God, Everlasting Father, Prince of Peace.
—**Isaiah 9:6**

In the Old Testament, the name "Mighty God" literally means "Hero God." In a world where heroes are in such short supply, it's great to have a God who is truly a hero!

It's important to remember that our God mightily conquered sin, death, and hell. He overcame every obstacle in life and death so that you and I can have just that—life. And eternal life at that!

Don't be fooled by the many opinions that exist today about who Jesus is. If you were to ask people on the street who they think Jesus is, you'd get a variety of incorrect answers.

But the Bible says "Jesus Christ is the same yesterday and today and forever" (Hebrews 13:8). He is the Mighty God... with all power... and He is available to you right now!

Through Him you can overcome anything in life. Whatever pain, crisis or challenge comes along, know that your Mighty God—your hero—will enable you to overcome it.

**JESUS CHRIST IS THE MIGHTY GOD...
THE "HERO GOD" AND HE HAS DONE, AND WILL DO,
GREAT THINGS FOR YOU!**

For to us a child is born, to us a son is given; and the government shall be upon his shoulder, and his name shall be called Wonderful Counselor, Mighty God, Everlasting Father, Prince of Peace.

—Isaiah 9:6

When Jesus came to this earth, part of His mission was to reveal what your heavenly Father is really like... the Everlasting Father.

This was important because God knew that you and I might compare Him to our earthly father... and that may not provide a true reflection of who He is.

Your heavenly Father is loving, wise, and faithful. He can be trusted, and He longs to spend time with you and to provide all of your needs. This may be a stark contrast to your experience with your earthly father... which is why God chose to reveal Himself to you through the living example of His Son.

Jesus said, "If you had known me, you would have known my Father also, and from now on you know Him and have seen Him... Believe me that I am in the Father and the Father in me..." (John 14:7, 11).

In the words He spoke and the acts of mercy He showed, Jesus was imitating His Father and showing you exactly what your Everlasting Father is really like.

He did this so you would come to your Father... with full confidence... and accept His love.

TO KNOW WHAT YOUR HEAVENLY FATHER IS REALLY LIKE, LOOK AT THE LIFE AND CHARACTER OF JESUS CHRIST.

Day 249

For to us a child is born, to us a son is given; and the government shall be upon his shoulder, and his name shall be called Wonderful Counselor, Mighty God, Everlasting Father, Prince of Peace.

—Isaiah 9:6

If you know the Lord, you can experience peace today.

No matter what you may be dealing with—whether it's a stressful family situation, work issues, or poor health—you can find what the Bible calls "the peace of God, which surpasses all understanding..."

Jesus is the source of peace, in fact, He is called the Prince of Peace! You need to run to Him in your time of crisis. Then you will find the peace you desperately need.

In John 14:27, Jesus said, "Peace I leave with you; my peace I give to you. Not as the world gives do I give to you. Let not your hearts be troubled, neither let them be afraid."

You have a choice in times of trouble to try to carry your burden alone, or to run to the Prince of Peace and allow Him to help you. And today, I want to encourage you to run to Jesus to let Him help you... no matter what you're going through!

IN TIMES OF ANXIETY OR TROUBLE, YOU CAN FIND SUPERNATURAL PEACE IN JESUS CHRIST.

"Not everyone who says to me, 'Lord, Lord,' will enter the kingdom of heaven, but the one who does the will of my Father who is in heaven."

—Matthew 7:21

Being a follower of Jesus Christ is a matter of the heart… it's not about following rules or rituals, or being "religious" as some people think.

Of course, it's important to obey the Lord's commands, and by doing so, you demonstrate your love for Him. But God has always been more interested in the state of your heart than what you can do to impress Him.

When your heart is humble and you genuinely seek to serve Him because of your relationship with Him, He is pleased by that.

But He sees right through the façade when a person is simply going through the motions, or doing their "good works" to receive applause from men. This kind of "religion" will never win God's favor.

That's the difference between being a disciple of Jesus and being "religious". Keep your heart engaged with Him and serve Him out of true devotion, and you will bring pleasure to the heart of God.

**GOD IS NOT IMPRESSED BY "RELIGION",
BUT BY HEARTFELT DEVOTION TO HIM.**

Day 251

For all have sinned and fall short of the glory of God, and are justified by his grace as a gift, through the redemption that is in Christ Jesus.

—Romans 3:23-24

The most important question a person could ever ask is found in Job 9:2, "How can a man be in the right before God?"

No one has been born righteous, and there is no religion or human effort that can make us right with God. Which is why we must look to the pardon and provision of God's grace for our salvation!

If you have placed your faith in Jesus Christ, God has declared you righteous. You have been forgiven of your sins through the shed blood of Jesus Christ. That's the Good News!

It can be easy to go through the day—or even many days—and not think about this powerful truth. But a heart of gratitude will constantly remember what God has done… and how our lives have been forever changed by the sacrifice of Jesus!

"For by grace you have been saved through faith. And this is not your own doing; it is the gift of God" (Ephesians 2:8).

EVERY DAY, BE THANKFUL THAT YOU ARE RIGHTEOUS IN GOD'S SIGHT BECAUSE OF JESUS.

Day 252

Jesus said to him, "I am the way, and the truth, and the life.
No one comes to the Father except through me."

—John 14:6

It's important to remember that we were all born into sin and charged with a spiritual debt from the moment we were born.

But God came to earth in the person of Jesus Christ and lived a perfect life... died a brutal death... was buried and rose three days later... to pay for our sins!

Sadly, many people put their sin debt off thinking they will deal with it later, or ignore it altogether. But there is a day coming soon when all charges will be brought to the table and by then it will be too late.

If you have not eliminated your spiritual debt by accepting Jesus as your personal Lord and Savior, call out to God right now and ask for forgiveness.

Then you will be able to start a fresh new life in Christ... free from the bondage of sin... and reconciled to the God who created you and loves you!

IF YOU HAVE UNRESOLVED SIN
IN YOUR LIFE, CALL OUT TO GOD RIGHT NOW
AND ASK FOR FORGIVENESS.

Day 253

No distrust made him waver concerning the promise of God, but he grew strong in his faith as he gave glory to God, fully convinced that God was able to do what He had promised.

—Romans 4:20-21

We learn in today's passage from Romans that Abraham lived a life of unwavering faith. He followed God before he knew where God wanted him to go or why. He obeyed even when he didn't understand. It wasn't easy for him to do... and it's not easy for us!

Abraham refused to allow distrust against God to lodge in his heart. He made a conscious decision to believe God, to trust Him and to obey Him... no matter what.

This can be a challenge when you are facing a seemingly impossible situation. But if you will trust Him, God will be faithful to you... just as He was to Abraham.

Don't allow doubts, fears, or the negative influence of others to cause you to distrust the promises of God. Like Abraham, make a choice to believe your heavenly Father, and you will see Him work on your behalf.

MAKE A DECISION TO TRUST THE PROMISES OF GOD IN EVERY SITUATION.

Day 254

So faith comes from hearing, and hearing through the word of Christ.

—Romans 10:17

Your faith pleases God and it releases His power in your situation. But too often we try to manage our lives without including faith in the equation!

When that happens, we can become burdened with worry and confusion, and then wonder why we're not living a victorious Christian life.

Faith is a must-have when walking daily with the Lord. It's like a muscle... the more you exercise it, the stronger it becomes. Faith isn't feelings or emotions; it's believing that God will do what He says He will do.

True faith can only come from a personal relationship with Jesus... and that relationship can only be deepened by spending time in God's Word.

So today, if you want to build your faith muscles, make time to read your Bible. As you do, your heart will be encouraged by God's promises and you can approach your daily life with the confidence that comes from your relationship with Christ!

**FAITH WILL GROW IN YOUR HEART
AS YOU SPEND TIME IN GOD'S WORD.**

Day 255

By faith Abel offered to God a more excellent sacrifice than Cain, through which he was commended as righteous, God commending him by accepting his gifts. And through his faith, though he died, he still speaks.

—Hebrews 11:4

The biggest lesson you and I can learn from the sacrifice of Abel is that he brought his best before the Lord… and he did so by faith.

Good works alone will never be the answer… nor will religion. But faith… acting on our trust in what God says is true… is the key.

Christian, the Lord deserves your very best. Are you giving everything over to Him… in your personal life, marriage, family, friendships? Are you offering it all up to Him by faith?

Romans 12:1 says, "Present your bodies as a living sacrifice, holy and acceptable to God, which is your spiritual worship."

Lay your life on the altar as a sacrifice before God… by faith… so that you can be used by Him. Your faith will demonstrate to others the way to Jesus, the worship of Jesus, and the witness of His grace and power in your life!

YOU BRING GLORY TO GOD
WHEN YOU OFFER YOUR LIFE TO HIM
IN OBEDIENCE AND FAITH.

By faith Enoch was taken up so that he should not see death, and he was not found, because God had taken him. Now before he was taken he was commended as having pleased God.

—Hebrews 11:5

Enoch faithfully walked with God for 300 years and received the special honor of being recorded in the Bible as "having pleased God."

Most importantly, Enoch lived out his Christian faith boldly and unashamedly in front of his family, and in the midst of a sinful generation.

Isn't that something you would like to be known for?

We too are living in perverted days and it is increasingly challenging for believers to live out their faith without compromise. But God is seeking men and women who will stand for truth and godliness, despite the opinions of others.

Will you make a commitment to live for Christ, no matter what other people think?

As you do, you will not only gain the favor of God, but your life will have a profound impact on those around you.

IT TAKES COURAGE TO LIVE OUT YOUR FAITH WITHOUT COMPROMISE... BUT IT PLEASES GOD.

By faith Noah, being warned by God concerning events as yet unseen, in reverent fear constructed an ark for the saving of his household...

—Hebrews 11:7

Noah demonstrated that his faith was real by believing what God had said and acting on it. And although that sounds simple, it's not always easy to do!

Noah had lots of reasons not to obey what God had asked. There were no signs of rain... it was too big a task for one person... and what would people say?

There were probably times when he felt fear, doubt, insecurity, and embarrassment... but he made a choice to believe what God had said and act on it. And then it happened.

The rain came. The people perished. And only Noah and his family survived!

On that day, Noah was thankful for the choice he made to believe what God had said and to act on it.

And when you make the same choice to obey God, let me assure you, you won't regret it!

WHATEVER SITUATION YOU ARE FACING TODAY, BELIEVE WHAT GOD HAS SAID AND ACT ON IT!

Day 258

By faith Abraham obeyed when he was called to go out to a place that he was to receive as an inheritance. And he went out, not knowing where he was going.

—Hebrews 11:8

The faith Abraham displayed is one of the greatest in all of Scripture... and we can learn so much from how he trusted God even in incredibly difficult circumstances.

And you know, God just may be calling you right now to do something great for His Kingdom. So let me ask you: Are you willing to step out, to leave that which is familiar to you, to follow His direction?

Abraham left everything he knew... his hometown and friends... to follow the call of God on his life. God may be calling you into the unknown. The question is, are you willing to go?

It can certainly be frightening to abandon what you know to follow the Lord in obedience. But if your faith is real and genuine... like Abraham's... and you trust God completely with your life... then any road you travel down will ultimately be a blessing!

**ARE YOU READY TO FOLLOW GOD BY FAITH
NO MATTER THE COST?**

Give ear, O my people, to my teaching… tell to the coming generation the glorious deeds of the Lord, and his might, and the wonders that he has done.

—Psalm 78:1, 4

The family today is under attack like it never has been before. If you're a parent, I strongly encourage you to be diligent in imparting a solid faith in Christ to your spouse and children.

As you build your home on the foundation of the Word of God, your children will grow in their own commitment to Christ. They will also be well equipped for their future life and become effective at leading others to the Lord.

If you want to pass along your faith to your children, then:

- Work to build a strong, healthy Christian marriage,
- Devote yourself to being a godly parent, and
- Train your children in Christian discipleship.

Then continue to make disciples of your children by giving them:

- Unconditional love, encouragement and praise,
- A genuine godly example to follow, and
- Godly leadership, discipline and wisdom.

Parents, God has called you to pass along your faith to your family. Make this one of your highest priorities!

BEFORE WE CAN INFLUENCE OUR CULTURE FOR CHRIST, WE MUST LIVE OUT OUR FAITH IN OUR OWN HOMES.

Day 260

For everyone who has been born of God overcomes the world.
And this is the victory that has overcome the world—our faith.

—1 John 5:4

Moses was a man of great faith. And one of the things that made his faith strongest was his willingness to make a break from the world… an example each of us should follow today.

When Pharaoh tried to oblige Moses by telling him to stay in Egypt to worship God, Moses adamantly refused. He knew Egypt was a land of bondage and that his people could never freely worship God there.

This is the same trick the devil tries to play on you and me today. He wants us to play the religious game… to look godly, but to really deny the power of God. To not really trust in Him.

You and I must learn to separate ourselves from the world's way of thinking and living, just as Moses did. We can do this by trusting in God and His Word. Only then will we develop an overcoming faith that will help us weather any storm we face!

WHEN YOU PERSIST IN TRUSTING IN GOD
AND HIS WORD, YOU CAN MAKE A BREAK FROM
THE WORLD'S WAY OF THINKING.

And the Lord said, "If you had faith like a grain of mustard seed, you could say to this mulberry tree, 'Be uprooted and planted in the sea,' and it would obey you."

—Luke 17:6

So many great men and women are mentioned in the Bible, not because of personal greatness, but because their faith pleased God. And as a result, God used their faith to miraculously change their lives and the lives of those around them.

You may be in a situation today that seems impossible. Perhaps your life is spinning out of control. Let me assure you, if you are a believer in the Lord Jesus Christ, then your faith can make the impossible possible!

To have the kind of faith that Jesus spoke about in today's verse, you need to do these three things:

- First, surrender your life completely to the Lord and worship Him in the way you live your life;
- Second, be completely obedient to what He calls you to do;
- And third, never stop believing and trusting in Him.

Faith is not just hoping that God will come through as He promised… it is knowing that He will, no matter how bleak your situation might look.

YOUR FAITH CAN MAKE THE IMPOSSIBLE POSSIBLE!

Day 262

...Time would fail me to tell of Gideon, Barak, Samson... who through faith conquered kingdoms, enforced justice, obtained promises, stopped the mouths of lions, quenched the power of fire, escaped the edge of the sword, were made strong out of weakness, became mighty in war, put foreign armies to flight.

—Hebrews 11:32-34

There are countless people from the Bible who displayed great faith and commitment to the Lord. They were from all different walks of life, most of them ordinary people just like you and me.

But they all had one thing in common: their trust in and commitment to the Lord.

It doesn't matter what kind of car you drive or where you live. God isn't limited by how much you do or don't have. He wants to use you right where you are!

Many believers in Christ claim to have faith in Him, but they don't follow through in their actions. They see obstacles or face trials and take off running in the other direction!

But I want to challenge you today, if you are a follower of Christ, to respond by faith to what the Lord is calling you to do. To live the life He is calling you to live through His Word... by faith!

AS YOU REMAIN UNMOVED IN YOUR TRUST AND COMMITMENT TO GOD, HE'LL DO SOMETHING EXTRAORDINARY WITH YOUR LIFE.

Day 263

"O Lord, God of Abraham, Isaac, and Israel, let it be known this day that you are God in Israel, and that I am your servant, and that I have done all these things at your word. Answer me, O Lord, answer me, that this people may know that you, O Lord, are God, and that you have turned their hearts back."

—1 Kings 18:36-37

If today's anti-faith, immoral culture has you concerned, you can do something about it!

As believers we can stand and say without hesitation, "We will serve the one true God! We will follow the Lord Jesus Christ!" We need a spiritual revival in this country… a spiritual revolution that will transform our culture.

And all it takes to make this happen is one person. Just one man… one woman… one student that God uses to bring about spiritual revival in His church, among His people, in a community, and even in a nation!

Yes, all it takes is one person. So let me ask you, will you be that person?

In 1 Kings Chapters 17 and 18, you can read about how Elijah took a stand for his God in the midst of that perverted generation. It wasn't easy. But it's never easy to take a stand in any generation for the Word of God and the testimony of Jesus Christ! It always has and always will require a bodacious faith and a bold commitment.

In what areas of your life could you take a stand for Christ today?

Perhaps for you, it might mean saying no to that unscrupulous deal. Or it might mean not going certain places on the internet. Or it might mean not repeating gossip when you hear it.

Whatever taking a stand for Christ means for you, I want to remind you that any kind of revival in our country must begin in you and me as believers.

Because God is the one and only true God, and because of what Christ has done for us on the cross, we can't give a half-effort any longer! The Lord Jesus deserves everything we have! That means standing up for Him through the power of His Holy Spirit that is at work within us.

I pray this challenges and encourages your heart today…

ASK GOD FOR THE STRENGTH AND COURAGE TO TAKE A STAND FOR CHRIST TODAY… AND EVERY DAY!

Day 264

Indeed, all who desire to live a godly life in Christ Jesus will be persecuted…..

—2 Timothy 3:12

C hristianity has become comfortable for too many people today. It's easy to be a "Sunday morning Christian" and live like the world the rest of the week.

Today's verse reminds us that all followers of Christ will face persecution. And while most believers in America don't face physical persecution for their faith, what this verse affirms is that Christianity is not easy. If you stand for Christ, you will be spiritually attacked and your faith will be tested.

This may mean you aren't accepted in every circle because you won't compromise your beliefs. Or you may not get invited to hang out in certain places with your coworkers because they know what you stand for as a believer.

But if your faith is genuine, then the persecution and spiritual attacks you face from the world won't matter! Keep in mind that a true Christian is someone who:

- has made a choice to follow Jesus Christ;
- is continually being transformed by God; and
- is challenged to pick up his or her cross daily and follow the Lord no matter the cost.

Have you made the decision to follow Christ? If so, I want to challenge you today to let Him continually transform your attitude and actions so that the world will see in you what a true Christian really is!

IF YOUR FAITH IS GENUINE, THE PERSECUTION AND SPIRITUAL ATTACKS YOU FACE FROM THE WORLD WON'T MATTER.

Day 265

… Jesus came into Galilee, proclaiming the gospel of God and saying, "The time is fulfilled, and the kingdom of God is at hand; repent and believe in the gospel."

—Mark 1:14-15

What is the gospel?

The word itself means "good news"—and it's the term used to describe the story of Jesus' life, ministry, death, and resurrection.

The fact that forgiveness, freedom from sin, and a new life are possible… for anyone who will believe in Jesus Christ… is certainly Good News!

Although there are lots of religious philosophies, there is only one gospel because God has chosen to reconcile people to Himself in one way—by believing in Jesus. This is the message you and I have been given to share with those around us. It's so simple… yet incredibly powerful!

Romans 1:16 says, "For I am not ashamed of the gospel, for it is the power of God for salvation to everyone who believes…"

I encourage you to share the gospel with someone in your world today!

THE STORY OF WHAT JESUS HAS DONE FOR YOU IS GOOD NEWS… SO MAKE SURE YOU SHARE IT WITH OTHERS!

Day 266

For the Son of Man came to seek and to save the lost.

—**Luke 19:10**

What is salvation?

Salvation is the term Christians use to describe being rescued from the power of sin and death.

Sin is in everyone's life. It controls us... shapes our destinies... separates us from God... and we cannot overcome its power by ourselves.

That's why God intervened on our behalf through Jesus and provided salvation. Jesus overcame sin's power and offers forgiveness freely to everyone as a gift of grace... and that gift is available for you!

So how do you receive salvation?

Romans 10:9 says, "If you confess with your mouth that Jesus is Lord and believe in your heart that God raised Him from the dead, you will be saved."

It's very simple—Jesus wants you to come to Him and place your faith in Him for salvation. Will you take this important step today and experience salvation through Jesus Christ?

**SALVATION IS FREELY AVAILABLE FOR YOU...
MAKE SURE YOU RECEIVE THIS
PRICELESS GIFT TODAY!**

Day 267

*You do not know what will happen tomorrow. For what is your life?
It is even a vapor that appears for a little time and then vanishes
away.*

—James 4:14

This verse is a challenging reminder to make every day count!

It can be easy to get distracted by problems or vain pursuits… or
even to get weighed down in the same routine from day to day…
and forget that God created you with specific plans in mind.

He wants your relationship with Him to deepen with every passing
day… He wants to develop your Christian character… and He wants
to use you to touch the lives of others.

God desires for you to experience a life of purpose and meaning here
on this earth… and to be spiritually prepared to spend eternity with
Him.

But time is short! And life can be filled with unexpected turns. So it's
important not to waste the days that God has given you but to make
every day count for Him.

**MAKE EVERY DAY COUNT IN FOLLOWING THE LORD
AND FULFILLING HIS PURPOSES!**

Therefore, since we are surrounded by so great a cloud of witnesses, let us also lay aside every weight, and sin which clings so closely, and let us run with endurance the race that is set before us.

—Hebrews 12:1

The Christian life is not a 100-yard dash—it's a marathon. It shouldn't be lived in stops and starts, but like a great marathon racer running hard all the way to the finish line.

Finishing a marathon requires a tremendous amount of discipline, hard work, and endurance... just like the Christian life.

And according to today's verse, one of the keys to being able to endure a long and challenging race is to lighten your load!

In daily life, it can be easy to take on unnecessary burdens. Maybe they are tasks or worries or negative attitudes... but they're things God doesn't want you to bear. Likewise, areas of sin will hinder your capacity to run the race.

So let me ask you, are you carrying any unnecessary burdens or weights of sin that you need to lay aside?

Freedom from these burdens will enable you to endure the race before you with joy... and get you over the finish line!

TO ENDURE THE MARATHON OF THE CHRISTIAN LIFE, YOU NEED TO BE FREE OF UNNECESSARY BURDENS AND WEIGHTS OF SIN.

Day 269

And let us consider how to stir up one another to love and good works, not neglecting to meet together, as is the habit of some, but encouraging one another, and all the more as you see the Day drawing near.

—Hebrews 10:24-25

D o you have a church family?

You know, as a pastor I often hear people say, "I'm a Christian, but I don't really need to go to church." Unfortunately, this attitude is contrary to God's will!

As we learn in today's verse, other believers need you... and you need them.

The fact is that life can be discouraging. Work can be stressful... home life can be draining... and sometimes we may feel like we're the only ones trying to live godly lives! But you and I are not alone!

God has given us His people... called His church... to strengthen our faith, grow our families, and encourage one another. In fact, when you become a believer in the Lord Jesus Christ, you're actually called to faithfully and regularly fellowship with other believers.

The Bible describes the church as the Body of Christ. As followers of Jesus, you and I are a part of His body on this earth. We're not in a civic club or a country club. We're part of a unique, living community of faith.

So, let me ask you again, are you a part of His church? Do you fellowship with a local community of believers? In the words of the writer of Hebrews, are you "stirring one another to love and good works" and "encouraging one another"?

If not, I want to urge you to find a local church that you can be a part of today. It's my prayer that you'll discover a thriving, Bible-believing, Jesus-proclaiming church where you can build your faith and you can inspire faith in others!

IF YOU DON'T HAVE ONE ALREADY, BEGIN LOOKING FOR A CHURCH FAMILY TODAY. BECAUSE OTHER BELIEVERS NEED YOU... AND YOU NEED THEM!

Day 270

Slaves, obey your earthly masters with fear and trembling, with a sincere heart, as you would Christ, not by the way of eye-service, as people-pleasers, but as servants of Christ, doing the will of God from the heart.

—Ephesians 6:5-6

D id you know that your job is part of God's divine plan for your life? Too many believers think it's only pastors, evangelists, or missionaries who are in full-time service to the Lord.

But the truth is, every believer is in full-time service to the Lord... and our daily efforts are valuable to God and to others!

Maybe you think your job is insignificant or that you're not able to impact the lives of those around you because of where you work. Let me challenge you to change your perspective.

In our verse today, the apostle Paul encourages us to serve as if "doing the will of God from the heart."

God has placed you exactly where you are. When you are a follower of Christ, things don't just randomly happen in your life. God is at work, unfolding His divine plans. He has placed you in that job... or raising those children... at this exact time for a reason.

Work is something the Lord has ordained for our good... it's not just something to be endured. And when you give yourself to your work with a great attitude, that brings pleasure to the heart of God... and it shows those around you what a true servant of Christ is like.

Also, your work is an opportunity for you to develop your character—which is of ultimate importance to the Lord—and to bless those around you. It's not just the money you earn that blesses others, but the very service you contribute is meeting a need, and you have the unique responsibility to fulfill it.

Don't let half-hearted work be a part of your day. Whatever the Lord has given you to do, do it with enthusiasm, commitment, and excellence! This will bring glory to the Lord and will give your life new meaning. Anything less is not fitting for a child of God.

And don't ever think that you can't mix religion with business. Every day is an opportunity to glorify God. So give each day your best and enjoy the satisfaction of hard work, an honest life, and bringing joy to those around you!

GOD IS CALLING YOU TO LIVE OUT YOUR FAITH IN THE MARKETPLACE... IN THE HOME... OR WHEREVER YOU FIND YOURSELF TODAY.

Day 271

... be filled with the Spirit, addressing one another in psalms and hymns and spiritual songs, singing and making melody to the Lord with your heart, giving thanks always and for everything to God the Father in the name of our Lord Jesus Christ, submitting to one another out of reverence for Christ.

—Ephesians 5:18-21

Today's Scripture gives us as believers a clear command—to "be filled with the Holy Spirit." But how do you know you're leading a Spirit-filled life? The Scripture goes on to provide three very simple and practical essentials.

The first mark or evidence of a Spirit-filled life is our speaking or singing of praise. The Spirit-filled man or woman is constantly bringing worship and praise to God. It's like their heart is overflowing with a melody or a declaration of heartfelt praise.

It doesn't matter if you don't have a good singing voice—it's the heart of worship behind your song that God delights in! The daily worship that comes from your heart is a precious offering to the Lord and is a sign that the Holy Spirit is living in you.

The second mark of a Spirit-filled life is giving thanks to the Lord. Spirit-filled believers are not complainers or fault-finders. They live with an attitude of gratitude!

The Scripture commands us to "give thanks always and for everything." That means to give thanks for our blessings... for the blessings we are yet to receive... and even to give thanks when we are in the midst of difficult circumstances.

Spirit-filled believers are in love with Jesus Christ and cannot help but give thanks... it's a heart-attitude... it's a "heartitude"!

Finally, the third mark of a Spirit-filled life is submitting to one another. A Spirit-filled believer never seeks the spotlight, but seeks to serve others with a genuine attitude of humility.

This was the example that Jesus gave us. He submitted to the will of God and He served those around Him. When you are filled with the Holy Spirit, this same attitude can be seen in your life... a submission out of reverence for God.

These three signs...the singing of praise to God... the giving of thanks... and submission to others... are marks of a Spirit-filled life and will demonstrate to others the reality of your faith in Christ. And it's my prayer that these qualities will mark your life as a believer more and more each day.

MAKE AN EFFORT TODAY TO LIVE OUT YOUR FAITH BY OFFERING PRAISE TO GOD... GIVING HIM THANKS... AND SERVING SOMEONE ELSE.

But you will receive power when the Holy Spirit has come upon you, and you will be my witnesses in Jerusalem and in all Judea and Samaria, and to the end of the earth.

—Acts 1:8

D id you know that, as followers of Christ, we have access to incredible power?

Our verse for today teaches that through the Holy Spirit, we receive power. But it's important to realize that while every believer is indwelled by the Spirit of God, not every believer is filled with the Spirit of God. So let me share how you can live a life filled by God's Spirit and power each and every day.

First, you must desire to be filled by the Holy Spirit. When you desire the Spirit of God to work within you and you invite Him to come and live in you, change you, and empower you, you will see radical changes in your life.

Secondly, if you want the Holy Spirit to fill you, then determine to seek Him every single day. As you become intentional about laying your life before the Lord, you will receive a fresh infilling of His Spirit to empower you for every new day.

Thirdly, permit the Holy Spirit to fill you. The Holy Spirit is ready and willing to fill your life and to help you become more like Jesus. He wants to empower you and give you the strength and wisdom you need. All that is needed is for you to permit Him to be a central part of your life and to work with you in living each day for the glory of God!

As you surrender yourself to the Holy Spirit, you'll begin to radiate the fruits of the Spirit… love, joy, peace, patience, kindness, goodness, faithfulness, gentleness and self control. These qualities are not easy to develop in your own power!

But as you allow the Holy Spirit to live through you, these qualities will grow in you, and demonstrate to those around you the reality of God's power in your life.

LIVING IN THE POWER OF THE HOLY SPIRIT IS A CRUCIAL PART OF YOUR CHRISTIAN LIFE. ARE YOU ACCESSING THIS POWER EVERY DAY?

Look carefully then how you walk, not as unwise but as wise,
making the best use of the time, because the days are evil.

—Ephesians 5:15-16

A re you making the most of every day? Or do you feel rushed with never enough time to get everything done?

God has given to each one of us a measure of time to live on this earth. Every day is a gift from God... and every breath you take is from Him.

And God has prepared a specific plan and purpose for your life that He wants you to accomplish during the time that you have. But in order to do so, you need to be a good steward of your time and not waste it away!

Our verse for today encourages us to walk carefully—with precision, purpose, and determination. This is important because you only have one life to live, and you don't know how long it will be. So it's crucial to seize the day and live every moment to the fullest.

The Scripture tells us to "redeem the time"... to use it up... not for yourself, but for the glory of God. That's what Jesus did. He was never hurried, but lived a life of purpose and He accomplished so much. He said, "I have come to do Your will" and He prioritized His time according to what He believed God had called Him to do.

You and I must do the same thing. It's easy to rush through life and think you don't have enough time for everything. But the truth is God has given you the time and ability to do all that He asks you to do. It's up to you to give yourself to the most important things in life.

You can't live in yesterday and you can't live in tomorrow... you can only live today. So make it count and maximize every moment!

MAKE YOURSELF A PRIORITY LIST FOR TODAY
AND BUDGET YOUR TIME ACCORDINGLY!

According to the riches of his glory he may grant you to be
strengthened with power through his Spirit in you inner being.
—Ephesians 3:16

Today, maybe you feel like you're in a prison. Maybe you feel shackled and chained to your past or to sin. Well, the power of God is available to lift you, strengthen you, and refresh you!

The apostle Paul was in jail when he wrote Ephesians 3:14-19. I call it a "prison prayer." But even though he was jailed, Paul never considered himself a prisoner of his circumstances. Whether he was in prison or being beaten or stoned or shipwrecked, Paul knew he was free in Jesus... no matter what his circumstances were.

In today's Scripture verse, Paul offers us the promise of strength. Then verse 19 says, "...that you may be filled with all the fullness of God."

Paul is talking about the power of the Holy Spirit who lives in every believer. And that includes you if you're a follower of Christ!

So how can you access this power? Through prayer!

When you pray, God begins to work in your life. And it's God in you that gives you power. Consider that a glove can't move or hold things on its own. It's only when you put your hand into the glove that it can be put to effective work. The strength of your hand becomes the strength of that glove. In the same way, Christ is the strength in you if you will allow Him to be!

You and I are empty without Christ. But when you allow Him to come and live in you, He fills your life. And when you access the power of God through prayer, He empowers you and strengthens you... no matter what your circumstances are!

PRAY RIGHT NOW FOR STRENGTH TODAY AND
ALLOW GOD TO FILL YOU WITH HIS SPIRIT!

Day 275

For he himself is our peace, who has made us both one and has broken down in his flesh the dividing wall of hostility.

—Ephesians 2:14

D o you remember those incredible images of the Berlin Wall coming down in Germany? The photos and footage show masses of happy people on the wall... chipping away at the wall... and eventually flooding through it.

The world celebrated the tearing down of this wall because it represented that which separated the east from the west... those who were barricaded from those who were free.

But there's another wall that is erected in the heart of every human being. It's a wall that separates us from God. It's a wall that many of us have built in our own lives that keeps us from knowing God and experiencing His amazing grace.

But our verse today gives us encouragement. The apostle Paul is giving us the Good News of the gospel... that if you're a believer, then Jesus Christ has torn down the wall that separates you from God!

So let me ask you today, is there a wall in your heart that's separating you from God?

If there is, I can help you tear down that wall... right now. If you're willing, why don't you repeat this short prayer...

Lord Jesus, I know my sin stands as a wall of separation between me and You. But I am grateful for Your sacrifice on the Cross that tears down that wall. And I accept You as my Savior.

If you prayed the prayer above and meant it in your heart, I want to welcome you into the family of God! You are free in Jesus Christ!

YOU CAN SHARE THIS ETERNAL HOPE FOR FREEDOM! EXPLAIN THE SIMPLE MESSAGE OF SALVATION TO A FRIEND OR LOVED ONE.

Day 276

Now to him who is able to do far more abundantly than all that we ask or think, according to the power at work within us, to him be glory in the church and in Christ Jesus throughout all generations, forever and ever. Amen.

—Ephesians 3:20-21

Would you like to live a life of abundance? You can! In the book of Ephesians, the apostle Paul gives us an amazing promise. He says that it is your birthright… as a believer… to live an abundant, blessed life.

Remember what Jesus said in John 10:10, "I came that they may have life and have it abundantly." His riches… His favor… His blessing… His unlimited grace and goodness are available to you!

So what is this blessed and abundant life that is promised to you and me? It's the supernatural transformation of God in your life.

When you are blessed by God, you are able to rise above your circumstances. You are given a greater vision for your life. You are able to live beyond the limits… and expect and receive things from God Almighty.

The Scripture tells us in James 4:2, "You do not have because you do not ask." God wants to give you so much more than you can ever imagine… if you will only ask.

My prayer is that you will begin to ask boldly. Ask God for the rich blessings of life that are promised to you… and are already provided for you in Jesus Christ.

Think about it. God delights to give His children good things! God enjoys pouring out His blessings upon us. Our God is not reluctant to give. It's His very nature to give.

So when you pray, you don't have to twist God's arm. Simply open yourself up to receive all that He desires to give you.

My prayer is that you will begin to expect great things from God today. Let your focus be on Him. Let your faith be in Him. And let your future be in Him.

I promise you… your life will never ever be the same.

ARE YOU LIVING THE ABUNDANT LIFE CHRIST PROMISED? GO THROUGH YOUR DAY TODAY WITH AN ATTITUDE OF EXPECTANCY.

Therefore take up the whole armor of God… and take the helmet of salvation, and the sword of the Spirit, which is the word of God, praying at all times in the Spirit, with all prayer and supplication.
—Ephesians 6:13, 17-18

When you think of the devil, do you imagine a cartoon-like character with horns and a pitchfork tail? Or do you see Satan as a very real enemy and a powerful force?

Too many people are deceived into thinking that the devil doesn't even exist!

Let me assure you, the devil is no figment of your imagination. He is real and he's on a mission of destruction. You cannot and must not attempt to defeat him in your own strength.

The devil is a master of deceit and he is constantly working to keep people in darkness and to lure believers away from the truth. And one of the primary ways he tempts people to sin is by attacking their minds!

It's important to stay alert to the fact that the devil is relentlessly trying to corrupt your thought life. If he can bring confusion, doubt, or lies into your mind, he can influence your behavior. He has drawn many people away from Christ this way.

But although the devil is a powerful opposing force, he is not as powerful as our God!

Remember, Satan is a created being. Unlike our God, he is not all-powerful… he is not all-knowing… and he cannot be everywhere at the same time. Furthermore, he has already been defeated by the finished work of Jesus on the cross!

Yes, we must still fight the devil and resist his attacks… but we fight with the knowledge of how his story will end.

And how do we fight this spiritual enemy we cannot see?

As we read in Ephesians 6, God has provided spiritual weapons for you and me to use as we fight in this spiritual battle. And, according to our verse today, two powerful ways you can defeat the enemy is by using the Word of God and prayer.

As you face challenges of various kinds, let the Scripture be in your heart and your mind… and also on your lips. And equally important, be faithful in prayer. This will not only strengthen your own spirit, but unleash the power of heaven against the devil!

In the midst of the battle, remember that Jesus Himself is praying for you. Don't be troubled by the devil and his efforts to destroy… just keep your eyes on Jesus Christ and the victory He has won!

MAKE AN EFFORT TO GUARD YOUR MIND TODAY BY TAKING TIME TO PRAY AND READ GOD'S WORD.

Day 278

No, in all these things we are more than conquerers through him who loved us.

—Romans 8:37

D o you ever feel like you are just struggling to make it through the day or to the end of the week?

The apostle Paul is living proof that as believers, we can actually thrive… not just survive… in the midst of tough times!

Paul's life is a great example to us. As we read in the Scripture, he endured hardship, abuse, pain, and persecution. But he never let his circumstances defeat him. In fact, hardships only made Paul stronger as a man and follower of Christ.

You and I know that life can be tough. We all face the pressures of day-to-day living. We all endure stress, uncertainty, fear, and anxiety. Tough times are just inevitable!

But Paul tells us that—through Christ—we can rise above it all. And through his words and his actions, Paul gives us courage that we can be triumphant in tough times!

Paul said in Romans 8:28, "All things work together for good, for those who are called according to his purpose." Then he went on to say in verse 37, "We are more than conquerors through him who loved us."

If you're a follower of Christ, then you are more than a conqueror. You're a super conqueror!

One of the greatest lessons we can learn from Paul is that a triumphant Christian life begins with a victorious attitude. You see, the difference between the average Christian life and the abundant Christian life is attitude.

We see today that Paul had an attitude that was indomitable. Even when he was chained and in prison, his attitude was always positive… uplifting… joyous… and hopeful.

Paul knew that even in prison his spirit was free. That's why he declared that he was a prisoner of Jesus Christ, not of Rome… or of his circumstances. That's why he could sing songs of praise to God in prison. And that's why he could write the Scriptures from his cell!

So let me encourage you today. If you're going through adversity… and if you're facing a problem or a crisis… as a follower of Christ, you're in the grip of His grace! And you can face anything… and everything… because Jesus Christ is on *your* side!

GIVE YOUR ATTITUDE A BOOST BY LISTING FIVE THINGS YOU CAN BE THANKFUL FOR TODAY!

Day 279

In him you also, when you heard the word of truth, the gospel of your salvation, and believed in him, were sealed with the promised Holy Spirit, who is the guarantee of our inheritance until we acquire possession of it, to the praise of his glory.

—Ephesians 1:13-14

Have you ever doubted your salvation? If so, you're not alone. But it's absolutely vital that followers of Christ understand that their salvation is secure.

Once you have truly repented of your sin and asked the Lord for forgiveness, there is no reason why you need to spend one more moment in doubt about your salvation.

God has fully forgiven you, redeemed you, restored you, and received you in Jesus Christ. And He has given you the Holy Spirit as the mark, the identity, the divine seal of approval that you belong to Him!

According to our Scripture verses for today, you can know with confidence that you "…were sealed with the promised Holy Spirit, who is the guarantee of our inheritance…" The Spirit Himself is your guarantee!

You not only have the Word of God telling you that you're saved by trusting in Christ, you also have the Holy Spirit testifying to your heart, reminding you, "You belong to Jesus. Live like a Christian and I'll give you the power to do it."

God guarantees to finish what He has started in you. He has already saved you from the penalty of your sin, so you are completely accepted in His sight. And He is continuing to work in you, to make you more like Jesus, so you'll be ready for that great day when you're with Him in heaven.

If you have made your decision to follow Jesus Christ, you can rest assured that your salvation is secure. So don't allow doubts or lies from the enemy to rob you of the joy of your salvation!

**REJOICE IN YOUR SALVATION BY
SHARING YOUR PERSONAL TESTIMONY
WITH A FRIEND TODAY!**

For we are his workmanship, created in Christ Jesus for good works, which God prepared beforehand, that we should walk in them.

—Ephesians 2:10

Wouldn't it be great if you could see into the future? Well you can... sort of.

In today's verse, we find that we are God's workmanship. And that He has planned "good works" ahead for our lives.

You can know today that the Lord has planned a lifetime of opportunities for you to serve Him through good works.

But in order for you to be able to fulfill those good works God has prepared for you, He is, through His grace, transforming you into the person He wants you to be.

But remember this doesn't happen overnight. As you continue to walk in step with God, His grace is constantly changing you.

Isn't that encouraging? The Lord not only saves you and creates great plans for your life... He also enables you to live out those plans!

This is something to celebrate. Sometimes we can deceive ourselves into thinking that everything depends on us. That somehow we can contribute to our own righteousness.

But in reality, every one of us is completely and utterly reliant on the grace of God to rescue us from sin... to change our hearts so that we become holy... to empower us to remain faithful to Jesus Christ... and to make something worthwhile out of our lives.

And of course, God's plan is not for your life just to be worthwhile—but to be glorious! He wants to use you in ways you could never imagine, and the way He will do it is by transforming you by His grace.

So today, I'd like to encourage you by reminding you that you are a trophy of God's grace. And the master Artist is continuing His work in you, whether you're aware of it or not... to create you into the person He has destined you to be.

He looks beyond who you are today and sees what you will become through His grace... and He smiles!

**TAKE JUST A FEW MOMENTS OUT OF
YOUR DAY TODAY TO DREAM AND THANK GOD
FOR PLANNING YOUR FUTURE.**

But God, being rich in mercy, because of the great love with which he loved us, even when we were dead in our trespasses, made us alive together with Christ—by grace you have been saved.

—Ephesians 2:4-5

Are you living the good life today? If you are a believer, you've not only been rescued from death... you've also been given abundant life!

In Ephesians 2:1 it says, "And you He made alive, who were dead in trespasses and sins..." This Scripture explains exactly what condition you were in before you met Christ—you were dead!

After Adam and Eve rebelled against God, they were separated from Him... and they experienced spiritual and physical death. In the same way, you and I were once separated from God because of our disobedience, and we were living in a state of spiritual death.

But that was never the way God wanted it to be! And so our verse today says in His great mercy, God made a way for you and me to be reconciled to Him. He laid upon Jesus the punishment that was due to us, and enabled us to experience abundant life once again.

Isn't that amazing? You may have heard the gospel message a thousand times... but let it touch your heart again every time you hear it!

It can be easy to forget how much God has saved you from in this life. But there are three sinister forces that once held you captive... the world, the flesh, and the devil. And Jesus has set you free from all of these!

Is it any wonder we call the Christian life the good life? You and I have been rescued from a life of darkness and now we're seated with Christ in the heavenlies! He is exalted and everything is under His feet... and He has chosen for you to share in His victory, not only now, but forever.

Remind yourself of that when you're having a bad day! In fact, I encourage you to remind yourself of what Jesus has done for you every day... by taking you from death to life—and abundant life at that!

TAKE TIME OUT OF YOUR BUSY DAY TODAY TO REMEMBER WHAT OUR LORD JESUS HAS SAVED YOU FROM!

Day 282

That I may know him and the power of his resurrection, and may share his sufferings, becoming like him in his death.

—Philippians 3:10

What is the most important pursuit of your life?

The Bible says, without a doubt, the most important pursuit for every believer is to know God. Not to know about Him... or to know others who know Him... but to truly know Him for yourself.

This was God's plan from the very beginning—that His children would live in intimate fellowship with Him. He created you to know Him and to find your greatest fulfillment in His presence... and that is still His greatest desire for you today.

In our Scripture today, the apostle Paul made it clear that his primary pursuit in life was, "that I may know Him...." Of course, Paul already knew Jesus Christ as His Savior. But Paul understood that knowing the Lord would be a continuous journey throughout his lifetime... and he was passionate that his relationship with Christ would grow closer every day.

As you know, all relationships take time. You can't meet someone once, or just spend time with them occasionally, and claim that you truly know that person. There is tremendous depth in a person's heart, and it often takes years of relationship to connect and understand another person, and to share your life with them in a meaningful way.

In the same way, it takes time to develop an intimate relationship with the Lord. It won't just happen. To really know Christ will require you to be intentional about spending time in God's Word and in His presence... and to make the pursuit of knowing God a priority in your daily life.

When you do, you will experience a depth of relationship with the Lord that will radically transform your life.

I love what Bill Bright said... "Everything about your life; your desires, your motives, attitudes, words and actions, is influenced by your perception of God." When you truly know the Lord, you will respond to life in an entirely different way!

So let me ask you today... what are you pursuing in life? Are you seeking to truly know the Lord... or is this an area that needs greater priority in your life? I pray that you will make knowing the Lord your greatest pursuit in life, and in doing so, experience the abundant life He has for you!

MAKE GETTING TO KNOW GOD A PRIORITY TODAY THROUGH PRAYER AND BIBLE STUDY.

I came that they may have life and have it abundantly.

— **John 10:10**

Are you enjoying all that God has given you?

God has promised you an abundant life… not a mediocre, run-of-the-mill kind of life. That was, in fact, the very reason Jesus came to this earth!

According to our verse today, Jesus says He "came that they may have life and have it abundantly." And in Ephesians 1:3, Paul continued by saying that God "has blessed us in Christ with every spiritual blessing in the heavenly places."

These promises of "abundant life" and "every spiritual blessing" are big promises. But sometimes, when the challenges of life are pressing in on you, it may not feel like you're enjoying abundant life!

What are the spiritual blessings that have been purchased for you through the blood of Jesus Christ?

The list of spiritual blessings is enormous. Forgiveness, healing, peace, wisdom, love… and the more you delve into God's Word, the more you will discover.

Knowing the spiritual blessings that have already been provided for you will radically change the way you respond to daily life. Instead of feeling depressed and defeated, you can say with confidence, "Thank you, Lord, that You have already given me what I need to deal with this situation…."

As you begin to remind yourself of what has been provided for you, and claim God's Word in your situation, you are suddenly in a position of strength! You are no longer struggling through the day, wondering what it means to live an abundant life… you're tapping into your spiritual blessings!

**LOOK IN SCRIPTURE FOR DIFFERENT
SPIRITUAL BLESSINGS AVAILABLE TO YOU… AND
THANK GOD FOR THEM!**

Day 284

For to the one who pleases him God has given wisdom and knowledge and joy....

— **Ecclesiastes 2:26**

We've all had days when we throw up our hands and ask, "What's the point?"

Maybe you've struggled lately with questions about the purpose of your life. Or maybe you've wondered if it's possible to find real joy and fulfillment in life. So did Solomon.

Solomon tried many things to gain fulfillment: laughter, learning, liquor, luxuries, lust, and labor.

He had it all, but he was still empty inside and dissatisfied with his life.

He eventually even said, "Vanity of vanities; all is vanity!" And he was right. None of the things Solomon tried could satisfy him. Only God could!

As our verse for today says, Solomon found that wisdom, joy, and knowledge comes from God. You can only have a life full of purpose and meaning when you live life sold out to the Lord Jesus.

And you know, Solomon was right about something else. He said, "Remember now your Creator... before the difficult days come, and the years draw near when you say, 'I have no pleasure in them.'"

Don't wait any longer to live with purpose. If you, like Solomon, have tried just about everything to find fulfillment in life, but are still empty inside, then look no further than Jesus Christ.

WE'RE ON EARTH ONLY A SHORT TIME.
MAKE TODAY COUNT BY LIVING IT
THROUGH CHRIST!

No temptation has overtaken you that is not common to man. God is faithful, and he will not let you be tempted beyond your ability, but with the temptation he will also provide the way of escape, that you may be able to endure it.

—1 Corinthians 10:13

Today's devotion is a special word of encouragement for men. If you want to be the kind of man who wins in the race of life, it's important to learn how to overcome temptation.

All of us naturally tend to either give in to temptation or try to fight it in our own strength. But God's Word tells us that the only way we'll ever overcome or defeat temptation is through Jesus Christ and His strength. That's the only way!

You may be thinking that's something only a preacher would say. But I deal with temptation just like everyone else! And if there's one thing I've learned over the years, it's that Jesus Christ is the only One who can help me overcome temptation.

Our verse today holds a great promise. God is faithful! He will show us how to overcome temptation.

I want to encourage you today: If you know Christ, you are not defeated! You are not a loser! God made you to win against temptation!

If you will only determine to be a man—or woman—of God, you can influence your family, friends, coworkers and communities for Christ. You can finish your race strong.

KEEP TODAY'S SCRIPTURE CLOSE BY
FOR ENCOURAGEMENT AND STRENGTH TO
OVERCOME TEMPTATION.

No temptation has overtaken you that is not common to man. God is faithful, and he will not let you be tempted beyond your ability, but with the temptation he will also provide the way of escape, that you may be able to endure it.

—1 Corinthians 10:13

I have an honest question to ask you today: What's your greatest weakness?

Even if no one else knows what it is, Satan knows. He is very real and very powerful... and believers should always be on the lookout for the physical, emotional, and spiritual temptations he throws our way.

But the great news is that you are not alone in this struggle! As our Scripture verse for yesterday and today promises, God will always be faithful to provide an exit strategy in the midst of temptation.

And He gives us three ways to overcome temptation:

- By FAITH. First John 5:4 says, "For everyone who has been born of God overcomes the world. And this is the victory that has overcome the world—our faith."
- By FLEEING. Second Timothy 2:22 says, "So flee youthful passions and pursue righteousness, faith, love, and peace, along with those who call on the Lord from a pure heart."
- And by FIGHTING. Because Ephesians 6:13 says, "Therefore take up the whole armor of God, that you may be able to withstand in the evil day, and having done all, to stand firm."

Every time Satan tries to discourage you or cause you to doubt, pray against him in the name of Jesus, and he will run from you.

You have victory as a child of God in your battle against evil!

IF TEMPTATION COMES YOUR WAY TODAY, PRAY IMMEDIATELY AGAINST SATAN AND ASK GOD FOR STRENGTH.

Our fellowship is with the Father and his Son Jesus Christ. And we are writing these things so that our joy may be complete.

—1 John 1:3-4

Want to be happy? There is no greater joy in this life than to have a personal, intimate relationship with Jesus Christ. Nothing!

Now, the world will tell you the exact opposite. Our culture screams at us that money... or a perfect physical appearance... or the right relationship... or sexual expression... are the only ways to find true joy.

But the only way to know an incredible, deep, and dynamic joy... an inner happiness that lasts forever... is through a personal relationship with Jesus Christ.

Having been a pastor for many years, I've met a lot of people who can't seem to get past the fact that they can have a relationship with God... Someone they can't see or touch. Maybe you even feel this way today.

But I want to promise you, Jesus really is the personal God! I've never met Him physically, but I know Him all the same. He's not just somebody I know about, He's somebody I truly know.

How? Through the Spirit of God Who makes Him alive in me and makes me sure of His existence in my heart and life. And because of this, I have a deep and lasting joy. And you can too if you will just place your faith in Him today!

SPEND SOME PERSONAL TIME WITH JESUS CHRIST TODAY. GET TO KNOW HIM BETTER!

Day 288

But Ruth said, "Do not urge me to leave you or to return from following you. For where you go I will go, and where you lodge, I will lodge. Your people shall be my people, and your God my God."

—Ruth 1:16

I f you ever want to see the picture of true commitment, read the book of Ruth.

Ruth's commitment to her family and God changed the course of her life. And the scene when Ruth made her commitment to God is one of the great confessions of faith in the Bible and all of history.

There on the road to Bethlehem, Ruth accepted God's grace. He had brought her to the road to Bethlehem... and she was persuaded in her faith, even though her own mother-in-law told her to "turn back."

Now, Orpah, Ruth's sister-in-law, came to the crossroads with her and cried and wept and was full of emotion. But she turned on her heel, and she went back into Moab and died without God.

Ruth came to that same crossroads at Bethlehem, and she clung to her commitment. And as a result, her entire life was changed forever.

You know, that's what commitment to Christ really is. It's not fence-straddling. It's cross-bearing! Jesus said, "It's not always going to be easy. If you're going to follow Me, take up your cross... don't take the easy way... take up your cross and follow after Me."

I challenge you to make your commitment to God total and final! Get rid of the escape clauses, the fine print, and the footnotes on the contract of your commitment to Him.

WRITE OUT A CONFESSION OF YOUR COMMITMENT TO GOD TODAY AND KEEP IT IN YOUR BIBLE AS A DAILY REMINDER.

Day 289

"She said, 'Please let me glean and gather among the sheaves after the reapers.' So she came, and she has continued from early morning until now, except for a short rest."

—Ruth 2:7

If you are wondering what God's plan for your life is, you can learn an important lesson from Ruth.

Ruth is an example for you and me because she was faithful where she was... to what God had assigned her to do. She went to the field and worked, and she worked hard. According to Ruth 2, verse 7, she arrived early and stayed late!

You see, Ruth didn't have ulterior motives. She didn't know about the future... about Boaz being her future husband. She didn't know she would become the great-grandmother of David and a direct ancestor of the Lord Jesus Christ.

She didn't have a clue about any of that! Ruth simply did what she was assigned to do that day, letting God lead her as she faithfully obeyed Him.

And that is how God leads you and me. We're called to "bloom where we're planted." We should work hard doing what we're called to do... right now!

That's the story of Ruth's life. She met success in a common hour by simply doing what God had directed her in her heart to do.

Are you doing the will of God in your life right now? Are you blooming where God has planted you today?

WHATEVER YOU DO TODAY, DO IT TO THE VERY BEST OF YOUR ABILITY!

Then Naomi her mother-in-law said to her, "My daughter, should I not seek rest for you, that it may be well with you?"

—Ruth 3:1

Maybe you've experienced tragic disappointment in your life. Naomi could relate. She was uprooted from her home and lost her husband and her sons. Life's troubles had darkened her spirit and turned her bitter.

But I'd like to remind you what Naomi did in the midst of her state of depression. In fact, it's one thing that helped get her out from under the dark cloud of bitterness she was living in.

Naomi stopped thinking about herself and started thinking about someone else.

I don't know where you may find yourself today, but if you're down, I have a word for you: If you can get outside of yourself and start serving others, you will find any depression you have will begin to lift.

If you're discouraged today, I encourage you to get interested in someone else! Get involved in your church. Adopt a family or find a child that you can share a gift with.

And certainly it's important to share your faith. Nothing will lift your spirits and enliven your heart like sharing the Good News with someone who needs to hear it!

When you're discouraged or depressed, the best thing you can do is to get your mind on the Lord Jesus Christ… to worship Him, to look to Him, to speak to Him, to open your Bible, and to ask the Spirit of God to mend your broken heart.

And when you will do that, watch God begin to restore and replenish and refresh your despondent spirit. To move your life from bitterness… to blessing.

BLESS SOMEONE ELSE TODAY. WHEN YOU OFFER A SMILE, A CUP OF COFFEE, OR PRAYER OF ENCOURAGEMENT, YOUR SPIRITS WILL BE LIFTED!

Now this was the custom In former times in Israel concerning redeeming and exchanging: to confirm a transaction, the one drew off his sandal and gave it to the other, and this was the manner of attesting in Israel.

—Ruth 4:7

O ur Scripture verse explains a very unusual custom in Ruth's day.

When a redeemer was unwilling to redeem or to transact the business, it was the custom of the man to take off his sandal and give it to the man who would redeem.

And the man who would redeem would slip on that sandal as a sign of his willingness to stand in that man's shoes and to redeem and purchase what was rightfully his.

Can you think of a more vivid illustration of what Jesus Christ has done for us?

We, the near kinsman, the flesh… we could not do it, and so we take off our shoe and give it to Christ. Salvation is Jesus standing in my shoes and me standing in His!

When you look at Ruth's husband Boaz, you can see how he is a picture of what Jesus Christ did for you and me on the cross. No one is too far gone for God's love… but no one is capable of redeeming themselves.

REJOICE TODAY THAT JESUS REDEEMED YOU
JUST AS BOAZ DID FOR RUTH!

Day 292

I rejoiced greatly to find some of your children walking in the truth, just as we were commanded by the Father.

—2 John 4

I s there really such a thing as absolute truth?

The United States Declaration of Independence opens with words that have echoed through history:

"We hold these truths to be self-evident, that all men are created equal, that they are endowed by their Creator with certain unalienable Rights, that among these are Life, Liberty and the pursuit of Happiness."

Yes, America was built upon certain foundational truths that have guided and governed our nation… truths that came from God almighty Himself.

Which leads me to ask you today… how valuable is God's truth to you?

The great King Solomon, one of the wisest men who ever lived, once said, "Buy truth, and do not sell it; buy wisdom, instruction, and understanding." Solomon knew that truth was valuable… that it was priceless. So what about you?

Do you love God's truth? Do you obey His truth? Do you stand for His truth? And… do you proclaim His truth?

More and more, our society is turning its back on anyone who believes in Jesus Christ and the claim that salvation is found only through Him. But for the sake of our beloved nation and for the people we care about, you and I must defend the truth of who Jesus Christ is in our generation!

That's why I hope you will recommit yourself to stand undaunted for the truth. God's truth. And that through your witness, many people will come to know the truth that leads to salvation!

DO YOU LOVE GOD'S TRUTH? DO YOU OBEY HIS TRUTH? DO YOU STAND FOR HIS TRUTH? AND… DO YOU PROCLAIM HIS TRUTH?

Blessed be the God and Father of our Lord Jesus Christ! According to his great mercy, he has caused us to be born again to a living hope through the resurrection of Jesus Christ from the dead, to an inheritance that is imperishable, undefiled, and unfading, kept in heaven for you.

— 1 Peter 1:3-4

In these troubling times, have you ever wondered if we can really be hopeful about the future? I want to assure you that it is possible to live with hope, despite what may be going on around us.

Because while hope is ultimately about the future, it's also about the present. And that's because we have a living hope.

Through the resurrection of Jesus Christ we have hope. It's because He lives that hope can reside in your heart if you're a Christian.

And because of that, there is no need to fear the future! If you are a child of God, you are chosen and called by Him. You're not an accident, an afterthought, or a mistake. You have been in the heart and mind of God forever, and He has already been planning and preparing your future.

In fact, God knows the end from the beginning... and everything else in your life. That's comforting when we face tough times and when we're tempted to give up. It's encouraging to know that we are never, ever without hope!

So today, if you're tempted to give up on your marriage, don't! If you're thinking about giving up on your kids, don't! If you want to give up on your dreams... or even life itself... don't!

Remember that you have a living hope that is working in your past, your present, and your future. And as the Scripture teaches us in Romans chapter 5, that hope does not disappoint!

TODAY, GIVE GOD THANKS FOR KEEPING YOUR FUTURE IN HIS HANDS!

Day 294

And after you have suffered a little while, the God of all grace, who has called you to his eternal glory in Christ, will himself restore, confirm, strengthen, and establish you.

—1 Peter 5:10

Are you struggling today?

God never tells us that we won't experience grief or sorrow in this life. There will be tears. And, to be honest, sometimes life will just suck the air right out of you.

But we must remember that trials do have a purpose. Trials can fortify us. They can prove us, test us, and prepare us.

As today's verse says, "And after you have suffered a little while, the God of all grace who has called you to His eternal glory in Christ, will Himself restore, confirm, strengthen, and establish you."

The fact is, if you're a Christian, you're in a spiritual battle. Which means you have a very real enemy. And trials prepare you for this battle and make you stronger. In fact, you may be going through a spiritual boot camp of sorts today, which is preparing you for the battle ahead!

Think about it this way. When gold is made, all the impurities must be removed. The same process of refining takes place in our lives before genuine gold can come forth.

Whatever you may be facing today, keep in mind that God is forming your character, bringing out the gold in you. Everything has a reason. You may not see it… you may not understand it… but God is working in your life.

Remember that no matter what you may be going through, you can build your life on the certainty and confident expectation that God is in the midst of it. Rejoice because He is working in your life and your future!

THINK ABOUT SOME OF THE TRIALS IN YOUR PAST. WHAT DID YOU LEARN FROM THEM? HOW DID THEY PREPARE YOU FOR WHAT WAS AHEAD?

Though you have not seen him, you love him. Though you do not now see him, you believe in him and rejoice with joy that is inexpressible and filled with glory.

—1 Peter 1:8

What's your definition of a holy life? You might be surprised to find out that God is not only holy; God is happy!

And when we talk about living a holy life, we are talking about living a life full of energy, life, power, and joy.

As our verse for today says, we have "joy that is inexpressible and filled with glory"! That's a joy that's so incredible you can't even express it! It is because of salvation through Christ.

So when I talk about holiness, I'm not talking about being pious or religious. Rather, pure holiness is a beautiful expression of the very character of God. We are separated unto God that we might live positive, joyful, exuberant lives… as well as disciplined and dedicated lives.

The upward call of every Christian is to live with a purity of heart and a purity of life that comes from the soul and is unpolluted because the presence of God is there.

You and I have been called to live a godly life… no exceptions. And it all begins with our minds. According to Proverbs 23:7, "As [a man] calculates in his soul, so is he." Have you ever thought about how so many of our spiritual struggles begin when we allow our minds to wander aimlessly?

Today, I want to encourage you to make sure your thinking is controlled by the grace of God. Exercise self-discipline. Second, eliminate anything that weakens your mind or distorts your thinking or your judgment. Third, stay focused on the purposes and plan of God. And fourth, continually put your future hope in God.

These four things will help you keep your mind focused on what is good, true, and right!

**KEEP YOUR MIND FOCUSED ON THE JOY OF GOD…
AND THE HOPE OF YOUR SALVATION TODAY!**

The LORD appeared to him from far away. I have loved you with an everlasting love; therefore I have continued my faithfulness to you.
—Jeremiah 31:3

Did you know that the most incredible love known to man can be yours? It's the unconditional, unchanging love of God!

The problem with most of us isn't that we don't love God enough. It's that we don't let God love us enough.

If we could only understand how much God loves us, we could be set free from disappointment in ourselves… and from the slavery of sin and rebellion.

God who is omnipotent and all-powerful loves you! His love is unconditional and unchanging. In Jeremiah 31:3, our verse for today, He said, "I have loved you with an everlasting love."

If you ever doubt that God loves you, just look at the cross and remember His love. Jesus defines and demonstrated the love of God. Calvary is the heart of God beating for you. He loved you enough to step out of heaven and offer His sacrificial blood.

Did you know that the precious blood of Jesus has the power to cleanse… to wipe away sin… and to conquer death and hell? The blood gives power for freedom and the power to love others.

And not only can the blood place God's love in us, but it can also share God's love through us.

Have you experienced that love? You can. Just say this prayer:

Lord, I know that I am a sinner and separated from Your love. I believe that You provided a way for me to experience Your unchanging, unending love through the death and resurrection of Jesus Christ. I believe in and I accept your love today.

If you prayed that prayer of faith, you have just accepted God's unending love. Congratulations!

SHARE THE UNCHANGING, UNENDING LOVE YOU HAVE FOUND WITH SOMEONE ELSE TODAY!

Like newborn infants, long for the pure spiritual milk, that by it you may grow up into salvation....

—1 Peter 2:2

I want to remind you today that not only is the Word of God perfect, living, and abiding forever. Not only is the Word of God unchanging and true. Not only does it have a saving purpose.

But the Scripture also has the power to transform your life!

Jesus said in John 17:17, "Sanctify them in the truth; your word is truth." If you want your life to change, saturate your soul and nourish your heart in the Word of God.

The Bible has power to save and sanctify, and it also has the power to strengthen. In our verse for today—1 Peter 2, verse 2—the Word of God is described as milk to strengthen and grow us in our faith.

Have you tasted the goodness of God from Scriptures? Have you experienced the grace of God found in His Word?

The Bible is not an ancient black book filled with theology about yesterday. It is a book that satisfies the longing of the human heart. The Word of God strengthens us every day and nourishes our spirit. Our very life depends upon this Word and truth!

So, let me leave you with some questions to consider. Do you love God's Word? Are you obeying God's Word? If you love it, you will read it. And if you read it, you will pray it... think it... live it... and share it.

**TAKE THE TIME TODAY TO STUDY GOD'S WORD
AND MAKE IT AN EVERYDAY COMMITMENT!**

Day 298

Like newborn babies, crave pure spiritual milk, so that by it you may grow up in your salvation, now that you have tasted that the Lord is good.

— 1 Peter 2:2-3

We all know that a well-balanced diet is essential to good health... but what about our spiritual health?

If we are going to grow strong spiritually, we need a constant diet of the Word of God.

To taste the goodness of God, to experience the reality of God in our lives through Jesus Christ, we must go to the Word of God. Scriptures provide everything we need for strength and success in life.

The mark of a growing Christian is someone who "abides" in the Word of God. Jesus said, "If you abide in my word, you are truly my disciples" (John 8:31).

The Word of God fills us with counsel for life... correction when we get off the path... and strength for the battle. And the Bible gives us encouragement and hope.

You see, when you open the Scriptures, Jesus walks out of the Word and right into your life!

So today I'd like to ask you this: Are you growing in Christ? Because if you are not moving forward, you are probably moving backwards in your Christian life. And that may be because you are in a weakened condition.

It is a signal that your spiritual life is sick if you have no appetite for the Word of God. Just like it is an instinct for a little baby to crave milk, believers should cry out for the milk of God's Word. It isn't an option!

We desperately need the Word of God in our lives that we may get stronger and grow up in our faith. So, let me leave you with one final question... got milk?

MAKE TIME TO READ AND STUDY GOD'S WORD TODAY.

For it stands in Scripture: "Behold, I am laying in Zion a stone, a cornerstone chosen and precious, and whoever believes in him will not be put to shame."

—1 Peter 2:6

D oes your life feel like it's falling apart at times? Maybe even today it seems as if the world is crumbling around you.

If so, let's take a moment to think about the life and living hope that we have because of Jesus, the chief Cornerstone.

Because of what Christ did for us on the cross, we've been set free from our past, fully and freely forgiven. Now, we've been given a life of purpose and significance.

In this life, we are no longer alone or isolated or living independently of God. We have been loved unconditionally and accepted into God's family. Which means we should live without fear of the future because we have this hope in Christ! He is sufficient for every hurt, for every habit, for every challenge and test in life.

But we must first choose to build our lives on the Rock. Our Scripture for today reminds us, "For it stands in Scripture: 'Behold, I am laying in Zion a stone, a cornerstone chosen and precious, and whoever believes in him will not be put to shame'".

Though rejected by others, if Jesus is the Cornerstone set in your life, there is consistence, strength, and significance.

Maybe you are wondering today why your life doesn't seem to fit together... why things aren't working out the way you had planned. If you're trying to build your life without Jesus, the Cornerstone, everything will ultimately fall apart.

As the old hymn says, "On Christ, the solid Rock, I stand, all other ground is sinking sand." Jesus is the solid Rock. So learn to consistently build your life upon Him... not on the things of this world!

PRAY AND ASK GOD'S GUIDANCE TODAY FOR THE CHALLENGES IN YOUR LIFE.

Day 300

Blessed be the God and Father of our Lord Jesus Christ! According to his great mercy, he has caused us to be born again to a living hope through the resurrection of Jesus Christ from the dead.

—1 Peter 1:3

Maybe today, you or someone you know is facing stress, anxiety, or a sense of defeat and despair. And if this feeling is making you want to give up on your life or trade it in for a new one, I want you to know this: You don't need a new start, you need a new heart!

Jesus came to earth to deliver you and me from our sins. He died and rose again to give you a brand new life! The power and passion of Jesus Christ is your hope! You can have a fresh start and a new day through Him!

According to our verse today, 1 Peter 1:3, we are "born again to a living hope through the resurrection of Jesus Christ from the dead."

Born again? In John 3:7, Jesus said we "must be born again" to begin living in this new hope. Life in Christ is such a radical transformation that it's like being born all over again.

When you go to the cross, it is more than a new start… it is a new life!

Jesus Christ, the living Savior, can take men and women discouraged by the world around them and give them not only hope now, but hope forever. It's a hope that dawns in the hearts of those who have been born again.

So if you would like to be born again today by the power of the resurrection of Jesus, why don't you say this simple prayer?

Dear Lord, I know I am a sinner born into a world of sin. But I want to be born again through Jesus Christ! Please forgive me through Christ's sacrifice and give me a new start. I accept your gift of hope and grace. Amen.

If you have prayed these words… and meant it in your heart… it is the dawn of a new day of hope in your life! And I want to be the first to welcome you into God's family!

**SHARE YOUR NEW HOPE WITH
SOMEONE YOU CARE ABOUT TODAY.**

Day 301

Now the works of the flesh are evident: sexual immorality, impurity, sensuality, idolatry, sorcery, enmity, strife, jealousy, fits of anger, rivalries, dissensions, divisions, envy, drunkenness, orgies and things like these. I warn you, as I warned you before, that those who do such things will not inherit the kingdom of God.

—Galatians 5:19-21

Did you know that your life is on display? Someone is always watching how you react, what you say and what you do. You are a living, breathing gospel story!

Sometimes, I think the church gets stuck thinking that proclaiming the gospel is all about talking… when it's really about walking.

In Matthew 5:16, Jesus said, "In the same way, let your light shine before others, so that they may see your good works and give glory to your Father who is in heaven." Being a true and effective follower of Christ also requires action!

God's ministry should be known for our muscles as much as our mouths as we work hard to serve people who need Jesus. It's one thing to talk about the joy, the grace, the hope, and the love of our Lord Jesus Christ. But the world really takes notice when somebody shows love.

What an incredible thing to lead the way in loving our neighbors… to show the love and grace of the Lord Jesus Christ through our actions.

So today, I want to challenge you to let your light shine before others! Demonstrate the living hope of Christ through your faithfulness and consistency… through your kindness and compassion… through your good deeds… and through your honorable acts.

Sometimes, it's the little moments of kindness that bring great results in people's lives. So often the shortest visit, the simplest word can make the difference between heaven and hell in a person's life.

Jesus said, "And whoever gives one of these little ones even a cup of cold water because he is a disciple, truly, I say to you, he will by no means lose his reward."

So let me ask you… how will you shine your light today?

LET YOUR ACTIONS TODAY REFLECT JESUS CHRIST.

Likewise, wives, be subject to your own husbands, so that even if some do not obey the word, they may be won without a word by the conduct of their wives, when they see your respectful and pure conduct.

—1 Peter 3:1-2

Our Scripture for today offers advice for wives who want to make their marriage not only survive... but thrive.

It also deals with a subject that culture often views as distasteful and dated—submission. In fact, many in our generation discard the biblical view of submission completely.

And yet, it is the definite counsel and command of the Word of God. We are to mutually submit to one another. We are to submit to God. And wives, specifically, are to submit to their husbands.

Now submission does not imply inferiority. As a matter of fact, in the language of the New Testament, it is a response... a voluntary reaction.

The example we are given in 1 Peter 2 is the Lord Jesus. Christ submitted Himself to us when He willingly and voluntarily laid down His life for us.

The goal for our relationship with Christ and in our marriage is oneness. You and your spouse are a team. To submit is not to be a slave or a doormat, but to willingly respond to the God-ordained leadership of your husband.

The Scripture says a gentle and respectful spirit can be a woman's most powerful influence. It is a way that you can radiate the beauty of Christ. And inner beauty keeps romance alive and grows love in a marriage.

Wives, stay attractive through a permanent kind of beauty... beauty that grows with time rather than fades... beauty that radiates from the inside out... and beauty that is precious in the sight of God.

Even though the world says you're crazy and culture says you are out of step, I want to encourage you today to let the countenance of Christ shine through you. Reveal a gentleness of spirit and a graciousness of heart today that is simply irresistible.

**REACT TO YOUR SPOUSE TODAY WITH
A GENTLE, RESPECTFUL SPIRIT.**

Day 303

Husbands, love your wives, as Christ loved the church and gave himself up for her.

—Ephesians 5:25

D o you know what the primary responsibility of a man in marriage is? According to God's plan, it's to love his wife.

Sounds simple enough, doesn't it? Not really!

Our Scripture today says, "Husbands, love your wives, as Christ loved the church and gave himself up for her." As men, our example of how to love our wives is the Lord Jesus Christ.

And what exactly does that kind of love look like?

First, it initiates. According to 1 John 4:19, Jesus "first loved us." If we take the first step in initiating an atmosphere of love at home, our wives will respond.

Second, it sacrifices. In the Scripture, we are commanded to love sacrificially just as Christ did when He laid down His life for us. Genuine sacrifice like this in a marriage fuels loyalty, godly submission, and acceptance.

And third, a Christ-like love is humble. It leads with humility. Remember, if you have to tell your wife that you're in charge… you're not in charge. Real authority comes from humility.

Christ's example of love is the biblical blueprint for success in marriage. So, how does a man love a woman? In the footsteps of Christ!

Men, it's a hard assignment. And we cannot do it alone. We need the Spirit of the living Christ to supernaturally make us more like Him as we assume the responsibility He has ordained for us as husbands.

ASK GOD TODAY TO FILL YOUR SPIRIT AND HEART WITH THE LOVE THAT COMES FROM SACRIFICE, HUMILITY, AND UNDERSTANDING.

Day 304

Yet you are holy, enthroned on the praises of Israel.

—Psalm 22:3

A re you missing out on the most important thing in the Christian life?

According to Scriptures, worship is the most important thing we're called to do as believers in Christ.

In our devotion today, I'd like to focus on one of the reasons why you should worship the Lord: Because it fortifies your faith.

Psalm 34:4-5 says, "I sought the LORD, and he answered me and delivered me from all my fears. Those who look to him are radiant, and their faces shall never be ashamed."

When your faith needs a boost, look up! Praise, worship, singing spiritual songs, and expressing adoration to God all strengthen your faith and draw you nearer to Him.

Remember what our Scripture verse today tells us: God is "enthroned on the praises of Israel." Wherever genuine praise is, so is God!

I am confident that taking your focus off of your troubles… and genuinely thanking God for what He has done in your life… will strengthen your faith and brighten your outlook on life!

**TODAY, IN SPITE OF WHAT HAPPENS
AT HOME OR WORK, FIND ONE THING FOR WHICH
TO PRAISE THE LORD.**

Day 305

I will bless the LORD at all times; his praise shall continually be in my mouth.

—Psalm 34:1

How do you worship? Even though there are many ways to worship God, we all need to remember that worship is an action.

It's not sitting and watching, it's something you do. It is participation. It is not mere emotion. It is not a feeling, not a thought process, but rather the active response of your heart, your life, and even your body to God!

If you go to a worship service and watch everyone else worship, you haven't worshipped… you have become a religious consumer rather than a spiritual communer. You've become a spectator rather than a true worshipper.

Perhaps you grew up in a church where you sang hymns and participated at some level. But, maybe… just maybe… you have never had a genuine experience of encountering the presence of God in true worship.

If not, I challenge you to take time even today to tell God you desire to be a genuine worshipper. He will honor your prayer because He has made you to worship Him! You were created that you might know Him and make Him known.

As a believer in Jesus Christ, worshipping Him intimately and intensely should be the driving force in your life. That's why I want to call you to become a true worshipper of the Lord Jesus Christ today… whether in or out of church!

TAKE AN ACTIVE ROLE IN WORSHIP BY OFFERING GOD PRAISE THROUGHOUT YOUR DAY!

It is no longer I who live, but Christ who lives in me..

—Galatians 2:20

Today, I want you to think about two of Jesus' disciples, Peter and John. These were two men who had been with Jesus, who for three years had looked into His eyes and heard Him pray.

They'd listened intently as He taught lessons of the Kingdom and what it meant to follow Him. They'd seen His tears in the Garden of Gethsemane. They even watched Him die. Then they saw Him in the glory of His resurrection!

Because they had been with Jesus, Peter and John acted like Jesus. In fact, their lives had been revolutionized so dramatically because of the time they spent with Jesus that when people—even their enemies—observed them, they knew there was something distinct, something uniquely different, about these men.

So let me ask you, when the world looks at you as a believer in Christ, can they say the same thing? Can a watching world tell when you have worshipped… when you have bowed in your own time of prayer? Do they see evidence that you've been with Jesus?

When you interact with your friends, your family, and your business associates today, I pray they will see that there is something different about you. Namely, that you have been with Jesus Christ!

**ASK GOD TO HELP YOU BE A LIVING EXAMPLE
OF OUR LORD JESUS CHRIST TODAY.**

Day 307

Mary therefore took a pound of expensive ointment made from pure nard, and anointed the feet of Jesus and wiped his feet with her hair. The house was filled with the fragrance of the perfume.

—John 12:3

God is seeking true worshippers. And friend, that includes you!

You know, there are few better examples of what a true worshipper looks like than Mary of Bethany. Her dedication and love for Christ is such an inspiration to me.

Mary was a living testimony to what Paul talks about in Romans 12:1, when he says to "present your bodies as a living sacrifice, holy and acceptable to God, which is your spiritual worship." Mary came with all that she had and with all that she was to worship Christ.

She was so focused on Him and centered on Him that she paid no attention to the many distractions around her. She absolutely and recklessly abandoned herself… and generously and extravagantly gave herself… all in worship to Christ!

Friend, that's how we're to worship Him each and every day.

So I want to ask you, as a believer, is there anything that's distracting you from worshipping the Lord? If so, I urge you to confess it to God and ask Him to help you refocus on what's truly important… becoming a true worshipper of Him!

**MAKE TIME TODAY TO FOCUS
COMPLETELY ON GOD. REMOVE ALL
DISTRACTIONS AND WORSHIP HIM!**

Day 308

All the earth worships you and sings praises to you; they sing praises to your name.

—Psalm 66:4

Today, I want to ask you, when God looks at your life, does He see genuine worship or does He see a counterfeit? Does He see something real or something phony?

The bottom line is that each of us was made to worship God. And until we realize the true purpose in life... which is to worship Him and enjoy Him forever... we'll always be floundering. We'll always be frustrated because worship is the central purpose of life!

It is impossible to be a productive, positive Christian without participating in meaningful, genuine worship!

And I'm not just talking about corporate worship. Worship is something more than what we do... worship is a lifestyle. It is an attitude that we carry with us day by day. It is an activity and an attitude that reveals the inner heart and recognizes the value we place on God in our lives. That's what worship is!

So today, let me challenge you to make your life a life of worship... an exclamation of the glory of our God!

EXAMINE YOUR LIFE TODAY... DO YOU HAVE AN ATTITUDE OF GENUINE WORSHIP?

Day 309

I will bless the LORD at all times; his praise shall continually be in my mouth.

—Psalm 34:1

Have you ever wondered why we are commanded to offer praise continually as believers?

First, when we praise the Lord, it encourages others. Psalm 34:2 says, "My soul makes its boast in the LORD; let the humble hear and be glad."

I think you'd be amazed at how people, Christian and non-Christian alike, respond to something as positive as honest and sincere praise to God when something good or bad happens to you.

Second, praising God naturally brings fellowship. Psalm 34:3 says, "Oh, magnify the LORD with me, and let us exalt his name together!" There is a closeness… a bond… that is created when you're praising God together.

And last, praising the Lord gives you power for your day-to-day life. Psalm 34:4 says, "I sought the LORD, and he answered me and delivered me from all my fears."

I don't know what you may be facing today, be it a temptation you can't let go of or a sin you can't escape. Whatever it is, praise will help bring you out of it!

God responds to your honest, genuine praise of Him. So I urge you to make praise a habit, like our Scripture verse for today suggests, no matter what you may be going through.

**START TODAY! GIVE GOD PRAISE FOR
THE GOOD AND BAD IN YOUR LIFE!**

Day 310

For God so loved the world, that he gave his only Son, that whoever believes in him should not perish but have eternal life.

—John 3:16

D o you know who Jesus really is?

The deity of Christ is constantly assaulted by our society these days. But in the midst of such cultural confusion, we as believers can stand on the biblical truth of who Jesus is… and what He did for us in coming to earth as a man.

Yes, He was a man… a perfect, sinless man. But He was also God… a God who loved us so much that He laid His life down so that we might be saved.

Take another look at our Scripture verse for today. "For God so loved the world, that he gave his only Son, that whoever believes in him should not perish but have eternal life."

Most believers have heard this verse since their days as baby Christians. But it's my prayer that God would give you a new perspective and fresh insight about just how much He loves you today.

And if you've never accepted the free gift of salvation that God is offering to you, just say these words:

Dear Heavenly Father, please forgive me of my sins. I accept the gift of grace and sacrifice Jesus Christ came to earth to give me. Thank you, Jesus, for what you did for me on the cross. Amen.

Friend, if you've just prayed this prayer and meant it in your heart, I want to welcome you into the family of God!

TELL SOMEONE TODAY WHO JESUS REALLY IS AND WHAT HE HAS DONE FOR YOU!

Day 311

Brothers, I do not consider that I have made it my own. But one thing I do: forgetting what lies behind and straining forward to what lies ahead, I press on toward the goal for the prize of the upward call of God in Christ Jesus.

—Philippians 3:13-14

Want to know how to win in life? The apostle Paul said the meaning of life was the pursuit of Christ. And Paul focused on that goal.

So often we don't win in life because we don't know the difference between what is good and what is best. There are many good things that we can do, but God has called us to higher things, to the better things, to the best things in our lives. We need to do those best things, rather than being constantly distracted by our own over-commitments.

In Hebrews 12:1, the writer encourages us to "lay aside every weight"… to take off the things that drag and pull us down.

So what is slowing you down? Work? A hobby? Channel surfing? A sin? Maybe it's just a distraction that's keeping you from focusing on your calling in God because you don't have the time to spend with Him. Is there something in your life today that's causing you to take your eyes off the prize?

Every successful person has a focus in life… and they opt for the best things over the good things. It's the passion of a winner's life to excel at the highest level and that's good because in the Christian life, God made you to win.

I hope today you'll lay aside your weights, you'll focus on the best things… the things of God… and you'll press toward the prize of your calling in Christ!

**TAKE A LOOK AT YOUR SCHEDULE TODAY.
ARE YOU FOCUSING ON THE "BEST" WITH
EVERYTHING YOU DO?**

Day 312

For many, of whom I have often told you and now tell you even with tears, walk as enemies of the cross of Christ. Their end is destruction, their god is their belly, and they glory in their shame with minds set on earthly things.

—Philippians 3:18-19

Have you ever thought about what makes you truly happy?

Our world today is all about self-fulfillment. We chase after pleasure. Our culture says, "Life's all about fun and games! It's all about the party! Live, love life, and be happy!"

But there's one big problem with a life that is on the road to pleasure. That road is a dead-end! While sin does gratify for a time, it will never satisfy.

It doesn't matter how much money you have… what car you drive… or how much fun you have. None of these things will ever satisfy you! They will never be enough. And here's the reason: We all have a God-shaped hole inside us that can never be satisfied by the things of this world.

Only God can fill that hole in your soul. A relationship with Jesus Christ is the only thing that will fill that deep-seated need within you.

How do you begin that relationship? You must receive God's free gift of salvation by placing your faith in the Lord Jesus Christ. That means you understand that you are a sinner and that the penalty for sin is death. But God sent His Son, Jesus Christ, to pay that penalty for your sin through His death on the cross.

Your sins will be forgiven… and you can have eternal life… by placing your faith in Jesus today! This is the only thing that will ever truly satisfy you in life.

A RELATIONSHIP WITH JESUS CHRIST IS THE ONLY THING THAT WILL FILL THAT DEEP-SEATED NEED WITHIN YOU.

Day 313

Rejoice in the Lord always; again I will say, Rejoice.

—Philippians 4:4

Think about today's Scripture verse for a moment, "Rejoice in the Lord always; again I will say, Rejoice." What wonderful Christian wisdom! This contagious, conspicuous, continuous joy should be the mark of every believer.

But you might be saying to yourself, "Well, I'm a believer, but I don't always feel joyful. My life's in chaos right now. How on earth do I rejoice in the Lord?"

Pay attention to the key phrase that the apostle Paul uses over and over again in the book of Philippians: in the Lord.

Now, why should that bring you joy? Because, if you're a believer, you are in Christ. And in Christ, there is security, there is strength, and there is peace. As a follower of Christ, you should find your joy in Him… not in your circumstances.

Now, I'm not talking about putting on a plastic smile and pretending to be happy or being superficial and phony. I'm talking about a joy deep within us that can't help but come out. It's what Chuck Swindoll calls "outrageous joy."

Wouldn't you love for the joy of the Lord to be so strong in you that it could be called outrageous?

Keep in mind that Satan knows there is joy in the Lord, and he diligently tries to steal it from you. He wants to rob you of that joy through disappointments, defeat, or discouragement. He wants to make you weak and vulnerable, because it's our joy in the Lord that keeps us strong and draws others to Christ!

Jesus is the source of all joy. So when your circumstances don't make you feel all that joyful, rejoice in the Lord. Praise Him, because when you exalt Christ in your life, you will find true joy.

**LOOK BEYOND YOUR CIRCUMSTANCES TODAY
AND REJOICE BECAUSE OF THE HOPE
YOU HAVE IN CHRIST.**

Day 314

Do not be anxious about anything, but in everything by prayer and supplication with thanksgiving let your requests be made known to God.

—Philippians 4:6

What do you worry about? Money? Your job? Your family?

If you worry, our Scripture verse today offers some good advice. "Do not be anxious about anything, but in everything by prayer and supplication with thanksgiving let your requests be made known to God."

You know, if you think about it, worry really is useless. It has never solved a problem, never dried a tear, and never changed anything.

And most of us spend most of our time worrying about things that will never happen or circumstances we can't change anyway! Worry saps your strength, destroys your spirit, and robs you of the joy in life. It takes its toll physically, emotionally, and spiritually.

Someone once said, "Worry is assuming responsibility that God never intended for you to have."

Yet it seems so much easier to worry about things instead of sharing those concerns with God. But that's exactly what He wants you to do! He wants you to offer your concerns up to Him in prayer.

Today, I want to encourage you to stop worrying about your future, because God's got your future! Don't worry about your life, because He has your life! Don't worry about anything, but rather, pray about everything! There's nothing too great for God. There's no problem too hard for God to solve and there is no problem too small for God.

Take comfort in His promises, like the promise in Philippians 4:19, which says, "And my God will supply every need of yours according to his riches in glory in Christ Jesus."

Pray confidently… and ask, seek, and knock continually. Because only in trusting God will you find peace!

IF YOU HAVE A WORRY OR NEED IN YOUR LIFE, DON'T WAIT! GIVE IT TO GOD RIGHT NOW THROUGH PRAYER.

Day 315

And my God will supply every need of yours according to his riches in glory in Christ Jesus.

—Philippians 4:19

O ur Scripture for today is so important. Because there are so many believers who are missing out being a blessing because they're so absorbed with trying to meet their own needs!

For example, how many people do you know who, instead of trusting God to meet their needs, go out and buy what they think they need... only to go into debt doing it?! Then, saddled with that debt, they can't be a blessing to others!

Can you relate? Are you missing out on being a blessing?

Well, you can change that! Begin trusting God, wait on Him, and just see if He will show you how He's going to supply what you need!

You'll never experience the power of God to meet your needs if you don't trust Him for what He can do. God's strength, grace, and power are available to you. Like Paul says in Philippians 4:13, "I can do all things through him who strengthens me."

God knows what you need even before you ask for it. When you pray, asking for God's provision, you put yourself in the position to receive from God all that He wants to give you. When you pray expectantly, you can pray confidently that you will receive from God what He desires to give you!

Today I want to challenge you to elevate your expectations of God. Believe Him for great things in your life. When you do, you will begin to see how your life can indeed become a blessing to others.

BEGIN TODAY AND EVERY DAY IN WORSHIP AND ASK FOR GOD'S PROVISION IN YOUR LIFE.

And you Philippians yourselves know that in the beginning of the gospel, when I left Macedonia, no church entered into partnership with me in giving and receiving, except you only.

—Philippians 4:15

The people that Paul wrote to in our Scripture today weren't rich. As a matter of fact, the apostle says these compassionate Christians gave out of their poverty so that his needs would be met.

But they were doing so much more than just meeting his needs. They were making a spiritual investment!

In the same way today, when you give to the work of the Lord, you too make a spiritual investment. Not a contribution, but an investment in something that will truly last.

Here's something to think about: If God doesn't really need your money, why should you give? Because He wants you to be a part of His redemptive work in the world today! When you give, your focus is on others and on His Kingdom work. And He knows that when your focus is on you, life gets very, very small.

Even if you think you don't have very much to give, look around! Do you have time? Then plant the seed of time. Even the smallest investment in others can make such a difference.

Remember this: The Philippian believers were not a rich people, but they were rich towards God and they sowed into the life and ministry of the apostle Paul. They gave—and God blessed them as a result!

TAKE INVENTORY OF WHAT YOU CAN INVEST SPIRITUALLY TODAY. YOU HAVE MORE TO OFFER THAN YOU THINK!

Day 317

And now, little children, abide in him, so that when he appears we may have confidence and not shrink from him in shame at his coming.

—1 John 2:28

The Scripture verse for today urges you and me to "abide" in Christ until His return. What does this mean? Part of what it means is to spend time in God's Word.

You know, one of the best habits we can have as believers is to memorize the Word of God and then make it our own. For example, if you find yourself worrying, remember Matthew 6:33, which says to seek first His Kingdom, and all these things will be added to you.

Or if you have an important decision to make, you might recall Proverbs 3:5-6, which says, "Trust in the LORD with all your heart, and do not lean on your own understanding. In all your ways acknowledge him, and he will make straight your paths."

Once you have memorized a verse, you can use it when you have a crisis or a need. You can recall it for strength and direction.

Remember too that abiding in God's Word is so much more than just reading the Bible here and there. It means really taking the time to study God's Word… to comprehend it and to meditate on it.

Make a commitment to spend time in His Word, and to make that a consistent habit. And strive to conform to God's Word, to know Him intimately, and to abide in Him each day… so you can be ready for His return!

HAVE YOU SPENT TIME STUDYING AND MEDITATING ON GOD'S WORD TODAY?

Day 318

See what kind of love the Father has given us, that we should be called children of God; and so we are. The reason why the world does not know us is that it did not know him.

—1 John 3:1

If you're a child of God, there are four things about the love of God that I'd like to remind you of today.

First, God loves you. Think about it: God… loves… you. He loves you more than anyone else could ever love you.

Second, God's love for you is eternal. In the Scripture, Jeremiah 31:3 says God loves you with an everlasting love. Time cannot erase it. God loves you and He will always love you.

Third, God's love for you is unconditional. This concept is hard to completely understand at times because of how conditional human love can be. Sometimes human love is dependent on how we feel about someone… or it's dependent upon someone loving us in return. But God's love is unconditional. Nothing you do or don't do can alter it.

Lastly, God's love is incomprehensible! It's immeasurable. I love the words of the old hymn that describe the love of God:

> "Could we with ink the ocean fill,
> And were the skies of parchment made,
> Were every stalk on earth a quill,
> And every man a scribe by trade;
> To write the love of God above
> Would drain the ocean dry;
> Nor could the scroll contain the whole,
> Though stretched from sky to sky."

And what's most wonderful about God's love is that in spite of your sin and my sin… despite our failure and brokenness and worthlessness… He reached down and showed us His love by sending His Son to die in our place on the cross.

It's my prayer that you'll remember just how much God loves you today… and that as a result, you'll be motivated to share God's love with others.

TELL SOMEONE TODAY ABOUT GOD'S LOVE FOR THEM!

Day 319

Little children, you are from God and have overcome them, for he who is in you is greater than he who is in the world.

—1 John 4:4

I want to share something with you that Satan doesn't want you to know: As a follower of Christ, you are victorious!

Yes, you have a very real and very deadly enemy. Yes, you're engaged in a spiritual battle with him every single day. But, you are victorious in Jesus Christ! According to our Scripture today, the battle is already won.

As believers, we fight from a position of strength, not from a position of weakness. We fight from victory... not for victory. When Jesus cried out "It is finished!" Satan was finished. And because of the cross, we have victory in Jesus.

When we came into the Kingdom of God, we were not only transformed, we were translated from the kingdom of darkness into the glorious Kingdom of God. We were born again into the family of God as His children. And because we're children of God, we are joint heirs with the Lord Jesus Christ. That means everything is ours because of Him!

You and I have been born into the family of God, and now the risen, resurrected Redeemer is living in us. The Holy Spirit has taken up residence in our lives and as a result, "he who is in you is greater than he who is in the world."

That is our victory in Jesus and that's why we can say we fight, not for victory, but from victory, from the strongest possible position of strength! According to God's Word, through Jesus Christ we are invincible against the attacks of the enemy... invincible.

For the Scripture says in 1 John 2:17, "Whoever does the will of God abides forever."

I want to leave you with one last thought today: Satan may frighten you, but he cannot hurt you. Because as God's child, you are in His omnipotent grip!

As it says in 2 Corinthians 4:8-9, "We are afflicted in every way, but not crushed; perplexed, but not driven to despair; persecuted, but not forsaken; struck down, but not destroyed"!!

It's my prayer that the Lord Jesus would encourage you with these words no matter what you may be going though today!

FACE THE CHALLENGES OF TODAY KNOWING THAT YOU ARE VICTORIOUS IN CHRIST!

Day 320

In this the love of God was made manifest among us, that God sent his only Son into the world, so that we might live through him.

—1 John 4:4

Jesus came to earth for one reason: to save YOU!

He came to be the Savior of your heart and mine. And why do you and I need a Savior? Because we've all sinned and we're all lost!

Now, I know this isn't a popular idea for our culture today. No one really wants to hear that they're a sinner, much less that they're lost on their own. We all want to believe that we're self-sufficient.

But that's not what the Bible tells us. In fact, if I could reduce the message of the entire Bible down to two words it would simply be, "Jesus saves." The Father sent the Son to be the Savior of the world. This was promised and provided in Christ only.

The Scripture says in Acts 4:12, "And there is salvation in no one else, for there is no other name under heaven given among men by which we must be saved."

And this salvation includes everyone. No one is excluded! Jesus didn't just die for a select few. He died for you and He died for me. Jesus came to be the Savior of the world and God's desire is that every man, woman, boy, and girl be saved. God is not willing that any should perish, but that all should come to repentance.

Romans 10:9 says, "If you confess with your mouth that Jesus is Lord and believe in your heart that God raised him from the dead, you will be saved."

It's that simple! So I encourage you… if you've never said those words and meant them… that you would do so today.

It will be the best decision you'll ever make!

**JESUS CAME TO EARTH FOR ONE REASON:
TO SAVE YOU!**

Day 321

And this is the confidence that we have toward him, that if we ask anything according to his will he hears us.

—1 John 5:14

You and I know that prayer changes things. It's a clear promise from Scripture.

But did you know that prayer also changes you and me? It changes our priorities, and it gets our lives in sync with God's plan.

There's a great formula for prayer I learned from my fellow pastor and friend, Dr. Ed Young from Houston. It's the acronym SELF:

> **S stands for surrender**. Each day, you and I must surrender our lives to the Lord. We must say, "Lord, I report for duty. I give You my life today. I am Your child and I want to be in Your will today."

> **E stands for empty**. Once you surrender your life to Christ each day, you must empty yourself of self and sin and any thing else that would keep you from fulfilling God's plan and purpose for your life.

> You must say, "Lord, I empty all my unresolved conflicts and issues. I want to get rid of everything that would keep me from connecting with You today."

> **L stands for lift**. Once you surrender your life to the Lord Jesus and empty yourself of everything that would hinder your relationship with Him, you must lift your heart in praise, petition, and thanksgiving.

> **F stands for fill**. This is when you ask God to fill you with His Holy Spirit so that you will live in the fullness of His power and His blessing.

So SELF is surrendering, it is emptying, it is lifting, and it is filling. And if you do theses things in prayer every day, not only is your relationship with Christ going to be that much sweeter, you'll make an eternal impact on the world for Jesus Christ!

**DURING YOUR PRAYER TIME TODAY,
GO THROUGH THE STEPS FOR "SELF."**

Day 322

"Are not two sparrows sold for a penny? And not one of them will fall to the ground apart from your Father."

—Matthew 10:29

In today's Scripture verse, Jesus tells us that not even a sparrow falls to the ground apart from God's knowledge. And if God cares about a sparrow, don't you think He cares about you as a believer?

Well, He does. It's an amazing thought that the God who made the stars and calls them all by name is the same God who knows the number of hairs on your head!

Not only does He know the number of hairs on your head, He knows your name. Your name is recorded in God's infinite mind and heart!

God knows you. He knows your past as well as your future. And the thing He knows better than anyone else is your heart.

Now, that might strike terror into your life at times when you realize that God sees the worst about you! But what's so wonderful is that even though God knows the worst about you… He loves you anyway!

Perhaps today you feel a little like you've let God down somehow. Perhaps you feel ashamed of something from your past… a failure that you can't seem to get over.

If so, remember that with Jesus, no failure is final. The Lord can restore you! God knows your heart. He knows all about you. He knows what you need… and He wants to meet you at the point of your need today. Will you let Him?

REJOICE IN THE FACT THAT GOD KNOWS YOU BETTER THAN ANYONE… AND LOVES YOU MORE THAN ANYONE!

Day 323

In the year that King Uzziah died I saw the Lord sitting upon a throne, high and lifted up; and the train of his robe filled the temple.

—Isaiah 6:1

Are you worried about the future… about our nation… about our leaders? You're not alone. According to today's Scripture, Isaiah and the rest of the Israelites were deeply troubled because their earthly king was dead. They were grieved… and they were concerned about the future.

But God gave Isaiah a vision of His glory and holiness. This prophet of the Lord describes how he saw Him "sitting upon a throne, high and lifted up." Isaiah saw the Lord sitting on the throne of the universe.

When Isaiah entered into the presence of the Lord, he realized that there was a greater One than any earthly king sitting upon the throne of the universe. His name is holy God, the Lord of Hosts!

Like the Israelites, it's easy to worry about the future… and wonder what's gone wrong and what will happen next in our world.

But as believers in the Lord Jesus, we don't have to wonder! We don't have to wring our hands worrying because we know that our God is sitting on the throne of the universe.

Remember that there is no panic in heaven… only plans. God never walks up and down the streets of heaven wondering about what He's going to do next.

So no matter what's going on in your world… no matter how out-of-control things may seem… remember that God is still on His throne!

Today, it's my prayer that you will get your mind off the earthly and temporary and fix your eye of faith on your Lord and Savior, Jesus Christ, who is gloriously reigning and ruling upon the throne of this universe!

TODAY, THANK GOD THAT HE IS STILL ON HIS THRONE!

Day 324

For I am sure that neither death nor life, nor angels nor rulers, nor things present nor things to come, nor powers, nor height nor depth, nor anything else in all creation, will be able to separate us from the love of God in Christ Jesus our Lord.

—Romans 8:38-39

I s there anything you can do to keep God from loving you? You can find the answer in today's passage. But the parable of the prodigal son is one of the most dramatic pictures of God's love in all the Scripture.

I love how Luke 15:20 says, "And he arose and came to his father. But while he was still a long way off, his father saw him and felt compassion, and ran and embraced him and kissed him."

What a picture of God Almighty! What a picture of God the Father! I like the way Phillips translates the last phrase of that verse. It says, "His father's heart went out to him while he was yet a long way off."

This is not a father who can't wait to punish his sinful son. This is not a father who has written his boy off as wasted and worthless. This is a loving, caring father who cannot wait to embrace his son and to welcome him home! So the father leaves the house and runs down the road to meet his son and to embrace him and bring him in.

What I hope you see here is a picture of God the Father's love for you. It's an aggressive love… a love that's eager and excessive. His love is approachable. And His love is abundant.

The prodigal son's father didn't hold back his emotions toward his child. And neither does God ever withhold His love from you!

REJOICE IN GOD'S LOVE FOR YOU!
THEN SHARE IT WITH SOMEONE ELSE TODAY.

He who calls you is faithful; he will surely do it.

—1 Thessalonians 5:24

Maybe someone has let you down recently. Or maybe you've let yourself down. Take heart! God is faithful. He will do what He says He will do.

And not only is God faithful and reliable, but He is committed to your spiritual growth and maturity. First Thessalonians 5:23-24 says, "Now may the God of peace himself sanctify you completely, and may your whole spirit and soul and body be kept blameless at the coming of our Lord Jesus Christ. He who calls you is faithful; he will surely do it."

I love that! Because it promises you and me that God is constantly working on us… creatively, constructively, and continually. The Spirit of God is working in your body and in your soul. And His purpose is to make you more like Him!

Remember when you were a teenager and you couldn't wait to grow up? That's how we feel sometimes as Christians. When will we ever grow up? When will we ever be responsible in the Christian life? When will we ever be obedient in the Christian life? It's so easy to become frustrated with ourselves!

But we need to remember that God is patient… and that God is persevering. And according to Philippians 1:6, "he who began a good work in you will bring it to completion at the day of Jesus Christ."

And when God gets through with you, you're going to stand complete, perfect in the glory of Jesus Christ. You shall arise in His likeness. You will be like Jesus. That's God's goal in your life and mine… and He will be faithful to perform it!

**ARE YOU TRYING TO STAND ON YOUR OWN TODAY?
OR ARE YOU DEPENDING ON GOD?**

Day 326

The heavens declare the glory of God, and the sky above proclaims his handiwork. Day to day pours out speech, and night to night reveals knowledge. There is no speech, nor are there words, whose voice is not heard. Their voice goes out through all the earth, and their words to the end of the world.

—Psalm 19:1-4

In our society of cell phones and text messages, communication with each other seems easier than ever. But how does God speak to you?

God speaks to us today the same as He always has… in the skies… through His creation. We can know God… we can see the light of God… by simply looking up at the sky.

The Greek word for "man" in the ancient world and in your New Testament is "anthropos," which means "the upper-looking one." Animals look down, but God created man to look up into the heavens to see His glory and to experience His power in creation. God speaks to us in the starry skies!

Indeed, the heavens declare the glory of God. As the psalmist says, "Day to day pours out speech, and night to night reveals knowledge."

Creation is constantly, continually, and eternally speaking. And when we look into the creation, we know that because there is a creation, there must be a creator!

Now, you may not be a morning person, but I'd encourage you… if you want to catch a glorious glimpse of your Creator… get up early one morning this week to watch the sun rise.

I can assure you, seeing His handiwork in creation will speak words of encouragement to your soul!

TAKE A WALK OUTSIDE AND REDISCOVER THE GLORY OF GOD'S HANDIWORK.

Day 327

Heaven and earth will pass away, but my words will not pass away.

—Luke 21:33

Does the Bible still have relevance for your life today? You bet!

According to our Scripture verse today, not one jot, one tittle, one mark, one abbreviation point... not one word will pass away!

God's Word is infallible. In all that it teaches and all it affirms, it is correct and right and perfect for any time period. And the Word of God is inerrant. There are no errors in the Scripture. Can you imagine a perfect, pure God breathing out error? Certainly not! God's Word is accurate!

So when you deny the authority of Scripture, you deny the authority of God. It's as simple as that. And in effect, when you deny the authority of Scripture, you deny the work of the Holy Spirit in giving us the Scriptures and you even defame the deity of Jesus Christ, who is described in the Bible as the incarnate Word of God. His very name is the Word of God!

You see, the Word of God and the God of the Word are inseparable. You cannot separate God from His Word. Even Jesus came believing and teaching and preaching the Word of God, affirming the Old Testament and proclaiming the new and the living way of salvation.

That's why you can trust the Bible through and through for your life today. From the very beginning of Genesis when God created the heavens and the earth until the closing chapters of the Revelation, we have the Word of God... consistent, clear, and concise... telling us how to go to heaven, how to know Jesus Christ, how to experience eternal life, how to know and worship God.

This is the Word of God! And you can trust it as your ultimate authority of life and truth for today.

**READ GOD'S WORD TODAY WITH ASSURANCE
IN ITS POWER AND AUTHORITY!**

Day 328

For I know the plans I have for you, declares the LORD, plans for welfare and not for evil, to give you a future and a hope.

—Jeremiah 29:11

God loves you and has a wonderful plan for your life. God has something significant that He wants to do in and through you. Do you really believe that today?

Despite what our culture says, you're not here by accident. You're here by divine Providence... and God has a plan and purpose for you. According to our verse for today, God has something significant for all of us to do... and that includes you.

Consider the story of Joseph in the Old Testament. The Scripture says that God gave Joseph great success. But beyond success, there's significance... which is something more important that Joseph had. He also had vision, courage, determination, character, ability, and perseverance—all the qualities of a leader.

Yet there is one quality that stands out in this great man's life. It's the quality of faith. Joseph trusted God throughout all of his days... in good times as well as bad times. And that faith is what gave Joseph significance!

In spite of the obstacles, against all the odds, this man persevered by faith. He started over many times in his life. He faced circumstances that would have defeated the average, ordinary individual. And yet regardless of the difficulties, he kept believing God. He kept following his Lord. He kept trusting his Master.

Why? Because Joseph believed that God had a plan for his life, and he was determined to discover his destiny. I mean, think about it: Joseph was despised and rejected by his own dysfunctional family. He was kidnapped and left for dead. He was sold as a slave. He was falsely accused and imprisoned. He was used and abused. He was failed and forgotten. And yet by faith he carried on.

And I want to encourage you to carry on by faith as well. Whether you're in good times or bad times right now, God has a perfect plan for your life.

**TRUST IN GOD'S PROMISE THAT YOU HAVE
TRUE SIGNIFICANCE IN HIM.**

And we know that for those who love God all things work together for good, for those who are called according to his purpose.

—Romans 8:28

Are you struggling today? If so, remember that in the midst of any storm, it's easy to forget that God's in control. It may not feel like it, but as a child of God, He's always in control, taking care of you.

As a follower of Christ, you are the object of God's persevering grace in your life. I'm talking about every step you take. All your hopes, your hurts, and your hallelujahs are being worked out together according to God's perfect plan for your life.

Our Scripture today is a glorious promise of God's power and concern for your life. "All things work together for good, for those who are called according to his purpose." What a comfort!

So today, if your dreams have been shattered, if your hopes have been dashed, or even if something you prayed for has been taken away, I want to remind you of two things.

First, don't demand to understand. You can't always understand. And just because it doesn't make sense now, doesn't mean that it doesn't make sense. God has a plan and a purpose.

Second, don't bow to bitterness. Some people break when their dreams are dashed. Then bitterness sets in and they spend the rest of their days in the sorrow of a long distant past.

Romans 8:31 says, "If God is for us, who can be against us?" Remember, no matter what you're going through in your life, no matter how much turmoil you're in today or tomorrow, no matter how deep the pit is you may be living in, God is for you.

And He's constantly working in your life—constructively and creatively—to bring about His purpose and the divine destiny of your life.

Stand on this promise today!

ALL YOUR HOPES, YOUR HURTS, AND YOUR HALLELUJAHS ARE BEING WORKED OUT TOGETHER ACCORDING TO GOD'S PERFECT PLAN FOR YOUR LIFE.

Day 330

Fear not, for I am with you; be not dismayed, for I am your God; I will strengthen you, I will help you, I will uphold you with my righteous right hand.

—Isaiah 41:10

Perhaps today, you are looking at your life and asking, "How did I get here?" Maybe life hasn't turned out the way you planned. Or maybe you're enslaved to your past and you wonder, "What do I do now?"

If this describes you or someone you love today, I want to remind you that God always preserves His own. Remember Joseph's many trials and challenges in the Old Testament? In Genesis 39:2, we read, "The LORD was with Joseph." Now, remember—Joseph wasn't preserved from his circumstances. He was preserved in and through his circumstances.

The fact is we can't change our circumstances. We can't control what happens to us at all times. But you know what? We can change how we respond to the circumstances of life. And that attitude is what God expects us to work on.

You know, God often allows circumstances and winds to blow against us in order to knock the rough edges off of our lives. Kind of like how sandpaper knocks the rough edges off of wood. God uses the circumstances of our lives in order to polish us and make us more like the Master.

For example, perhaps God had to deal with Joseph's pride and ego before He could ultimately use him for His glory. So God allowed him to be sold into slavery and sent into Egypt. But remember this: While Joseph left his father back in Canaan, his heavenly Father went with him to Egypt.

If you find yourself in a difficult circumstance that you never imagined or never dreamed of, claim the promise from the Lord found in today's Scripture: "Fear not, for I am with you; be not dismayed, for I am your God; I will strengthen you, I will help you, I will uphold you with my righteous right hand."

When you claim that promise, you can be joyful in any circumstance, knowing that God is protecting you, preserving you, and holding His hand upon you.

YOU CAN'T ALWAYS CONTROL WHAT HAPPENS TO YOU, BUT YOU CAN ALWAYS CONTROL HOW YOU RESPOND.

Day 331

Therefore let anyone who thinks that he stands take heed lest he fall.

—1 Corinthians 10:12

I f you think you are above sexual sin... look out!

As Christians, each of us must recognize our potential for moral and sexual failure. Now perhaps you'd say, "Pastor, I don't know about you, but I'd never cheat on my wife." Or, "I'd never be unfaithful to my husband."

As our verse for today says, no one is above sexual sin. That's why Jesus tells us in Mark 14:38, "Watch and pray that you may not enter into temptation. The spirit indeed is willing, but the flesh is weak."

I mean, think about it. The Scripture calls David a man after God's own heart... something that wouldn't be said of very many of us today. Yet even David yielded to the temptation of sexual sin. He knew God, he walked with God, he had been exalted by God to a position of great spiritual responsibility. And yet, even David failed!

I don't care who you are or what position of spiritual leadership you're in. Not ONE of us is exempt from the possibility of giving in to moral impurity if we fail to guard our hearts. That's why Proverbs 4:23 says, "Keep [or guard] your heart with all vigilance, for from it flow the springs of life." You always have to be on guard!

What I hear again and again from couples who've found themselves in the fracture of infidelity is, "I never dreamed this would happen to me. I never planned it. I never envisioned it. I never even thought about it, that I'm aware of. I can't believe this actually happened to me... to us."

It can happen to you if you're not watchful and prayerful. So today, I encourage you to guard your heart by running from sin into the grace and mercy of the Lord Jesus Christ and by surrounding yourself with godly people who will keep you accountable.

**PRAY FOR GOD'S PROTECTION FROM
SEXUAL SIN IN YOUR LIFE.**

Day 332

When he was reviled, he did not revile in return; when he suffered, he did not threaten, but continued entrusting himself to him who judges justly.

—1 Peter 2:23

Want to know the difference between winners and losers? It's attitude!

Whatever the circumstance, your attitude helps determine whether you succeed or fail.

No, I'm not talking about just a Pollyanna-type, pie-in-the-sky kind of attitude. I'm talking about dealing with disappointment and disillusionment by trusting and having faith in God!

Romans 5:3-5 says, "Suffering produces endurance, and endurance produces character, and character produces hope, and hope does not put us to shame, because God's love has been poured into our hearts through the Holy Spirit who has been given to us."

So the way to keep from being disappointed in life is to allow God to build your character. And if you want God to build your character, you have to learn to deal with the problems and the disappointments of life with a good attitude.

Here are three tiny, but valuable words that will help you: Let…it… go. Let it go! It might even be a good idea to write these words on a Post-it note and stick it to the mirror in your bathroom or on the dashboard of your car.

Rather than living in and grinding on the injustices in this life, turn loose and let it go. According to our Scripture verse for today, that's what Jesus did.

Follow His example. Don't seek revenge. Let God take care of those who mistreat you. Because He'll do a much better job than you can!

**ASK GOD TO HELP YOU LET GO
OF A PAIN FROM YOUR PAST TODAY.**

Day 333

And I am sure of this, that he who began a good work in you will bring it to completion at the day of Jesus Christ.

—Philippians 1:6

J ust as today's Bible verse says, you can be sure that God has good things planned for your life.

Not only are you and I to wait actively, patiently, and silently for God's best in our lives, we're to wait expectantly. We're to live in eager anticipation of what God is going to do next.

Don't ever say, "God, when are You going to start working in my life?" Because He already is working in your life. It's just a matter of believing it.

Now, the world says seeing is believing. But the Bible says believing is seeing. You and I can begin to see how God is working as we wait on Him and trust Him.

So often you and I want an explanation for what's going on in our lives. We ask God why. It's not wrong to ask God why. Jesus Himself asked God why on the cross. And there are times when we are to ask for wisdom and direction. God may choose to give us an answer.

But for the most part, the question is not why. It is how.

How are we going to respond to what God is doing in our lives? How are we going to respond to the circumstances of life? How are we going to allow God to work in us, forming our character?

You know, most Christians are like photographs, they develop best in the dark. And character is what we are in the dark.

You and I need to learn to look past our problems to see the promises of God today. When we do, we'll become the men and women that God has called us to be!

THANK GOD FOR HIS PLAN FOR YOUR LIFE, EVEN IF YOU DON'T KNOW WHAT IT IS YET!

Day 334

The steps of a man are established by the LORD, when he delights in his way.

—Psalm 37:23

Is there a way for you to live a life that's over the top? Yes!

First, you need to understand the "mode" you're living in now. Are you simply in survival mode, just getting by and trying to make it to Friday? Maybe you live in success mode, always striving for personal and financial achievement.

A better choice is to live in significance mode, knowing who you are in Christ and discovering His destiny for your life.

Sadly, most people live in survival or success mode. But living in significance mode is the only way to see God's plan for your life fulfilled before your very eyes.

Joseph of the Old Testament was a man of significance. Yet what gave his life significance? Purpose. Joseph was a man of purpose. And the person that God uses is someone who lives life with purpose.

God put a dream in Joseph's heart when he was a young man. And he never forgot God's dream for his life. Joseph would not let that dream die. He was driven by that dream and consumed by the call of God upon his life.

Because of this driving purpose, Joseph saw every problem as an opportunity for God to work in his life.

So let me ask you today, does an obstacle that you're facing seem bigger than God?

Remember that it's not! Nothing you face in life right now is bigger than God. Jesus tells us in Mark 10:27, "With man it is impossible, but not with God. For all things are possible with God."

People of purpose are not paralyzed by their problems. Because people of purpose who know the Lord Jesus Christ, know there's no panic in heaven… only plans!

REMEMBER THAT GOD IS BIGGER THAN ANY OBSTACLE YOU'RE FACING RIGHT NOW.

Day 335

Be kind to one another, tenderhearted, forgiving one another, as God in Christ forgave you.

—Ephesians 4:32

Do you have any bitterness in your life today? Are you harboring any negative feelings, animosity, or even hatred towards another person?

Perhaps you have been hurt greatly. Perhaps you were sexually, physically, or verbally abused as a child. Maybe you've been devastated by rejection in a relationship. Perhaps you've been unsuccessful in school or in your current career. I know that every one of us faces hurt and rejection in life.

But I also know that Satan laughs when there's a conflict that's caused by bitterness. Why does he laugh? Because he knows that a spirit of bitterness gives him a foothold in your life, which will make you unable to pray, unable to witness, and unable to serve God effectively.

You say, "Well, Pastor, you don't understand how much I've been hurt. You don't know how deeply I've been wounded. You don't know my story." And you know what? You're right. I don't.

But I do know what happened to Jesus when He was taken into the hands of cruel and violent men. He was handed over to Roman soldiers who saw Him as nothing but a piece of flesh to be executed. They beat Him, mocked Him, pulled out His beard, spat in His face, and they nailed Him to a cross.

And yet Jesus said, "Father, forgive them, for they know not what they do" (Luke 23:34).

That's what Christ has done for you! And as a believer, the Spirit of Christ lives within you, enabling you by His power to respond to others with forgiveness.

You know, if you will ask God to take away your bitterness, He'll do it. He will bring you to a place in your life where His grace and peace replaces the animosity, hurt, and anger that you feel.

**PRAY AND ASK GOD FOR THE COURAGE TO
FORGIVE A PERSON WHO HAS HURT YOU DEEPLY.**

Day 336

I came that they may have life and have it abundantly.

—John 10:10

Jesus loves you! That's one of the first phrases children learn in Sunday school. But the full impact of it can be hard to grasp. He came to give you life!

As our Lord Jesus Christ says in the verse for today, "I came that they may have life and have it abundantly."

It's been said that Jesus will not only add years to your life, but life to your years. The cross of the Lord Jesus Christ is God's plus-sign to the world to say, "I love you and I've come to give you this abundant, overwhelmingly good life."

Some people think if they give their life to Jesus Christ, He's going to take away all those things that they enjoy.

But remember, the only thing God asks you to give up are those things that harm and hurt you. Psalm 84:11 promises us, "For the Lord God is a sun and shield; the LORD bestows favor and honor. No good thing does he withhold from those who walk uprightly."

You know, we don't deserve and we didn't earn the favor and the love of the Father. But by His mercy and grace, and because of His great love, He sent us His Son to die in our place on the cross.

And through Christ, we have everything we need as believers! So why should we ever be disappointed? Why should we be discouraged? Why should we be distressed? Who minds the journey if the journey leads home?

The old hymn says, "Tis so sweet to trust in Jesus." And how sweet it is to be loved unconditionally and to be provided for now and for eternity!

**GIVE THANKS TODAY FOR THE
UNCONDITIONAL LOVE OF JESUS CHRIST.**

Day 337

I appeal to you therefore, brothers, by the mercies of God, to present your bodies as a living sacrifice, holy and acceptable to God, which is your spiritual worship.

—Romans 12:1

You may not realize it, but we all worship something.

Why? Because God made us that way. He designed us to worship, but not to worship just anything. He hardwired us to worship Him!

Solomon tells us in Ecclesiastes chapter 3 that God "has put eternity into man's heart." We're made for beyond the here and now. We're made to experience and enjoy the living presence of our God today and every day.

And how do you experience the presence of God in your life today? Paul tells us in today's verse to "present your bodies as a living sacrifice, holy and acceptable to God, which is your spiritual worship."

Worship is so much more than the songs you sing in church—although praising God in song is vitally important.

Remember those two men who walked with the risen Christ along the road to Emmaus? They didn't recognize Him at first. But after they had experienced His presence and realized that they had been with the living Lord, they said, "Did not our hearts burn within us while he talked to us on the road?"

You see, that is worship! Worship is giving yourself to God each step of the way, every day. It's surrendering yourself to the Lord in every area of your life.

Can you truly say that you're surrendered to the Lord in every area of your life? In your thought life? In your work life? In your family life?

It's my prayer that you will learn what it means to become a dynamic worshiper of the Lord Jesus Christ by giving yourself as a living sacrifice. When you do, you will experience His power and His presence in your life each day.

CAN YOU TRULY SAY THAT YOU'RE SURRENDERED TO THE LORD IN EVERY AREA OF YOUR LIFE?

Day 338

All Scripture is breathed out by God and profitable for teaching, for reproof, for correction, and for training in righteousness.

—2 Timothy 3:16

In Ephesians 6:10-12, the apostle Paul reminds us that you and I are in a daily battle against evil.

He says, "Finally, be strong in the Lord and in the strength of his might. Put on the whole armor of God, that you may be able to stand against the schemes of the devil. For we do not wrestle against flesh and blood, but against the rulers, against the authorities, against the cosmic powers over this present darkness, against the spiritual forces of evil in the heavenly places."

Putting on the "armor of God" includes taking up the sword of the Spirit, which is the Word of God. Becoming a fully committed follower of the Lord Jesus Christ begins by picking up your sword each day!

As we see in today's verse, the Bible is not a human book. It's a God-given book! And it is sufficient for your every need.

That's why I want to encourage you to have a daily time of devotion and discipline where you open God's Word and ask God to speak to you through the Scriptures.

I want to also encourage you to take your Bible with you when you gather with other believers in worship. And take a pen with you so you can underline or highlight some Scriptures, take a few notes, and really engage.

Taking up the sword of the Spirit each day is the only way you'll be strong in the Lord and in the power of His might, able to withstand the attacks of our enemy, the devil.

It's the only way you'll be able to stand strong in the spiritual battle you face every day!

HAVE YOU SPENT TIME IN GOD'S WORD TODAY? IF NOT, TAKE SOME TIME, ASKING HIM TO SPEAK TO YOU THROUGH THE SCRIPTURES.

Behold, I am doing a new thing; now it springs forth, do you not perceive it? I will make a way in the wilderness and rivers in the desert.

—Isaiah 43:19

It's easy to get in a rut at times.

In fact, maybe today, you find yourself in a rut in your own life. Maybe you're in a place where you're thinking, "Well, this is as good as it gets." And perhaps you've settled for mediocrity. Mediocrity in your marriage, mediocrity with your children, mediocrity in your career.

But God has so much more for you! He wants to do supernatural things in you, things you could never imagine.

Think about what God tells us in our Scripture for today: "Behold, I am doing a new thing; now it springs forth, do you not perceive it? I will make a way in the wilderness and rivers in the desert."

In other words, God is saying, "Look! Can't you see it? Can't you taste it? Can't you feel this new thing that I'm doing?"

God takes barren places and barren people and uses them for His glory when He does the brand new thing in their lives. And God wants to do something new in you.

Do you believe that God can do greater things in your own life, right now, than you ever imagined possible? I believe God can and will do what you believe He can do.

Now, you say, "That's impossible!" Let me remind you what the Scripture says in Romans 8:31, "If God is for us, who can be against us?"

If you're a child of God, He is for you. So don't doubt that He wants to do great things in your life!

**GOD WANTS TO DO SOMETHING NEW IN YOU.
ARE YOU WILLING?**

What does the LORD your God require of you, but to fear the LORD your God, to walk in all his ways, to love him, to serve the LORD your God with all your heart and with all your soul.

—Deuteronomy 10:12

Are you making a living, or are you making a life? God has called you not to just take up space in this world, but to make our world a better place in which to live.

Yes, God wants you to make a difference.

And the people God uses to make a difference in this world are people who are vulnerable to Him, who are dependent on Him, and who are available to Him. If you seek a courageous faith and ask God to give you a compassionate heart, then anything is possible.

I believe it's time to make an impact on this generation and the coming generations for Christ. It's time for us to fulfill our calling before He comes again. It's time for God's Church to rise up and shake off the past and shake the world for Christ.

It's time for God to do a brand new thing in the hearts of His people. And that means you!

Someone put it this way: "A zealous man in religion is preeminently a man of one thing. It is not enough to say he is earnest, hardy, uncompromising, thoroughgoing, wholehearted, firm in spirit. He only sees one thing. He cares for one thing. He lives for one thing. He is swallowed up in one thing. And that one thing is to please God."

Let that be the passion and the prayer of our hearts and of our lives! God is looking for men and women who have a heart for Him… men and women who want to take their lives to the next level, who want to live beyond all limits.

That's my prayer for you and me today. That we will want to move out of the maze of mediocrity in our lives and live for something bigger than ourselves. That we will move out of our comfort zones into the life God has called us to live!

THE PEOPLE GOD USES TO MAKE A DIFFERENCE IN THIS WORLD ARE PEOPLE WHO ARE VULNERABLE TO HIM, WHO ARE DEPENDENT ON HIM, AND WHO ARE AVAILABLE TO HIM.

Day 341

I rejoice, because I have perfect confidence in you.
—2 Corinthians 7:16

More than likely, you'd like to pray with more confidence.

If so, remember that to pray with confidence, we must pray with concern, we must pray with confession, and we must pray with conviction.

What does it mean to pray with conviction? In Nehemiah 1:5-6, Nehemiah prays, "O LORD God of heaven, the great and awesome God who keeps covenant and steadfast love with those who love him and keep his commandments, let your ear be attentive and your eyes open, to hear the prayer of your servant...."

In this passage, Nehemiah is praying with conviction because he knows that his God is in control.

When it seemed like everything was out of control in Jerusalem, Nehemiah knew that God was still on His throne. Nehemiah knew that the Lord would answer his prayer because He was a great and awesome God. Because He was a wonderful God. Because He was a faithful God. Because He was a God who could meet all of Nehemiah's needs.

And in just the same way, God can handle any problem in your life. Do you believe that today?

God is bigger and greater than any situation or crisis in your life. And the first thing Nehemiah did is the first thing that you ought to do when you have a problem, a crisis, or a need: You need to turn it over to God. You need to give it to God, not as your last chance, but as your first choice!

When you know God's place, you can find your place in the work of Jesus Christ. When you know that God is above all and that He has everything under control... and when you know that your place is surrendered under the lordship of Christ, then you can find your place and know your prayers will be answered!

GOD *CAN* HANDLE ANY PROBLEM IN YOUR LIFE. DO YOU BELIEVE THAT TODAY?

Day 342

Trust in the LORD with all your heart, and do not lean on your own understanding. In all your ways acknowledge him, and he will make straight your paths.

—Proverbs 3:5-6

Do you think of yourself as a leader? If you think you could never lead anyone, let me remind you about Nehemiah in the Old Testament.

Nehemiah was one of the great leaders of the Bible. Yet he wasn't a prophet. He wasn't a priest. He wasn't even a preacher!

Nehemiah described himself as a cupbearer to the king. He was just a guy who worked hard and had risen to some prominence in his day and time. Nehemiah was just a man, but he was a man who God raised up!

There were some steps Nehemiah took that insured his success, steps that made him a very effective leader. They're the same steps you can take as a follower of Christ to ensure you're an effective leader in your sphere of influence as well.

Step number one is to pray fervently. We see this trait over and over again in the life of Nehemiah. He was a man of prayer. Real leaders understand that opportunity swings on the hinges of prayer.

Step number two is to proceed confidently and courageously. You accomplish this by living what today's verse says: "Trust in the LORD with all your heart, and do not lean on your own understanding. In all your ways acknowledge him, and he will make straight your paths."

Step number three to being an effective leader is to plan wisely. Too often we have an idea or dream and we just blindly go for it rather than taking time to plan. But there's a beautiful balance here. There's the divine side of praying and then there's the human side of planning. There is agonizing and then there is organizing.

This is why Nehemiah was such a great leader. Because he not only prayed, he proceeded with confidence and trust in the Lord. And he not only proceeded with confidence and trust in the Lord, he planned effectively.

These same steps, when applied to your life as a Christian, will help you become the effective leader God intends for you to be.

WHAT STEP DO YOU NEED TO TAKE TODAY TO BECOME THE LEADER GOD HAS CALLED YOU TO BE?

Day 343

For the body does not consist of one member but of many. But as it is, God arranged the members in the body, each one of them, as he chose.

—1 Corinthians 12:14,18

Y ou have a job to do in the body of Christ. Every member is a minister. You don't have to resign from your job for God to have a ministry for you.

And when we work together, cooperating in God's church among God's people, the impact is amazing.

Now, Nehemiah leaves a very sad commentary in Nehemiah chapter 3 when he talks about a group of people called the Tekoites. These people were farmers who helped repair the wall of Jerusalem. In Nehemiah 3:5, Nehemiah says, "And next to them the Tekoites repaired, but their nobles would not stoop to serve their Lord."

The nobles thought they were too good! They wouldn't stoop down. They didn't want to get their hands dirty. They thought they were above working on a wall, just shoving bricks around. So what did they do? They sat out while others worked!

It's always been an amazing thing to me that some believers watch while others work. How some believers sit while others serve! To me, a non-serving Christian is a contradiction in terms.

Perhaps today, you'd admit that you've been sitting on the sidelines, watching while others get their hands dirty doing the work of the Lord. And who knows, maybe you have a list a mile long as to why you're not involved in some kind of ministry in your church or elsewhere. Or maybe you don't think there's a place of ministry for you.

If so, I want to ask you to perform an experiment this week. I want you to call your church and ask them if they need help in any area of ministry. Whether it's ushering, parking cars, working with children, or sweeping floors, just ask if there's some place where they need help. If you do this, I can promise you that God will use you in a mighty way… a way you never thought possible!

In addition to that, I'm confident that God will bless your life as you make yourself available in service to Him.

**GET IN THE GAME! SERVE SOMEONE
IN CHRIST'S NAME THIS WEEK.**

Day 344

Let us run with endurance the race that is set before us, looking to Jesus, the founder and perfecter of our faith, who for the joy that was set before him endured the cross, despising the shame, and is seated at the right hand of the throne of God. Consider him who endured from sinners such hostility against himself, so that you may not grow weary or fainthearted.

—Hebrews 12:1-3

Maybe you've experienced disappointment in your life lately. Possibly a challenge faces you just around the corner.

If so, how do you get up when you're down? Look up! That's what Nehemiah did when there was opposition to the rebuilding of the wall of Jerusalem.

Listen to his prayer in Nehemiah 4:4: "Hear, O our God, for we are despised. Turn back their taunt on their own heads and give them up to be plundered in a land where they are captives."

Nehemiah didn't waste time or divert from the task at hand dealing with all the criticism he received from those who opposed him rebuilding the wall. Instead of trying to handle it all on his own, you know what Nehemiah did? He went straight to the throne of God. Nehemiah recognized that God could do a better job of dealing with his enemies than he could, so he just gave it all to God!

The next time you're down or discouraged, let me give you the best piece of advice that you could ever hear: Run to God! Cry out to Him! Now, how simple is that?

And yet, so often we try to figure everything out on our own. We try to fix things ourselves. And then we come to the end and we say, "Well, I guess it's come to this; I guess I'm just going to pray now."

Don't make prayer your last chance... make it your first choice!

Somebody said if you look behind you, you'll be defeated. If you look ahead of you, you'll be distressed. If you look around you, you'll be discouraged. But if you look above you, you will be determined.

As our verse for today says, when problems come, take them to the top! Go to the Lord and tell Him all about it. Look to Him to overcome the disappointments you face in life.

ARE YOU WORRIED? DISAPPOINTED? STRESSED? TELL GOD ABOUT IT, AND HE WILL HELP YOU TODAY!

Day 345

The plans of the diligent lead surely to abundance, but everyone who is hasty comes only to poverty.

—Proverbs 21:5

Are you in financial bondage?

If you're not sure, here's what financial bondage looks like...

1. You charge daily expenditures for the lack of funds.
2. You put off paying a bill until next month.
3. You borrow money to pay fixed expenses such as your mortgage, insurance, or energy payment.
4. You are unaware of how much you owe your creditors.
5. You have creditors calling or writing you about past-due bills.
6. You take money from savings to pay your current bills.
7. You take out new loans to pay off old loans.
8. You and your spouse argue about money.
9. You consider being dishonest about your finances.
10. You find it difficult to tithe.

If any one of these markers describes your life today, I want to offer you a word of encouragement: There is a way to escape financial bondage!

Number one, you need to confront the problem. When you have a problem, you have to be willing to be honest about it.

Number two, you need to take decisive action. As our Scripture today says, you need to have a plan if you're going to escape financial bondage. It's not just going to take care of itself on its own! This will probably involve such things as reducing your spending, putting up or tearing up your credit cards, and budgeting your income.

The last way to escape financial bondage is to focus on what you can give—not on what you can get. In Luke 6:38, Jesus says, "Give, and it will be given to you. Good measure, pressed down, shaken together, running over, will be put into your lap. For with the measure you use it will be measured back to you."

If you find yourself in financial bondage, I encourage you... make the decision to free yourself today!

YOU WILL NEVER BE THE BLESSING AS GOD INTENDS AS LONG AS YOU ARE IN BONDAGE TO MONEY.

Day 346

We obligate ourselves to bring the firstfruits of our ground and the firstfruits of all fruit of every tree, year by year, to the house of the LORD.

—Proverbs 21:5

I want to ask you some important questions that every follower of Christ should ask themselves from time to time.

- If every member of your church were just like you, what kind of church would your church be?
- If every member prayed like you pray, what kind of prayer life would your church know?
- If every member served as you serve, what kind of ministry would your church have to hurting and broken people?
- If every member worshipped as you worship, what would the dynamic of your church's worship look like and feel like?
- If every member witnessed, invited, and encouraged others to come just like you witness, invite, and encourage others to come, what would the outreach of your church look like?
- Lastly, if every church member gave as you give, would your church have buildings to worship and serve our God?

Now, I know that asking people about money is a very touchy thing. When you get close to people's money, people get nervous! But the fact is that every follower of Christ has a duty before God and an accountability to one another to be a part of what He is doing in His Church.

And with this accountability comes a commitment of our finances to God. In today's Scripture verse, the people of Israel committed to give God the very best, something we call "sacrifice."

So I want to ask you today, are you giving God the "firstfruits" of everything you have? Are you giving to His Church like He would have you to? Because it takes your sacrifice and stewardship to help the Church successfully and effectively reach others for Christ.

CONSIDER YOUR GIVING RECORD. IF IT'S NOT YOUR BEST, DO SOMETHING ABOUT IT STARTING TODAY.

You make known to me the path of life; in your presence there is fullness of joy; at your right hand are pleasures forevermore.
—Psalm 16:11

Can you really live in the presence of God every day of your life? According to our Scripture verse for today, you can.

You and I can enjoy the presence of God when we open His Word and let it speak to us, when we gather with fellow Christians and worship, and when we pray with open hearts to Him.

That's when God revives our spirit and Jesus gives us joy that fills our lives.

There's the joy of the Scripture... there's the joy of the Savior... and there's the joy of salvation. In fact, Jesus said in Luke 10:20, "Rejoice that your names are written in heaven."

Yes, the greatest joy of all is knowing that you're saved!

But today, perhaps you realize that you're not saved. Maybe you don't know the joy of salvation in Jesus Christ.

If you would like to know that joy and accept the salvation that Jesus offers, I invite you to pray this prayer:

Lord Jesus Christ, I want to live in the joy and presence of God without sin. I know you made that possible when you paid the price for my sins with your blood. Please come into my life. Forgive my sins and take me into God's presence. Thank you for your grace and joy. Amen.

Second Corinthians 5:21 says, "For our sake he made him to be sin who knew no sin, so that in him we might become the righteousness of God." If you've just prayed this prayer, rejoice that you have been declared righteous by God!

THE GREATEST JOY OF ALL IS KNOWING THAT YOU'RE SAVED!

For everyone who calls on the name of the Lord will be saved. How then will they call on him in whom they have not believed? And how are they to believe in him of whom they have never heard? And how are they to hear without someone preaching?
—Romans 10:13-14

Did you know that God is calling you to the mission field? As followers of Christ, you and I have a mission to take the gospel to the world.

We must be on a mission to share the gospel because it is universal in its application. It's for all people, all cultures, and all countries. All people need to know Jesus as Savior! We all face the problem of sin! And the only solution is Jesus.

We must be on a mission to share the gospel with the world because it is universal in its invitation.

Romans 10:13 says that "everyone who calls on the name of the Lord will be saved" (emphasis added). The gospel invitation is universal because all of us have the same need and we all need the same Savior.

Finally, we must be on a mission to share the gospel because it is universal in its proclamation. We must go and be messengers. In Acts 1:8, Jesus tells His apostles, "you will be my witnesses in Jerusalem and in all Judea and Samaria, and to the end of the earth."

Now, you may say, "What can I really do about world missions?" I'll tell you what you can do: Get available! Get usable! Get expendable!

The gospel can't go from land to land until it goes from life to life and from lip to lip. And you're not only to go into the world at large, but you are to go to the world nearby—across the street—with the message of Jesus Christ.

It's my prayer that you will take this challenge from the Lord seriously today and every day!

**PRAY THAT GOD WILL HELP YOU SEE
YOUR PERSONAL MISSION FIELD.**

Day 349

Those who sow in tears shall reap with shouts of joy! He who goes out weeping, bearing the seed for sowing, shall come home with shouts of joy, bringing his sheaves with him.

—Psalm 126:5-6

I have two questions for you today. Do you care? And, do you dare?

God has called every Christian to share Jesus. It is plain and simple. You and I have the responsibility to share the love of Jesus Christ one-on-one with our friends and family members who don't know Him.

But the sad and tragic fact is that most Christians never lead another soul to Christ. When was the last time you individually shared Christ with someone else? How many people are going to be in heaven because you cared and because you dared to share the gospel?

Let me break this down into three parts for you: task, tears, and treasure.

Our task is bringing people to Jesus. The psalmist is saying in today's passage that sharing Jesus Christ is like planting a crop. And the only way to plant this crop is by sharing Christ personally with someone else. This is our task; this is our priority as followers of Jesus.

Next is our tears. Great men of God have always wept tears over the "lostness" of people.

In Romans 9:2-4, Paul says "I have great sorrow and unceasing anguish in my heart… for the sake of my brothers, my kinsmen according to the flesh. They are Israelites, and to them belong the adoption, the glory, the covenants, the giving of the law, the worship, and the promises."

What drove Paul was his deep burden because people are lost without Jesus Christ. This burden should continue to drive us today. And our concern for those lost around us should drive us to tears.

Then, finally, there's our treasure, for it says in Psalm 126:6, "He who goes out weeping, bearing seed for sowing, shall come home with shouts of joy, bringing his sheaves with him."

The seed is the Word of God, and if we're faithful to take the Word of God to people, it's the Spirit's responsibility to drive it home to their hearts. We don't win people to Christ by our theories or opinions. We bring people to Jesus Christ by the seed of the Word of God.

I pray you will care enough… to dare to share the gospel with someone you know today!

I CHALLENGE YOU TO TELL SOMEONE ABOUT JESUS TODAY!

Day 350

A man once gave a great banquet and invited many. And at the time for the banquet he sent his servant to say to those who had been invited, "Come, for everything is now ready."

—Luke 14:16-17

If you are a Christian, I know that you agree: people need the Lord. But how can they find Him?

Simply put, the answer is you and me. People will never know the Lord unless you and I are willing to share Jesus with our world. It's what God has called every one of us to do.

In Luke 14, Jesus tells a story, or parable, of a beautiful banquet that has been prepared. But when the master of the house says, "Invite the guests," all the guests begin to make excuses. They all reject the master's invitation.

So the master says, "Fine, go tell the blind, the lame, the maimed; go into the highways and hedges, go into the streets, the lanes, the back alleys and invite all of those folks to come in."

This parable gives us important insight into our responsibility to share the gospel. First, verse 21 shows who is to go and extend the invitation to the banquet—the servants. If we are servants of the Lord Jesus Christ, it's our job to share Christ and to issue the invitation to his "banquet" of salvation.

Next, it shows how we are to go. Verse 22 says, "And the servant said, 'Sir, what you commanded has been done, and still there is room.' And the master said to the servant, 'Go out to the highways and hedges and compel people to come in.'"

We're to go and share the gospel in every form and every fashion with every kind of method that we can use that honors God!

Third, we are shown who are we to go to. Verse 21 again shows us that we're to go and reach the poor—the physically poor, materially poor, spiritually poor. All are poor without the Lord Jesus Christ.

And when are we to go? Again, verse 21 says we're to go quickly. There's never been an opportunity better than right now.

Finally, we are told in verse 23 why are we to go…"That my house may be filled." Jesus is talking about His heavenly house, and He is looking for us to reach more and more people who need to hear the invitation of the Lord Jesus Christ to spend eternity with Him.

God has prepared the banquet of salvation. Are you willing to be His servant—going to a spiritually hungry world and extending His invitation to come and dine with Him for eternity? I hope your answer is YES!

PUT YOURSELF IN THE PARABLE OF LUKE 14. WHO WOULD YOU INVITE TO THE BANQUET?

Day 351

All have sinned and come short of the glory of God.

—Romans 3:23

If you had the opportunity, could you lead someone to Christ?

Many of us don't know how to share our faith, one on one, with someone else. I want to share with you quickly the ABCs of doing just that.

A—there's something to **admit**. Romans 3:23 says that, "All have sinned and come short of the glory of God." And Romans 6:23 tells us, "The wages of sin is death." Before someone can be saved, they have to recognize that they're lost. They have to understand their condition without God.

B—something to **believe**. And what people need to believe if they're going to be saved is that Jesus is Lord. In Acts 16:31 Paul made it clear: "Believe on the Lord Jesus Christ and you shall be saved." To believe in Jesus means to trust Him, to really give your life to Him.

C—something to **consider**. You need to consider what it means to give your life to Christ. As Paul says in Ephesians 4:21-24, "You... were taught... to put off your old self, which belongs to your former manner of life and is corrupt through deceitful desires... and to put on the new self, created after the likeness of God in true righteousness and holiness." This means a new way of living. And it means repenting and turning from those things that bury you spiritually.

D—something to **do**. And that something is to receive Jesus as your Lord and Savior. John 1:12, "To all who believed in his name, he gave the right to become children of God."

Admit, believe, consider, and do. You can share that little message, as I have, in just a few minutes.

WRITE THE ABC'S OF SALVATION DOWN ON A SMALL CARD AND KEEP IT IN YOUR WALLET OR PURSE.

"But you will receive power when the Holy Spirit has come upon you, and you will be my witnesses in Jerusalem and in all Judea and Samaria, and to the end of the earth."

—**Acts 1:8**

Do you get weak in the knees when you think about sharing your faith? Are you clueless about how to even begin witnessing?

According to our Scripture for today, witnessing is not a question of "if" but of "when." Christ made it clear that God's plan for every Christian is a life of faithfulness to be a witness for Him.

Unfortunately, a lot of Christians have this fear, or maybe a reluctance to share their faith. The good news is that you can overcome these obstacles!

I believe there are two simple principles that will help you be the witness God desires you to be.

First, recognize the adequacy of Jesus Christ in you through His Holy Spirit. Jesus said, "You will be my witnesses when the Holy Spirit has come upon you." See, the work of the Holy Spirit in our lives makes us more than adequate for everything we need as a witness. And when we recognize who we are in Christ, we can overcome our reluctance to share our faith.

Second, you and I must also develop certain skills that will help us share our faith. Now, God can use even the most limited witness, but you and I should want to fully develop our evangelism skills as followers of Jesus Christ. And as you learn the skills to share your faith with others, God will use you under any circumstances, wherever you are.

BEGIN PRACTICING YOUR EVANGELISM SKILLS BY THINKING ABOUT YOUR OWN PERSONAL TESTIMONY. WHAT HAS GOD DONE IN YOUR LIFE?

Day 353

For it is God who works in you, both to will and to work for his good pleasure.

—Philippians 2:13

Do you know that God wants to use you to accomplish His purposes on the earth? Yes, YOU!

"But, Pastor," you say, "you don't know my past. You don't know what I struggle with. How can God ever use someone like me?"

I'm here to tell you today that God can and will use you. How do I know? Because His Word is chocked full of men and women who would have never thought God would use them! These are people like Noah. When God called him to build the ark, we might have heard him say, "Do what, God? Build an ark? That's impossible!"

Or what about Nehemiah? When the call of God came upon his life, he might have said something like, "Wait a minute, God. I'm comfortable here in Persia. I've got a great job. Why would you want someone like me to give up everything to rebuild a wall?"

Or think about Paul. When Jesus called him, we might have heard him say, "Wait a minute, Lord, I'm your chosen instrument? Do you know my past? Have you seen what I've done?"

Yet God called each of these men to do great things for Him! And not only did He call them, but God equipped them to do what He had called them to do.

And you know what? God can do the same for you! As our Scripture verse for today says, "For it is God who works in you, both to will and to work for his good pleasure" (Philippians 2:13).

So let me ask you, are you willing to let God use you? If so, I urge you to echo the words of Isaiah, who said to God, "Here am I! Send me"!

IT'S TRUE! GOD WANTS TO USE YOU TO ACCOMPLISH HIS PURPOSES HERE ON EARTH.

"But you will receive power when the Holy Spirit has come upon you, and you will be my witnesses in Jerusalem and in all Judea and Samaria, and to the end of the earth."

—Acts 1:8

Do you know what it means to be a global Christian?

Becoming a global Christian starts with a personal commitment. Each of us—every Bible-believing man, woman, and young person—needs to make and take our personal witness for Jesus Christ personally.

Our verse today says, "But you will receive power when the Holy Spirit has come upon you, and you will be my witnesses in Jerusalem and in all Judea and Samaria, and to the end of the earth" (Acts 1:8).

If you want to live under the Lordship of Christ… if you want to be an obedient, Spirit-filled Christian… then you must take seriously the commandment of Christ to be a personal witness for Him.

Now, everyone's a witness, of course. You're either a good witness or a bad witness. You're either witnessing positively for Christ or negatively for Christ. But we're all witnesses of Jesus Christ!

But we're not only to witness with our lives, we're to witness with our lips. If we want to live a significant life and get beyond ourselves and our own little world, we will do what Jesus said to do and that is to be salt and light.

Salt penetrates and light illuminates. And every one of us can be salt and every one of us can be light right where we live. "Well," you say, "I don't really have a witness. I really don't have that great of a testimony."

Christian, it doesn't matter how small you think your life is. You can penetrate the darkness for Jesus Christ. And besides that, you're called to do it!

Today, it's my prayer that you will make and take your witness for Jesus personally so you can be the global Christian that God has called you to be!

**PAY ATTENTION TO YOUR ACTIONS TODAY.
ARE YOU REFLECTING THE CHARACTER
OF JESUS CHRIST?**

Day 355

And we know that for those who love God all things work together for good, for those who are called according to his purpose.

—Romans 8:28

If you are a Christian, you've probably heard the concept that God has a specific plan and purpose for your life. But do you really trust Him to accomplish it?

D. Elton Trueblood, the noted 20th century American Quaker and theologian, wrote, "Faith is not belief without proof, but trust without reservation."

For you and for me, there are times when we can't fully understand all that's going on in our lives. There are things that don't make sense to us. There are painful times that make us question God's plan for us.

But it is in those times that we must fully trust God. To have a faith that is without reservation!

And how do you do that? By understanding the truth of Romans 8:28-29: "And we know that for those who love God all things work together for good, for those who are called according to his purpose. For those whom he foreknew he also predestined to be conformed to the image of his Son, in order that he might be the firstborn among many brothers."

We get the word *synergy* from the word *work* in this passage. God is working synergistically in your life, taking the forces and circumstances and situations of your life and working them all together for your good. That's why you can fully trust God even when things are not going as you had hoped.

Yes, God does have an incredible plan for your life and that plan is your purpose. Trust Him today to work everything together for your good and to accomplish that purpose!

WRITE OUT OUR SCRIPTURE VERSE FOR TODAY AND PUT IT ON YOUR REFRIGERATOR OR BATHROOM MIRROR FOR DAILY ENCOURAGEMENT.

Day 356

There is laid up for me the crown of righteousness, which the Lord, the righteous judge, will award to me on that Day, and not only to me but also to all who have loved his appearing.

—2 Timothy 4:8

Did you know that you can live with God's protection and provision? You can live every single day in His love! How do you do that?

One way is to embrace your future by living for eternity. Or, as Steven R. Covey says, "Begin with the end in mind." That's how you and I are to live our lives as followers of Christ.

When everything around you is crumbling, when you're facing danger and difficulties and deception of all kinds, your outlook on life will be determined by your "up-look."

And if your up-look is to love Christ's return and to long for His appearing, knowing that at any moment He could come for you, then you are living in His love.

As today's verse says, "There is laid up for me the crown of righteousness, which the Lord, the righteous judge, will award to me on that Day, and not only to me but also to all who have loved his appearing."

When we are daily embracing our future with God, that keeps us in His love!

WHEN EVERYTHING AROUND YOU IS CRUMBLING, WHEN YOU'RE FACING DANGER AND DIFFICULTIES AND DECEPTION OF ALL KINDS, YOUR OUTLOOK ON LIFE WILL BE DETERMINED BY YOUR "UP-LOOK."

Day 357

"If anyone serves me, he must follow me; and where I am, there will my servant be also. If anyone serves me, the Father will honor him."

—**John 12:26**

This is a good day for you to have a spiritual DTR—Defining The Relationship—with Christ. In fact, I believe every person who calls themselves a Christian should take stock and evaluate where they are with Jesus Christ on a regular basis.

Jesus is constantly calling us to commitment and to define our relationship with Him. He wants to know, as He often said, "Are you with Me or are you against Me? Are we really a thing or do you just date Me on Sundays? Am I just a friend with benefits or do we really have something that's real, something that's relational and something that's forever?"

So many people treat God as though He is a distant relative rather than a vital part of life. But Jesus refuses to let us get away with that in our relationship with Him!

You know, when people in the Bible came face-to-face with Jesus they didn't walk away the same people. They were dramatically transformed... for good or for bad. Some received Him, some rejected Him, but every one who came in contact with Christ was powerfully impacted by Him.

The Bible tells us of a rich young ruler who had a DTR with Jesus when Jesus called him to follow Him fully (Matthew 19). But that man went away sorrowfully, rejecting Christ because he couldn't handle the commitment.

So what about you? Is it time that you had a DTR with Jesus Christ?

Just like Jesus asked the disciples after He fed the multitudes in John chapter 6, He's asking you, "Are you with Me? Are you willing to walk with Me every day of the week... not just on Sundays?"

It's my prayer that you will define your relationship with Jesus Christ today... that you will commit your love and life to His Lordship, His will, and His ways.

CONSIDER YOUR LIFE AT WORK AND AT HOME FROM MONDAY TO SATURDAY. IS JESUS A PART OF IT?

Restore to me the joy of your salvation, and uphold me with a willing spirit.

—Psalm 51:12

If you're not really happy with your life today, maybe you think a change would be good.

So many of us fall into the trap of thinking that changing our jobs, changing our appearance, or changing our environment will make us happy. But it just isn't true!

All of these external changes may temporarily improve your life but none of them can change your life. None can make you truly happy. You may move around. You may change cars. You may even change jobs. But you know what? Wherever you go, it's the same old you, right?

It's not that your circumstances or your surroundings need to change. It's your heart that needs to change. It's your heart that needs a new birth.

The Bible is pretty clear when it talks about our hearts. In Jeremiah 17:9, it says, "The heart is deceitful above all things, and desperately sick." The heart, according to the Bible, is not good!

Which means your heart needs a spiritual change. I'm not talking about a resolution—promising to be better, do better, or live better. I'm talking about a revolution!

It's something so radical, so dramatic, that it's like beginning life all over again! It's a new beginning! It's an inward change! Your heart undergoes a spiritual transformation when God takes it and transplants it with His love and His heart.

So my challenge to you today is to let God transform your heart. Realize that no external change can truly make you joyful or fulfilled. Only a heart transformed by God will. So let Him create a new beginning in you today!

ASK GOD TO RESTORE THE JOY OF YOUR HEART TODAY.

Day 359

As Jesus passed on from there, he saw a man called Matthew sitting at the tax booth, and he said to him, "Follow me." And he rose and followed him.

—John 12:26

In our Scripture verse today, Jesus says, "Follow me." The words were written in Matthew 9:9 as a command. Jesus didn't ask Matthew to follow Him if he felt like it. No. Jesus said, "Follow me. Start today... and follow me for the rest of your life. Don't ever stop following me."

But what does that mean for your life today? Notice that the words follow me actually mean "to walk along side the road with me." Jesus, the great God of the universe, told Matthew, a social outcast, to walk with Him!

And you know what? Jesus says the same thing to you today! The great God of the universe is saying to you, "Follow me." Not "Walk way behind me," but "Walk with me." God wants to be your friend!

"But Pastor," you say, "there are things in my past, things that God could never forgive me for. It's too late for me."

No it's not. Jesus Christ is passing your way. And He's calling your name and saying, "Follow me!" This is a great deal! You can leave your sin and your past and walk into a brand new life and a brand new future with the Lord.

Do you want to take Jesus up on His offer to follow Him today? If so, I want to invite you to say this prayer:

"Lord Jesus, I know that I am a sinner. My life is full of mistakes. But I also know that You died to take away all my sin and bad choices and give me a new start. I accept Your offer today. I will walk with You!"

If you said this prayer, I want to welcome you into the family of God! Get ready for an incredible journey with Jesus Christ!

IF YOU MADE A DECISION FOR CHRIST TODAY, TELL SOMEONE ABOUT IT!

Day 360

Therefore, if anyone is in Christ, he is a new creation. The old has passed away; behold, the new has come.

—2 Corinthians 5:17

Have you ever felt like you were trapped? Maybe you feel that way today—trapped by addictions, bad habits, a painful past, or broken relationships.

If so, you can find freedom! When you accept Jesus as your personal Savior, you have access to the power to overcome what has you bound up. You're no longer on your own!

The apostle Paul reinforces this in today's Scripture verse. You become a "new creation" not by getting the evil out, but by getting the power of God in! That's what changes you.

If you are desperate for freedom today, start by asking Jesus Christ into your life. Repeat this prayer:

> *Heavenly Father, I know that my sin keeps me bound. But because You love me, You sent Your Son, Jesus Christ, to set me free. I accept Your gift of freedom and welcome Jesus into my heart and life. Amen.*

If you've just said this prayer and believe what you prayed, you now know the source of power for victory over addictions, habits, a broken heart, and more.

When Christ comes to live in you, then the love of sin is replaced for a love of God. The love of sinful passion and sinful pleasure is replaced with a love for holy purposes and passions that honor God.

The old you passes away and the new you takes its place!

**ASK GOD FOR THE STRENGTH TO OVERCOME
WHAT BINDS YOU TODAY.**

Day 361

"Ask, and it will be given to you; seek, and you will find; knock, and it will be opened to you."

—Matthew 7:7

How great is your faith? Are you hungry for God? Do you pursue Jesus Christ?

In Matthew chapter 15, we see how a Canaanite women relentlessly pursued Jesus, and how her faith in Christ was daring, desperate, and determined.

She also had to overcome many obstacles to get to Jesus. She was a social outcast. The religious people of her day had turned their backs on her. More than likely, she was responsible for her daughter being possessed by a demon. And not only that, Jesus didn't respond to her the first time she called out to Him!

Yet she still came to Jesus. She still pursued Him. She still sought His blessing in her life. And as a result, Jesus said, "O woman, great is your faith!" And forever she is an example in God's Word of a person of relentless faith.

Maybe today, your kids have turned their backs on you or on God. Maybe your parents are far from God with no desire to know Him personally. Maybe your friend doesn't know the Lord and is making all the wrong decisions in life. And maybe Satan is saying to you, "It's a lost cause! Give up! I've got them now!"

Don't you believe a word of it! Keep running relentlessly to Jesus! Keep crying out to the One who said, "Ask, and it will be given to you; seek, and you will find; knock, and it will be opened to you." Literally, keep on asking, keep on seeking, keep on knocking!

Psalm 37:4 says, "Delight yourself in the LORD, and he will give you the desires of your heart." Trust in this promise today as you relentlessly pursue Jesus Christ!

RUN AFTER JESUS CHRIST TODAY THROUGH PRAYER AND BY READING HIS WORD.

Day 362

"But whoever drinks of the water that I will give him will never be thirsty again. The water that I will give him will become in him a spring of water welling up to eternal life."

—John 4:14

I s there a limit to God's mercy? Can you deny Him one too many times?

It doesn't matter who you are, what you've done, or where you've been, no one is too far gone for Jesus. No one! And there's no better evidence of this than the woman that Jesus met at the well in John 4.

She had been used and abused. She had been divorced five times and was living with her boyfriend. She was a mess! But Christ reached out to her with the living water of eternal life. And her life was instantly transformed.

This woman who was ravaged by regrets, failures, and brokenness was made brand new because of the power of Jesus Christ. She wasn't too far gone for the Lord Jesus!

The same is true for you and me. No one—no matter how wasted, burned out, or strung out they may seem—is too far gone for Jesus Christ.

In our Scripture today, Jesus says whoever drinks of the water that He gives will have eternal life! That means you.

**IT DOESN'T MATTER WHAT YOU'VE DONE,
YOU'RE NEVER TOO FAR GONE FOR GOD.**

Day 363

Do not withhold good from those to whom it is due, when it is in your power to do it.

—Proverbs 3:27

Did you know that what you say can build up or tear down others? Especially your children.

That's why I want to encourage you to speak words of faith, affection, and encouragement into the lives of your kids or grandkids. Bless them with words!

How do you do this? By telling them how special they are! Make sure you tell your children every day that they are a gift from God, a gift with amazing potential.

Even if your children are adults now, it's not too late. Your words of love, encouragement, and faith will have a tremendous impact on your children now.

Every kid wants encouragement from Mom and Dad no matter what age they are. So whether your children are young or old, start blessing them with your words today.

Proverbs 3:27 says not to "withhold good from those to whom it is due, when it is in your power to do it." So today, I'd encourage you to sit your child down in your lap or call your child on the phone and tell them how special they are.

They will feel loved and appreciated, and most importantly, God will be glorified as you build them up in faith, hope, and love.

TELL YOUR CHILDREN TODAY THAT THEY ARE GIFTS FROM GOD.

Day 364

No, in all these things we are more than conquerors through him who loved us.

—Romans 8:37

If you are suffering, I want to encourage you with our Scripture verse today.

No matter what you may be going through, Jesus is your ultimate answer. Because He died not only for your sin, He died for your suffering.

Does this mean that the pain you feel when you experience loss should be any less? No. Does this mean that you shouldn't feel sad when your heart is broken? Not at all! Remember that Jesus Himself cried when His friend Lazarus died.

Because of sin, you and I live in a fallen world. And in a fallen world, bad things happen to everyone, even God's people.

But take heart! You have a Savior who lives. And because you have a Savior who lives, because you have a Savior who endured and conquered suffering, you have a hope that lives.

It's a hope that knows that challenges and trials don't last forever and that Jesus can give you peace and confidence.

Yes, Jesus, the conquering Christ, is your answer, no matter what you may be going through today. And because He is a conqueror, you as His child, are a conqueror as well.

IF YOU ARE STRUGGLING, TAKE YOUR PAIN TO JESUS CHRIST. ASK FOR HIS STRENGTH TODAY.

Confess your sins to one another and pray for one another, that you may be healed.

—James 5:16

In today's devotional, I want to focus on a very sensitive subject, but one that needs to be addressed from a biblical standpoint—internet pornography.

More than likely, your life has been affected in some way by internet pornography, either directly or indirectly. Perhaps you'd even admit today that you struggle with viewing pornography on the internet, and that you don't how to stop looking at it.

If so, I want to let you know two things. One, you're not alone. And two, there is hope.

There is hope because the Lord Jesus Christ can set you free from the bondage of pornography addiction. But it will take action on your part to truly experience that freedom.

Maybe the first step for you is admitting that you have a problem, that you have an addiction. As today's verse says, "Confess your sins to one another and pray for one another, that you may be healed."

Maybe for you it means seeking help in a Bible-based recovery program like Celebrate Recovery. My church in Dallas has a Celebrate Recovery program, and I can tell you that lives are being set free every day as a result of it.

Remember, your sin struggle doesn't define who you are if you are a child of God.

But at the same time, you will need to seek help to truly experience the freedom from sin that you desire, and that God has made available through the death and resurrection of His Son.

TAKE THE FIRST STEP TO HEALING—ADMIT THAT YOU HAVE A PROBLEM.